ADVANCE PRAISE

for

Open Networks, Closed Regimes

"Many hope that information technology will generate new opportunities for global communications, breaking down national barriers even in dictatorial regimes with minimal freedom of the press. Kalathil and Boas provide a path-breaking and thoughtful analysis of this issue. A fascinating study, this should be widely read by all concerned with understanding and promoting democratization, regime change, and new information technology."

—**Pippa Norris,** John F. Kennedy School of
Government, Harvard University

"Through a country-by-country analysis, Kalathil and Boas shed light on practices formerly known only by anecdote, and their findings chip away at the apocryphal notion that going digital necessarily means going democratic. Their work answers a number of important questions, and frames a worthy challenge to those who wish to deploy technology for the cause of political openness."

—**Jonathan Zittrain,** Berkman Center for
Internet & Society, Harvard University

Open Networks
Closed Regimes

Open Networks
Closed Regimes

The Impact of the Internet on Authoritarian Rule

Shanthi Kalathil
Taylor C. Boas

CARNEGIE ENDOWMENT FOR INTERNATIONAL PEACE
Washington, D.C.

Carnegie Endowment for International Peace
1779 Massachusetts Avenue, N.W., Washington, D.C. 20036
202-483-7600   www.ceip.org

The Carnegie Endowment normally does not take institutional positions on public policy issues; the views and recommendations presented in this publication do not necessarily represent the views of the Carnegie Endowment, its officers, staff, or trustees.

To order, contact Carnegie's distributor:
The Brookings Institution Press
Department 029, Washington, D.C. 20042-0029, USA
1-800-275-1447 or 1-202-797-6258
Fax 202-797-2960, E-mail bibooks@brook.edu

Text set in Sabon. Composition by AlphaWebTech, Mechanicsville, Md. Printed by Malloy Lithographing of Ann Arbor, Mich., on acid-free paper (85% recycled content).

Library of Congress Cataloging-in-Publication Data

Kalathil, Shanthi.
Open networks, closed regimes : the impact of the internet on authoritarian rule / Shanthi Kalathil and Taylor C. Boas.
    p. cm.
Includes bibliographical references (p.) and index.
    ISBN 0-87003-194-5 (pbk.)
1. Authoritarianism—Case studies. 2. Internet—Political aspects—Case studies. I. Boas, Taylor C. II. Title.
    JC480 .K35 2002
    320.53—dc21   2002013713

---

10 09 08 07 06 05 04   5 4 3 2 1   1st Printing 2003

320.53
K14

Contents

Foreword

As the information revolution rapidly unfolds, Internet use is profoundly affecting governments, corporations, and societies around the world. Many of these effects, while widely assumed to be significant, have yet to be fully explored.

In the absence of thorough analysis, unexamined assumptions about the Internet's likely impact have become conventional wisdom. Tales of wired dissidents toppling strong-armed leaders, along with long-held beliefs about the medium's inherently democratic nature, have lent credibility to the idea that the Internet inexorably undermines authoritarian regimes. Having outlasted the initial euphoria surrounding the information age, this notion has now solidified into a truism. It is an assumption that informs the speeches of politicians, creeps into policy debates, and pops up as fact in press reports.

Few serious studies have yet tested this view. While new research has focused on individual countries or particular types of users, none has looked for patterns of effects across a broad sample of authoritarian regimes, giving equal consideration to Internet use by government, business, and civil society groups.

In this book, Shanthi Kalathil and Taylor C. Boas carefully examine the full range of Internet use under eight authoritarian regimes. They demonstrate how the Internet's net impact on authoritarian rule has often been obscured by conventional wisdom. In China, for instance, the Internet-enabled protests of the Falun Gong must be weighed against the government's efforts to channel online discourse and extend its own authority through Internet use. In Cuba, independent journalists may post their stories on web servers outside the country, but most citizens are shielded from the global Internet and encouraged to use a national computer network with government-authorized content. In some Southeast Asian countries, globally wired activist networks square off against governments who use the Internet to drive economic development and boost standards of living. And in many parts of the Middle East, the Internet increases access to Western images and ideas but also offers a soapbox for Islamic fundamentalists who oppose broadening civil liberties.

Overall, as Kalathil and Boas note, the Internet is challenging and helping to transform authoritarianism. Yet they also argue that information technology alone is unlikely to bring about its demise. Their study is a valuable corrective to the blind optimism equating the Internet with freedom, and it invites readers to realistically reflect on how the Internet might be better leveraged for democratic aims. This book builds on research conducted over the past three years at the Carnegie Endowment. It will serve as an innovative and useful guide for policy makers, activists, and anyone else who wants to use the potent information tools of the twenty-first century to promote greater global integration and understanding.

Jessica T. Mathews
President
Carnegie Endowment for International Peace

Acknowledgments

This book could not have been written without the support of a number of individuals and organizations. We would like to thank Jessica Mathews, Paul Balaran, George Perkovich, and Thomas Carothers for creating a welcoming institutional environment at the Carnegie Endowment and for steadfastly encouraging our research efforts in an emerging field. Maria Carlo and Pavani Reddy deftly handled the administrative and research assistance that we needed to keep the project organized and on track. Trish Reynolds, Sherry Pettie, and Catherine Wigginton guided us through the publication process, while Carmen MacDougall and Scott Nathanson expertly publicized our research. Carnegie librarians Kathleen Higgs and Chris Henley and former librarian Jennifer Little amassed many of the sources upon which this study relies. We are also indebted to the Ford Foundation, the John D. and Catherine T. MacArthur Foundation, and the Rockefeller Foundation, whose generous support of the Carnegie Endowment's Global Policy Program made this project possible.

In particular we wish to recognize William J. Drake, founding director of the Information Revolution and World Politics Project at the Carnegie Endowment, for his key role in launching this initiative and guiding it through its early stages. Our frequent discussions with Bill helped shape the framework and argument of this study in countless ways. We absolve him of responsibility for any shortcomings in the final product, but he can deservedly take credit for opening many of the doors that have helped make this book a reality.

We owe a special debt of gratitude to colleagues who read portions of the manuscript and offered feedback during the revision process, including Jon Alterman, Thomas Carothers, Peter Ferdinand, Will Foster, Nina Hachigian, Veron Hung, Philip Peters, Garry Rodan, and Deborah Wheeler. In addition, we would like to thank the numerous individuals around the world who generously provided us with information and insight during on- and off-the-record interviews. Their contributions proved invaluable in shaping the conclusions of this study.

Last but certainly not least, we are grateful to all those who have offered intellectual guidance, moral support, and encouragement during this research endeavor. They include David Collier, Terry Karl, Laura Krejsa, James Mulvenon, Helen Oliver, Minxin Pei, P. J. Simmons, Jon Wolfsthal, John Zysman, the members of the Chinese Internet Research Group, and our families.

Acronyms

When the letters of an acronym correspond to words in a foreign language, the English translation is listed.

ACWF	All-China Women's Federation
AOL	America Online
APEC	Asia Pacific Economic Cooperation
ASEAN	Association of Southeast Asian Nations
ASP	application service provider
BBC	British Broadcasting Corporation
CCP	Chinese Communist Party
CDA	Cuban Democracy Act (United States)
CDLR	Committee for the Defense of Legitimate Rights (Saudi Arabia)
CENIAI	National Center for Automated Data Exchange (Cuba)
CEPAL	United Nations Economic Commission for Latin America and the Caribbean
CIA	Central Intelligence Agency (United States)
CITMA	Ministry of Science, Technology, and the Environment (Cuba)
CNNIC	China Internet Network Information Center
CPV	Communist Party of Vietnam
CSO	civil society organization
ETECSA	Telecommunications Corporation of Cuba, S.A.
GDP	gross domestic product
GNI	gross national income
ICEI	Cuban Institute of Independent Economists
ICP	Internet content provider
ICT	information and communication technology
IDA	Info-communications Development Authority (Singapore)

IDSC	Information Decision Support Center (Egypt)
IMF	International Monetary Fund
ISP	Internet service provider
ISU	Internet Services Unit (Saudi Arabia)
IT	information technology
ITT	International Telephone and Telegraph
ITU	International Telecommunications Union
LAN	local area network
MCI	Ministry of Culture and Information (Vietnam)
MEI	Ministry of Electronic Industry (China)
MIC	Ministry of Computing and Communications (Cuba)
MII	Ministry of Information Industry (China)
MIRA	Movement for Islamic Reform in Arabia (Saudi Arabia)
MPT	Ministry of Posts and Telecommunications (China)
NDI	National Democratic Institute (United States)
NGO	nongovernmental organization
NII	National Information Infrastructure (Singapore)
NLD	National League for Democracy (Burma)
OECD	Organisation for Economic Co-operation and Development
PAP	People's Action Party (Singapore)
PLA	People's Liberation Army (China)
RITSEC	Regional Information Technology and Software Engineering Center (Egypt)
SARFT	State Administration of Radio, Film, and Television (China)
SBA	Singapore Broadcasting Authority
SIME	Ministry of Steel, Mechanics, and Electronics Industries (Cuba)
SMS	short message service
SOE	state-owned enterprise (China)
SPDC	State Peace and Development Council (Burma)
SPH	Singapore Press Holdings Ltd.
UAE	United Arab Emirates
UNDP	United Nations Development Program
UNEAC	Cuban Union of Writers and Artists
URL	uniform resource locator
USAID	United States Agency for International Development
VDC	Vietnam Data Communications
VNPT	Vietnam Post and Telecommunications Corporation
VOA	Voice of America (United States)
WTO	World Trade Organization

Open Networks
Closed Regimes

CHAPTER ONE

The Conventional Wisdom:
What Lies Beneath?

Technology will make it increasingly difficult for the state to
control the information its people receive. . . . The Goliath of
totalitarianism will be brought down by the David of the
microchip.

—Ronald Reagan, speech at London's Guildhall,
June 14, 1989

The world has changed a great deal since Ronald Reagan spoke these
words in 1989. To many, subsequent events have borne witness to the
truth of his prediction: authoritarian regimes have fallen around the world,
while the power of the microchip has risen. The connection between these
two phenomena has taken on a powerful, implicit veracity, even when it
has not been explicitly detailed.

A link between technological advance and democratization remains a
powerful assumption in popular thinking, even amid a decline in the general "information age" optimism that characterized much of the 1990s.
Specifically, there is now a widespread belief in the policy world that the
Internet poses an insurmountable threat to authoritarian rule. Political
leaders often espouse this notion: President George W. Bush has asserted
that the Internet will bring freedom to China, while Secretary of State
Colin Powell has stated that "the rise of democracy and the power of the
information revolution combine to leverage each other."[1] President Bill
Clinton was also a prolific proponent of the idea that the Internet is inherently a force for democracy.[2] Business leaders and media commentators
generally concur: former Citicorp chair Walter Wriston has argued in *Foreign Affairs* that "the virus of freedom . . . is spread by electronic networks to the four corners of the earth," and journalist Robert Wright
claims that "in all probability, resistance to the Internet's political logic
will plainly be futile within a decade or two."[3]

This conventional wisdom on the Internet and democracy has deeper roots than the ebullient pronouncements of recent politicians and pundits. In part, it draws upon the strong libertarian culture that prevailed among the Internet's early users—a sentiment epitomized by cyberguru John Perry Barlow's "Declaration of the Independence of Cyberspace."[4] In this statement, delivered at the World Economic Forum in 1996, he declared "the global social space we are building to be naturally independent of the tyrannies [governments] seek to impose on us."[5] A faith in technology's potential to challenge authoritarian rule also emerged out of a particular reading of the fall of communism in Eastern Europe, where the Soviet Union's inability to control the flow of electronic information was seen as crucial to its demise. Ronald Reagan's 1989 statement was typical of early sentiments about the democratizing potential of computer-based communications. As the diffusion of the Internet increasingly facilitates the globalization of communication, culture, and capital, there is a clear desire among the proponents of the process that all good things (including democracy) should go together.

As is often the case with conventional wisdom, this view has several problems. First, it often imputes a political character to the Internet itself, rather than focusing on specific uses of the technology. The Internet, however, is only a set of connections between computers (or a set of protocols allowing computers to exchange information); it can have no impact apart from its use by human beings. The conventional wisdom also tends to be based on a series of "black-box" assertions that obscure the ways in which the use of technology might truly produce a political outcome. Proponents see the Internet as leading to the downfall of authoritarian regimes, but the mechanisms through which this might occur are rarely specified. Instead, popular assumptions often rest on anecdotal evidence, drawing primarily on isolated examples of Internet-facilitated political protest. Subsequent assertions about the technology's political effects are usually made without consideration of the full national context in which the Internet operates in any given country. Hence, they fail to weigh politically challenging uses of the Internet against others that might reinforce authoritarian rule. Last, the conventional wisdom assumes a relatively static Internet whose early control-frustrating characteristics are replicated as it diffuses around the world.

In this study we seek to critically examine the impact of the Internet in authoritarian regimes, adopting an approach that avoids the pitfalls of the conventional wisdom. First and foremost, we aim to break down and analyze Internet use, taking a comprehensive look at how the Internet is employed by a broad range of political, economic, and social actors. So as not to contribute to the rash of black-box explanations, we examine the causal mechanisms that might connect these forms of Internet use with political impact. We also situate the potential effects of Internet use in their full national context, repeating this process for a diverse sample of authoritarian regimes. Such an approach avoids the problem of making inappropriate generalizations from isolated pieces of anecdotal evidence. Finally, we acknowledge that the Internet is not inherently free from government control, especially in those countries where governments have been in charge of its development since the beginning. As Lawrence Lessig has convincingly argued, governments (democratic and authoritarian alike) can most certainly regulate the Internet, both by controlling its underlying code and by shaping the legal environment in which it operates.[6]

Based on a systematic examination of evidence from eight cases—China, Cuba, Singapore, Vietnam, Burma, the United Arab Emirates, Saudi Arabia, and Egypt—we argue that the Internet is not necessarily a threat to authoritarian regimes. Certain types of Internet use do indeed pose political challenges to authoritarian governments, and such use may contribute to political change in the future. Still, other uses of the Internet reinforce authoritarian rule, and many authoritarian regimes are proactively promoting the development of an Internet that serves state-defined interests rather than challenging them. We do not seek to prove definitively that the Internet will not help to undermine authoritarian regimes, nor do we argue that the medium is merely a tool of repressive governments. Rather, we set forth a framework that allows for methodical thinking about limited evidence, and we consider what this evidence suggests in the short to medium term. As the Internet develops further in authoritarian regimes and more evidence accumulates in the future, we hope this framework will prove useful in assessing more long-term political impacts.

Existing Studies

Despite the prevalence of popular punditry on the Internet's democratizing effects, little attention has been paid to the issue in academia. Most of the scholarly literature on democratization does not explore the role of the Internet or even the information and communication technologies (ICTs) that predate it. Modernization theorists of the 1950s and 1960s considered the role of the mass media in promoting political and economic development, but the media and ICTs have generally received much less attention in more recent works.[7] Several democratization scholars have given brief mentions to the influence of ICTs on authoritarian rule, mostly in reference to the role of television in the "demonstration effect" in Eastern European transitions.[8] A few studies (mostly region-specific) have addressed more centrally the question of the media and democracy or democratization.[9] Few studies of democratization, however, have considered the potential role of the Internet and related technologies. As Daniel Lynch has argued, "On the question of telecommunications, the silence of the transitions literature is deafening."[10]

A growing literature has begun to examine the role of the Internet in the politics of advanced industrial democracies. Many of these studies have examined such issues as Internet use in party competition, the potential for online voting and "direct democracy," and the use of the Internet for political activism.[11] Another set of arguments revolves around the question of online social capital, whether virtual communities contribute to civic engagement in a manner that invigorates and strengthens democracy, or whether they promote social fragmentation and weaken associational life.[12] A number of scholars have also weighed in on the new policy issues and political debates surrounding such issues as online privacy, intellectual property, electronic commerce, Internet taxation, and competition policy.[13] Each of these strains of literature explores issues that are increasingly important to the politics of advanced industrial democracies. As Internet use becomes more common in the new democracies of the developing world, these questions will matter there as well. Yet the ideas advanced in this literature are much less relevant to the political dynamics of authoritarian regimes.

A few large-scale comparative works have begun to plug holes in the scholarly literature by examining the issue of the Internet in authoritarian regimes. Several of these involve the statistical analysis of democracy and Internet diffusion, but none has produced convincing evidence of a causal relation between these two factors.[14] Moreover, consistent and reliable data for such studies are hard to come by. A few important works engage in comparative case studies of the Internet across a variety of developing countries, including many authoritarian regimes.[15] Such studies are invaluable for examining the determinants (political or otherwise) of Internet diffusion in the developing world, but they pay less attention to the question of the political impact of Internet use. Several cross-national surveys by Human Rights Watch, Freedom House, and Reporters sans Frontières have examined restrictions on the Internet in authoritarian regimes, but these likewise engage in little comparative analysis of the medium's political impact.[16]

Finally, a number of individual case studies and news reports have examined Internet use in authoritarian regimes around the world. The best of these are balanced and well-informed studies, providing an essential foundation for the comparative work that we have undertaken in this book.[17] Many more, however, are impressionistic and anecdotal, falling prey to the pitfalls of the conventional wisdom.

In presenting a systematic, cross-regional comparative study of the impact of Internet use in authoritarian regimes, we seek to fill the gaps in the existing literature. While this is not an academic study per se, we seek to contribute to scholarly debates as well as to policy discourse on the Internet in authoritarian regimes.

The Framework of This Study

This study's framework for analysis provides a blueprint for examining a comprehensive range of Internet uses, specifying the ways in which those uses might produce political impact and situating such impacts within the full national context of each country. Within each case study, Internet use is divided into categories, but we do not interweave evidence from a number of cases in a general discussion of, for instance, the impact of e-commerce. Such an approach ensures that isolated examples of particular types of Internet use are not taken out of context, and it allows each case to stand on its own in addition to supporting the study's general argument.

While focusing on the use of the Internet, we consider state Internet policy as an important factor influencing Internet use. Obviously the role of the state is extensive in authoritarian regimes, and in many cases this is particularly true with respect to the media and ICTs. In such countries early experimentation with the Internet usually occurs in the scientific or academic sector, but the central government is generally the major player in any Internet development beyond the experimental level. Like their counterparts in advanced industrial democracies, many authoritarian governments have instituted ICT development plans, created special Internet governance committees, or reorganized bureaucracies to deal most effectively with the Internet. Furthermore, state Internet policies and governance structures are often outgrowths of older regulatory regimes for the mass media and traditional telecommunications, and a consideration of these historical roots is often valuable in understanding current Internet policy. As in any country (and especially where the role of the state is stronger), state policy will have an important influence on the myriad ways in which the Internet is actually used.[18]

Furthermore, in assessing the political impact of the Internet in any country, one must consider the full national context in which that impact occurs. For this reason, we survey the basic political, economic, and social dynamics of each country, considering such factors as the strength of the authoritarian regime; the major roots of its stability; the nature of the economy and the state's role in economic growth; the presence and strength of political opposition forces; the demographic characteristics of the population; and the importance of foreign relations and geopolitical concerns in domestic politics. Only with such contextual factors in mind can one proceed to analyze the actual political impact of Internet use in each case.

To gain a broad and balanced picture of the Internet's impact in each country, we examine Internet use in four comprehensive categories: civil society, politics and the state, the economy, and the international sphere. In each of the categories, one should presume no particular impact on authoritarian rule; a combination of both challenging and reinforcing uses of the Internet likely exists, though the balance may well tilt in one direction or another.

Civil Society

Internet use in the sphere of civil society includes use by the public and by civil society organizations (CSOs). Although the Internet is far from being a mass medium in many of the cases we examine, analyzing the impact of public Internet use (and how that impact may evolve with increased access) is still an important task. Here we consider, for example, whether public access to information on the Internet contributes in any way to a gradual liberalization of the public sphere.[19] Alternatively, the government may channel computer networking through such closed systems as national intranets, allowing for much greater state control over content. Even with unrestrained access to the Internet, users' choices of the information they consume (for instance, entertainment versus international news) will largely determine whether the mass public's Internet use has any political impact. Where relevant, we also consider public participation in online chat rooms, looking at whether such discourse is liberal and civic, nationalist and jingoistic, critical or supportive of the regime, or some combination of these characteristics.

In examining Internet use by CSOs, we adopt a loose definition of the term "civil society," looking generally at organizations in the public sphere that operate at least semi-autonomously of the state. This does not mean that they are entirely free from state influence in their activities or the positions they take on public policy issues. Nor should one assume the presence of a vibrant civil society in the country in question; in many of our cases precisely the opposite is true. We do examine the Internet use of prominent organizations in society, considering how they employ the medium to coordinate activities, network with other CSOs, and communicate with the domestic and international public. One should note that CSOs may support the regime as well as oppose it, or that they may take an essentially neutral political stance. Furthermore, Internet use may not actually make a difference in the political impact of CSOs. We also include in this category Internet use by political dissidents, both in groups and as individuals.

Politics and the State

In this category we examine Internet use by political parties (where relevant) and by the government. In most of our cases, legal opposition parties do not exist. Where they do, we consider the use of web sites for communication with voters, as well as web and e-mail use for logistic coordination by party activists. Much more common are state uses of the Internet, which can be divided into two main categories: e-government and propaganda. In many cases, e-government measures are likely to work to the benefit of the regime since they increase the state's capacity to provide citizen services effectively, thus increasing public satisfaction with the government. E-government may also increase transparency, which can expose corruption; this could cause a crisis of legitimacy for the regime (especially if corruption is widespread), but it might also bolster the regime's legitimacy if an honest central government is seen to be rooting out endemic corruption. State uses of the Internet for propaganda may be directed primarily at a national or international audience; both are likely to work to the benefit of the regime.

The Economy

In the economic sphere, we consider Internet use by domestic entrepreneurs, state promotion of Internet-driven economic development, and the issue of foreign investment in the Internet industry. The Internet may present significant opportunities for entrepreneurship in a developing economy, possibly leading to the invigoration of an independent private sector or the emergence of a new domestic business elite. Where that is the case, the political preferences and political influence of this group of entrepreneurs may be either favorable or opposed to the regime in power. Further, the state promotion of Internet-driven economic development in general may have a variety of different impacts. If government-promoted Internet use helps deliver economic development, it could benefit the regime by increasing popular satisfaction. Promoting Internet development in certain key industries may bolster the state's intake of hard currency or contribute to economic diversification, both of which are likely to improve the regime's stability. In the long term, however, the rise of a middle class associated with Internet-driven economic growth may pose challenges for authoritarian rule. Finally, the dynamics of foreign investment in a country's Internet industry may result in either pressure for political reform or investors' cooperation with the government on its own terms.

The International Sphere

The international sphere includes Internet usage that is outside the regime's immediate purview but still relevant for its political stability. A major component of this category is Internet use by transnational advocacy networks that are pushing a political agenda regarding the country in question.[20] Such advocacy networks generally have an impact by influencing the actions of others (such as consumers, corporations, foreign governments, and international organizations), and the success of their efforts depends in part on nontechnological factors. Just as with domestic CSOs, transnational advocacy networks do not necessarily oppose the regime in question; their agendas may actually support the regime in certain ways. In addition to transnational advocacy networks, we consider Internet use by diasporas, those members of a nation who are living abroad and who may be engaged in discourse with people in their home countries.[21] Here (as with domestic participation in Internet chat rooms) we examine the nature and potential political impact of that online discourse.

Case Selection

Since we aim to investigate the impact of Internet use on authoritarian rule, the majority of the cases we examine are full-fledged authoritarian regimes, where the leadership of the country is unelected and there are no legal opposition parties. When elections and legal opposition parties are present but elections are rigged, rules are manipulated, or power is wielded so that there is no real competition for elected office, the political regime is best described as semi-authoritarian.[22] Two semi-authoritarian regimes are included among the cases in this study, partly for variation on the type of regime and partly because each is an important case of Internet development in its respective region.

This study's framework for analysis was built around the cases of China and Cuba, which are presented in chapters 2 and 3, respectively. The analysis of those cases is based on a combination of in-country interviews, secondary literature, and an examination of such online material as laws, Internet development plans, and transcripts of chat room discourse. We chose to present China and Cuba as central case studies partly because of our personal knowledge of these cases and our experience in analyzing them.[23]

In addition to their offering the practical advantage of expanding upon previous research, China and Cuba are useful as framing cases for this study because they represent two different types of authoritarian regime, both seeking to manage the political ramifications of Internet use but doing so in very different ways. China is a massive country in both size and population, with a rapidly growing economy and increasing ties to the rest of the world. Cuba is much smaller, less economically dynamic, and less engaged with the global economy, partly by its own choice and partly because of the current U.S. embargo. Although both share a communist history and maintain strict authoritarian political regimes, China is much more committed to economic liberalization and to the development of a market economy, while Cuba clings to socialism in ways China has abandoned. China's approach to the Internet has involved the promotion of rapid, market-driven technology diffusion while controlling Internet use through content filtering, monitoring, and deterrence and by encouraging self-censorship. Cuba, on the other hand, has eschewed a market-led model of Internet development, viewing the technology as a limited resource to be centrally allocated, and it has carefully controlled the public's access to the Internet.

In chapters 4 and 5, we extend the framework for China and Cuba to examine six other cases: Singapore, Vietnam, Burma, the United Arab Emirates, Saudi Arabia, and Egypt. An analysis of these cases is based upon secondary literature and country-specific resources available on the

Internet. We have taken a regional approach to the selection of these cases, choosing three each from Southeast Asia and the Middle East. In adopting this approach, and in presenting the cases from each region in a separate chapter, we do not presume to generalize about the region as a whole. Too much has already been written about the Internet in the Middle East and Asia without acknowledging the variation that exists within each region or appreciating the national context of individual countries.

Rather, a regional approach to case selection is advantageous for both practical and substantive reasons. Much of the secondary literature on the Internet in authoritarian regimes, upon which these cases studies rely, is organized regionally. In addition, regional institutions (such as the Association of Southeast Asian Nations, or ASEAN) and region-specific geopolitical concerns matter in government approaches to Internet regulation and the impact of the technology in each country. Our choice of specific regions was influenced by the availability of data and the extent of Internet diffusion and use. The other regions with a large concentration of authoritarian regimes are Africa and Central Asia; in general, Internet development in those regions is sparse, and less secondary literature covers them. As more data become available in the future, we hope that others will take up the task of examining cases in Africa, Central Asia, and elsewhere.

We chose cases within each region so as to provide variation in size, wealth, the nature of the economy, and the approach to dealing with the Internet. The Southeast Asian cases are quite different on each of those measures. Singapore, a semi-authoritarian regime, is small, extremely wealthy, and highly interconnected with the global economy. It has been a leader in Internet development in ways that many other authoritarian (and some democratic) regimes have sought to emulate. Vietnam is a much poorer and more authoritarian country, with a communist history and an ambivalent relationship with the West. However, its population is young and relatively literate, and its government has shown an interest in leveraging ICTs for development. Burma is governed by a strict military regime; it is poor, economically stagnant, and more isolated than any other country in the region. It has taken the most reluctant stance toward the Internet, and little diffusion of the technology has occurred thus far.

The cases in the Middle East exhibit similar variation. The United Arab Emirates is comparable to Singapore in many ways—it is a small, wealthy country that serves as a regional financial center, has extensive ties to the global economy, and has enthusiastically promoted ICT development. Oil is also extremely important to the economy of the United Arab Emirates, and its overwhelming foreign national population creates a distinct political dynamic. Saudi Arabia is a large but sparsely populated country governed by a traditional monarchy. The political consequences of its extensive oil wealth and the strong influence of Islam in its politics are both important factors that mediate the impact of the Internet. Saudi Arabia has taken a cautious approach to Internet development thus far. Egypt is a large, highly populous, and poorer country governed by a semi-authoritarian regime. Officially, it is a secular state, but Islam is an important factor in its politics. Egypt is unique among our cases in that it has placed no real restrictions on the Internet.

Our focus on current authoritarian regimes means that we have not selected known historical cases where certain uses of the Internet may have facilitated political challenges. We have chosen, for example, not to look at e-mail use in Russia during the 1991 coup attempt, at Internet use by supporters of the 1994 Zapatista uprising in Mexico, or at the use of e-mail by students coordinating the protests that contributed to the 1998 fall of Suharto in Indonesia. These cases are frequently offered as anecdotal evidence of the Internet's threat to authoritarian regimes (even though analysts have had difficulty drawing a direct causal link between Internet use and eventual political change in each case).[24] We avoided these and similar cases for two reasons: we were wary of selecting cases based on anecdotes, and we wished to focus on current authoritarian regimes rather than cases of transition in the past. Had we taken a more historical approach to case selection, we would not have been able to examine a full range of Internet use in each country. The Internet is a new phenomenon throughout the developing world, and it was only a nascent technology in Indonesia, Mexico, and Russia at the time of the events in question.

The issue of the Internet's impact on authoritarian regimes is a subset of the larger question of ICT use in developing country politics. Thus, we do not consider many cases that fall only within the latter category, such as the use of the Internet for environmental activism with regard to the Brazilian rainforest or the use of mobile text messaging to coordinate political demonstrations in the Philippines before the ouster of the Estrada government in January 2001. Some analysts have suggested that Internet use may have a greater political impact in new or weak democracies such as these, a point we do not dispute.[25] We feel, however, that conventional wisdom on the Internet in authoritarian regimes is prevalent enough to justify our more narrow focus in this study.

Policy Implications

We hope that one of the main impacts of this study will be to challenge conventional wisdom on the Internet's impact on authoritarian regimes and to provide a framework for systematic thinking about this issue. Conventional wisdom is most prevalent at the level of high rhetoric. Admittedly, democracy promoters at such organizations as the National Democratic Institute (NDI) and the United States Agency for International Development (USAID) have a more realistic view of what contributes to the downfall of authoritarian regimes. Conventional wisdom, however, forms part of the gestalt in which policy is formulated, and a better understanding of the Internet's political effects should lead to better policy. Beliefs about the Internet's inevitable challenge to authoritarian rule imply that policy makers can simply encourage free trade and promote technological development, letting the positive political consequences flow naturally from those actions. The analysis that we present in this study suggests that such thinking is oversimplified. In reality, specific concrete actions are most important for the promotion of democracy, in both the technological and nontechnological spheres.

Therefore, in addition to challenging the conventional wisdom about the Internet's political impact, we call for increased attention to how the different uses of the Internet are likely to affect authoritarian regimes. To the extent that policy makers *can* encourage particular uses of the Internet in authoritarian countries, they may wish to do so. We believe, however, that it is not always in the interest of the United States to demand immediate change from authoritarian regimes. As Catharin Dalpino has argued, openness in authoritarian regimes is a good thing in and of itself, and insisting on rapid change rather than gradual liberalization can be counterproductive.[26] It may be important to support some uses of the Internet—such as e-government measures that increase transparency and reduce governmental corruption—even if they pose no challenge to authoritarian rule in the short to medium term. Our study should help policy makers to think about how the Internet can best be used to support political changes that are in the interest of both the United States and the citizens of existing authoritarian regimes.

CHAPTER TWO

Wired for Modernization in China

Imagine if the Internet took hold in China. Imagine how freedom would spread.

—George W. Bush, Phoenix, Arizona, December 7, 1999

Most followers of international affairs are now familiar with assertions of the Internet's potential to change China drastically. Certainly, access has grown exponentially since the country's first connection to the Internet in 1993. Domains and web sites have proliferated, while growing millions access the Internet from personal computers at home and the office. In major cities, cafeteria-sized Internet cafés host a generation accustomed more to cell phones and consumerism than to communist dogma. Chinese Internet companies seek and attain listings on U.S. stock markets, while foreign investors hail China's entry to the World Trade Organization. Beijing's municipal government boasts a web site where citizens can e-mail their mayor with grievances. Jiang Zemin, the leader who presided over much of this transformation, has spoken glowingly of "a borderless information space around the world."[1]

Yet tugging at the rhetoric is another reality. China's own information space is restricted by regulations inherited from prereform years. Its expansion is driven by five-year plans. Even as the so-called wired elite mushrooms and gains influence, growing numbers are arrested for expressing antigovernment views online. Falun Gong followers who use the Internet to spread information are sent to reeducation camps. Meanwhile, millions outside China's urban centers still lack telephones, much less Internet access.

Clearly, the hype over China's experience with the Internet belies a far more complicated scenario, one that does not lend itself easily to pat characterizations of political impact. Yet many have tried. A number of inter-

13

national observers have suggested that the technology poses a potent threat to China's political system, that a tide of forbidden images and ideas will simply sweep away half a century of outmoded thinking. Others believe that the Internet will become a tool of the Chinese regime, which will use increasingly powerful monitoring and surveillance technologies to stay one step ahead of the democracy-seeking masses.

The truth is considerably more complex than either extreme and difficult to discern. In part this is because the government's attitude has been contradictory, leading to uneven and sometimes unintended policy outcomes. The population of Chinese Internet users also defies easy labeling, especially as it expands in scope and scale. Perhaps what is most important is that China's approach to the information revolution is forged by its historical approach to modernization, which itself has warranted volumes of exposition.

Here, we paint a nuanced picture of China's Internet evolution, tracing its beginnings in ministries and inefficient bureaucracies to its myriad current uses in China's government, economy, and society. Even as competing sources of information broaden the public sphere of debate, the Chinese government has pursued a number of measures—from web site blocking to punitive deterrents—designed to shape the physical and symbolic environments in which Internet use takes place. The state is also vigorously encouraging Internet-driven development, harnessing the Internet for specific political and economic aims. Choosing a proactive approach, China has sought to use information technology, and in particular the Internet, to address such high-level issues as corruption, transparency, local government reform, and the development of poor areas. It has incorporated concepts of information-age warfare into its rethinking of military affairs. China has looked abroad for guidance on how to balance ICT promotion with authoritarian political control. Meanwhile, its state-led model of Internet development has served as a model for other authoritarian regimes, such as Cuba's (see chapter 3).

Hence, we argue that the state's attempts to direct and define the political impact of Internet use are, for now, succeeding. By its very nature, however, China's market-led approach is designed to increase popular access to the technology substantially, potentially increasing the government's vulnerability to challenges from Internet use.[2]

From the Iron Rice Bowl to the World Trade Organization

The People's Republic of China is a one-party authoritarian state that has been ruled by the Chinese Communist Party (CCP) since October 1, 1949.

The CCP controls all top government and military positions, as well as the media and security apparatus. It is headed by Hu Jintao, the hand-selected successor to former party chief Jiang Zemin.[3] The National People's Congress, a unicameral legislature that follows party dictates, elects the president and vice president and appoints the State Council, or cabinet. The president appoints the premier.

With nearly 1.3 billion people, China is the largest country in the world, a factor that makes the question of its development globally relevant. Its economy, officially pegged as growing by 7–8 percent a year, is the world's seventh largest. Despite recent growth and development, China is ranked a lower-middle-income country by the World Bank: 18.5 percent of the population lives on less than a dollar a day.[4] While the eastern urban centers have been rapidly modernizing, the vast majority of the population still lives in the countryside. An urban per capita disposable income of $759 in 2000 contrasted sharply with a rural per capita net income of $278.[5] Addressing the significant development gap between the country's eastern and western provinces will be a top economic and political priority in the years ahead.

After decades of inefficient and sometimes disastrous central planning, reforms begun in 1978 at the behest of leader Deng Xiaoping started the country on the slow path to a more market-based economy. Ministries and other government organs were forced to reorganize and adopt competitive practices. State-owned enterprises began the painful transformation from "iron rice bowls," which provided lifetime worker security, to the desired goal of efficient profit-seeking corporations. Sectors such as transport, power, aviation, and telecommunications were encouraged to attract overseas investment, initially seeking cooperation through turnkey and equipment-manufacturing projects rather than the foreign operation of key infrastructure. Although *guanxi,* the system of personal connections used to grease wheels in politics and business, remained important, the government made an effort to institutionalize market reform. National legislation was devised to eliminate favoritism and to attract overseas capital. More recently, the government has begun a five-year legislative work program to develop and revise laws relevant to World Trade Organization entry, including those pertaining to corporations, bankruptcy, trust, unfair competition, telecommunications, and trademarks and patents.

In 1992, Deng Xiaoping undertook a groundbreaking trip to the southern provinces to spur further economic growth. In the wake of that trip, capitalist fervor began to build and reached a fever pitch, particularly in the southern and eastern coastal provinces. With the aid of special economic zones to attract foreign investment through favorable investment and tax policies, growth in these regions began to outpace inland and rural areas rapidly. In the early 1990s, the largest, most well-connected (and occasionally well-managed) state-owned enterprises (SOEs) were chosen to attract foreign equity capital through listings on the Hong Kong and New York stock exchanges. Meanwhile, the country set up its own domestic stock markets in Shanghai and Shenzhen. The flurry of capitalist activity helped to create an unprecedented crop of Chinese millionaires and has led to a growing symbiosis between the party and formerly reviled private entrepreneurs.[6] At the same time, SOE reform continues to throw millions out of work, causing job seekers to migrate in huge numbers to the cities. With unofficial unions forbidden, labor advocates say scores of factory employees work in unsafe and unsanitary conditions. Peasant and worker protests have erupted in rising numbers. Against this backdrop, the government has highlighted Internet-driven economic activity and education as vehicles to accommodate more of the country's labor force. The CCP leadership also realizes that the development of a knowledge-based economy that significantly boosts standards of living can pay significant dividends in the form of broader support among the population.

Fears of social unrest and anarchy, underscored by personal experience of the chaotic Cultural Revolution during the 1960s and 1970s, have motivated the current generation of Chinese leaders to proceed more cautiously with political than with economic reforms, and at times the leaders have reacted harshly to perceived threats to stability. The government has embarked on an intense crackdown on crime and particularly corruption, seen as an endemic and high-priority problem. Such crackdowns usually involve large-scale capital punishment for convicted offenders: China executes more prisoners each year than all other countries combined. According to some estimates, at least 2,468 people were put to death in 2001 alone.[7] China has dealt with other perceived threats swiftly and harshly, including the pro-democracy uprising in 1989, the more recent emergence of the China Democracy Party, and the rise of the Falun Gong spiritual movement. Increasingly, dissidents and even ordinary citizens who express controversial views on the Internet are detained and punished. Viewed in this context, China's authoritarian system seems to have undergone little significant change in recent years.

Yet political reform has not been wholly absent. As Minxin Pei notes, many important political (although not necessarily democratizing) reforms have taken place since the late 1970s: the strengthening of national and local legislatures, legal reform, mandatory retirement for government officials, meritocracy, and (limited) rural self-government. Such actions have helped to build the institutional infrastructure necessary to safeguard economic reforms. At the same time, these changes have not addressed the Communist Party's continuing monopoly on state power, which limits the effects of continuing civil service reform and grassroots experiments in self-government.[8]

While conventional wisdom tends to envision political change driven by grassroots political pressure, a significant impulse for reform comes from within the government itself. Many current leaders possesses "technocrat" credentials stemming from backgrounds in economics and engineering. These credentials have helped to shape China's current approach to the information revolution. A new generation of leaders, promoted for merit-based reasons as well as party loyalty and communist credentials, is gradually taking command of an increasingly professional bureaucracy. In 1980, only 4 percent of China's ruling elite had a college degree; now more than 90 percent do. Members of this so-called fourth generation—the "baby boomer" crop—have earned degrees from U.S. universities and are more comfortable with non-Chinese culture than are previous generations, although many retain a strong nationalistic orientation.

In the coming years, as WTO–linked reforms take effect, China is likely to experience increasing social and political turbulence. Much depends on the attitude of the new leadership toward political reform. Should such reforms stagnate, leaving an increasingly unemployed population with little outlet for frustration, the prospect of wide-scale unrest is possible. Moreover, increased engagement with the world in general may leave China open to pressure from transnational advocacy networks and other nonstate actors. At the same time, China may push harder for a stronger hand in regional decision making and leadership, through such vehicles as the Asia Pacific Economic Cooperation (APEC) and alliances with central Asian nations. Essentially, China is entering the information age during a period of heightened domestic turbulence and an increased emphasis on foreign policy.

Centrally Planning an Information Age

Control of information has been central to the Chinese Communist Party's governing strategy ever since it came to power. Present-day discussions of the Internet in China often emphasize the tension the technology high-lights between economic modernization and political control. Yet this delicate balance has been historically addressed by state strategies toward earlier ICTs. Current attempts to guide the birth of China's information age can be better understood within this context.

Under Mao Zedong's command economy, the media's function was to serve the state through imposing ideological hegemony. This goal was accomplished by overwhelming the citizenry in every aspect of daily life with official information and interpretations of reality.[9] Mao's regime was characterized by the vertical control of communication, exemplified by a media system that acted as a conveyer belt carrying party thought from the leaders to the masses. This was complemented by a telecommunication network that was accessible only to elites, discouraging the public from communicating with one another.[10]

The necessity of inculcating revolutionary values meant that propaganda work was allotted its own powerful ministry. While the media (radio, television, and newspapers) were seen as propaganda tools, telecommunications were classified bureaucratically under the division of finance and economy. Meanwhile, the policing of telecommunication networks was the responsibility of the public security apparatus.[11] This division can be seen to this day: Internet content providers have been artificially divided from Internet service providers and will be allowed different foreign ownership limits under the WTO.[12] Meanwhile, control over broadband development has become a battleground between the propaganda-affiliated State Administration of Radio, Film, and Television (SARFT) and the telecommunication regulator, the Ministry of Information Industry (MII).

With the advent of economic reforms in the late 1970s, the role of the media began to change. No longer defined as instruments of class struggle, media organs were promoted as tools of economic and cultural development, emphasizing business information and entertainment.[13] Since then, the responsibilities and functions of media have continued to evolve, shifting in response to both domestic and global pressures. Lynch notes that commercialization, globalization, and pluralization have all combined to break down state control over "thought work," or the state's ability to shape the ideological environment.[14]

Certainly, commercial pressures have been a primary factor behind the diversification and continuing professionalization of media. With fewer state subsidies and heightened profit concerns, state-controlled media are trying to boost their audiences by increasingly exploring previously taboo areas, such as investigative journalism.[15] This more aggressive style of reporting is especially visible in local and provincial publications far from the eyes of Beijing. By making available a wide range of official news in one place, Chinese Internet portals have been encouraging competition between news organizations. This competition is heightened because news at times appears on the Internet either exclusively or before other traditional media outlets can publish it.

Yet commercialization and diversification are viewed with ambivalence by the Chinese leadership. Although Premier Zhu Rongji exhorted the media in 2001 to act as the watchdog of government, encouraging the exposure of corruption and government misdeeds, state regulations and actions have presented a conflicting image. Progressive publishing houses have been reined in, while journalists continue to be harassed and imprisoned for exposing official wrongdoing. An August 2001 campaign to clamp down on the media included a list of "Seven No's," banning media involvement in seven broad areas. These include the revelation of state secrets, interference in the work of the party and government, and the negation of "the guiding role of Marxism." Similar rules exist for news and information on the Internet; many are simply new iterations of past media regulations.

Convergence and Control in Telecommunications

Increased competition and commercialization have also characterized recent developments in telecommunications in China that have been crucial in shaping the current diffusion of the Internet. While public network construction was not a policy priority from the 1950s to the 1970s, in the early 1980s telecommunications was redefined as a key infrastructure essential to economic development. As Yuezhi Zhao puts it, central planning combined with local market incentives contributed to the fastest telecommunications build-up in history.[16] At the same time, supervision of the network fell to several different ministries. Although the Chinese public telecommunication sector was a state monopoly, in practice several administrative bodies carried out regulation. While general operation and oversight fell under the purview of the powerful Ministry of Posts and Telecommunications (MPT), the State Council served as the highest central authority for the telecommunication sector. The State Planning Commission approved the MPT's tariff policy, and the State Economic and

Trade Commission administered such state enterprises as the Directorate General of Telecommunications (the precursor of China Telecom).[17]

In essence, the fragmented regulatory regime foreshadowed the current competition between ministries to stake claims in the developing Internet sector. Although the MPT harmonized policies up until the late 1980s, technological convergence posed increasing complications. While the State Council attempted to manage conflict between ministries, a lack of concrete legislation meant that policy coordination was often left to negotiation and administrative measures.[18] During this period several ministries were campaigning for their own networks to bypass the inefficient MPT–operated public network. These ministries, which included the Ministry of Railways, the Ministry of Electronic Industry (MEI), and the Ministry of Power, eventually succeeded not only in establishing private networks, but in creating the basis for increased competition in the sector. In 1994 the central government formally created Unicom, a network backed by the aforementioned ministries, intended to compete with the MPT's Directorate General of Telecommunications. This branch was renamed China Telecom, responsible for operating and managing the MPT's fixed and mobile networks, while the MPT was left as a regulator.[19]

While partially introducing competition in the sector and establishing an independent telecommunications regulator, the changes also proved cosmetic in some ways since China Telecom remained directly under the regulatory authority's control. During subsequent years, despite continuing attempts to promote competition and standardize the telecommunication sector, bureaucratic sniping and confusion in the chain of oversight caused further policy paralysis. Finally, in 1998, the MPT and MEI were merged into the superministry MII. The MII was charged with administrating and regulating the entire information industry and was organized into departments responsible for policy making, administration, market regulation, and internal affairs.[20]

Throughout all the years of internal fighting and ministerial-level competition, the Chinese telecommunication sector remained nonetheless shielded from outside competition. During much of its history, the CCP has insisted on tight restrictions on foreign investment in what it sees as its most strategic sectors; until recently, therefore, foreign businesses were not allowed to own, operate, or manage telecommunication networks or services. Some analysts point to China's need to bargain for WTO accession as the driving force behind its eventually agreeing to allow foreign investment, while others see the decision as an inevitable by-product of globalization.[21] Whatever the reason, heightened competition is being hailed by many in China as a new force in standardizing and developing China's telecommunication landscape, although the sector's history suggests that future challenges lie in the realization of that goal.

A New Piece of Turf: The Internet

Just as in other countries, China's academic community established the first computer networks, sending the country's first international e-mail through a gateway in Germany in the late 1980s. In the early 1990s, the State Education Commission began building a more comprehensive academic network with funding from the central government. At the same time, the MPT began building its own packet-switching network, establishing its early dominance in voice and data communication. Its competitor, the Ministry of Electronics Industry, also began a set of new networks, known as Golden Projects, to link customs and financial networks.[22] These Golden Projects formed the basis for "informatization," originally used to refer to the use of information technology to streamline government processes and allow the central government better oversight of administrative processes at the periphery. The MEI's involvement in the process also highlights the early competition between various arms of government that persists to this day.

By 1995 the Internet had begun expanding in a somewhat uncoordinated manner, although the State Council still placed controls on organizations involved in its development. In an attempt to recentralize network development, the State Council subsequently set up a steering committee on national information infrastructure to consolidate Internet policy making and assume responsibility for issues related to informatization in China. In 1996 this committee made a key decision to establish an Internet access scheme that featured two tiers: users would connect to the first level, while that level itself connected to the Internet only through a second tier of state-controlled interconnecting networks. Therefore, all international Internet connections were to be made through a small number of state-controlled backbone networks.[23] To this day, the number of these backbone networks—now run by ministries and other competing collections of powerful interests—remains limited, even while Internet service providers (ISPs) and Internet content providers (ICPs) proliferate in the thousands. The future success of the backbones is often predicated on the strength of their political clout: the rising China Netcom, for example, is partially backed by the Chinese Academy of Sciences, the State Administration of Radio, Film, and Television, and by Jiang Mianheng, a Shanghai information-industry player and the U.S.–educated son of Jiang Zemin.

Despite attempts to centralize administrative oversight, the Internet continued to serve as the battleground for turf wars between various ministries, chiefly the MEI and the powerful MPT. Even though their merger has helped to eliminate much of the bureaucratic paralysis, overlaps as well as gaps in oversight remain. The policing and supervision of the Internet, for example, still fall to the Ministry of State Security. At present, at least nine party and government organizations see the Internet as part of their bureaucratic domain, and both the local and national arms of the bureaucracy have commercial interests in promoting the new technology.[24] In 2000, for instance, the Shanghai Foreign Investment Committee licensed a wholly foreign-owned company to operate as an Internet content provider, an act expressly forbidden by national rules. To this day, various "camps" within the MII still identify with their pre-merger ministries and attempt to stake claims accordingly. Inefficiencies and lack of communication between bureaus also hamper the effective centralized control of the Internet.

Moreover, technological convergence still causes various complexities. The Internet was originally seen as a tool of mass communication as well as an outgrowth of the telecommunication network. As such, it did not fit neatly into either the state's propaganda apparatus or its telecommunication branch, both of which were vertically controlled and separate from each other.[25] The State Administration of Radio, Film, and Television, which falls under the propaganda structure and controls the cable networks, is feuding with the MII over the right to develop and provide broadband capabilities. Although the feud has certainly encouraged the simultaneous and thus more extensive construction of the information infrastructure, at times the bureaucratic battles have led to street battles, complete with wire cutters, armed gangs, and casualties.[26] A line in China's 2001–2005 Five-Year Plan states that convergence will happen, but gives little guidance on its structure or timeline.[27]

Entry in the World Trade Organization has posed further challenges. China has agreed to allow 49 percent foreign investment in value-added services one year after entry and 50 percent foreign ownership two years after entry. It has also agreed to allow, incrementally, the foreign ownership of up to 49 percent of domestic and international packet and circuit-switching services six years after entry. Chinese officials have orally stated that Internet content providers fall under the category of value-added services, and Internet service providers under the category of switching services, but it is still unclear how much foreign equity participation will be permitted in such areas as the key backbone networks.[28] Many anticipate protracted post–WTO negotiations and disputes.

Regardless of such disputes, Internet diffusion is expected to continue at a fast clip over the next several years. According to the official survey of Chinese Internet users conducted by the China Internet Network Information Center, the number of users reached 33.7 million people by January 2002, a jump of 11.2 million people from 2001.[29] Although growth in user numbers now appears to be slowing, marketing firms still predict that by 2004 China will overtake Japan as the Asian country with the most Internet users.[30] Surveys also indicate that usage is beginning to increase beyond the wealthy, educated elite and that the average age of users will continue to drop. The typical home Internet user, according to a survey conducted by marketing research firm Iamasia, is thirty years old, earns about $221 a month, and is university educated.

Informatization and Its Discontents

Initially conceived of as a far less sweeping concept, informatization has grown to encompass a complete rethinking of how information technology factors into economic, political, and social development. The Tenth Five-Year Plan specifies ambitious targets for China's ICT industry growth, devoting an entire section to "accelerating national economic development and popularizing information technology throughout society."[31] Officials envision ICT implementation and innovation in sectors ranging from education and health to agriculture and industry. Just as the "Four Modernizations" of the late 1970s formed the basis for Deng Xiaoping's comprehensive economic reforms, so the thrust to enter the information age colors much of the country's current approach to political reform and economic development.

The pressures brought on by economic reform underscore the urgency of modernization through informatization. As state enterprises fire millions of workers, China desperately needs to find new ways to employ its huge workforce productively. Many economists see the development of a knowledge-based economy as key to ameliorating the effects of wide-ranging industrial reform. As such, in contrast to some other authoritarian countries, the commercial growth of the Internet is strongly encouraged, albeit under a mass of oft-confusing regulations.

Yet it is obvious that not everyone is benefiting immediately from informatization. A poor telecommunication infrastructure in the impoverished western provinces has led to increased dialogue within China about how to bridge the country's internal "digital divide," or the gap between the technological haves and have-nots. The promotion of the Internet thus forms part of a larger strategy to bridge uneven development between the rich eastern provinces and poor western ones. Government officials also emphasize the potential to leapfrog stages of development and close the gap, not only between the country's east and west but between China and the developed world. At various levels of government, innovative initiatives are being taken to improve rural life through use of ICTs. Many of these initiatives increasingly involve the input of nonstate actors and the private sector, relying on lessons from other developing countries.

Economic development is not the only goal of Internet promotion. Some government officials also see informatization as changing the very scope and structure of government processes, spearheading the campaign for "reform and openness." While some question the sincerity of such efforts, many party cadres and others genuinely desire some level of political reform, even though initiated from within the state. These officials see informatization as a force that will break down dusty hierarchies within the state structure and foster new organizations in a middle layer between the state and society.[32] Those who benefit personally from a less transparent bureaucracy, as well as those who favor a more authoritarian environment in which information resources are restricted, may be wary of the changes that informatization promises.

Finally, the promotion of the Internet is important in the context of China's long, complicated history with the West. As many analysts have noted, underlying much of the rhetoric about informatization lies the hope that by using, adapting, and improving upon a technology originally conceived in the West, China will have finally overcome past humiliations to achieve its rightful place among the pantheon of developed, modern nations.[33] Moreover, despite its WTO entry, China is ambivalent about the effects of economic globalization. In particular, it is worried about challenges to its sovereignty through an excessive dependence on Western ICT products and systems. This has led to the official encouragement of the open-source Red Flag Linux operating system over Microsoft products and the promotion of a domestic information technology industry that shares the leaders' vision of an online landscape with "Chinese characteristics."

All this means that China's leaders recognize the need to nurture a technologically savvy, well-educated, and informed populace that will both benefit from and enhance a knowledge-based economy. Therefore, unlike other authoritarian regimes that carefully mete out access, the Chinese government has chosen to encourage mass Internet usage and education in an environment that it is able to shape if not wholly control. Yet the leadership is also wary of the potential effects of an unfettered flow of information. The networked, decentralized nature of this new medium means Chinese leaders must constantly work to balance ICT promotion with political control. The central leadership must also constantly struggle to construct and maintain a coherent, unified vision for Internet development, even as various ministries and other organs battle to assume control over an increasingly strategic sector.

Areas of Use

A "Healthy and Orderly" Public Sphere

Much of the speculation about the Internet's political effects in China has centered on its impact on the mass public. Because the medium allows unprecedented access to multiple sources of images, news, and ideas, some believe it can challenge state hegemony over the distribution of information and ideologies.[34] As more and more of China's educated urban professionals and youth gain access to the Internet, they are becoming increasingly aware of foreign products, culture, and political norms.

New commercial web sites, featuring topics ranging from pollution to homosexuality, place formerly taboo issues solidly in the realm of public debate. Even official media organs use their web sites to post news that is unavailable in print or on the air.[35] For less than the price of a long-distance phone call, ordinary people can use e-mail to communicate with friends and acquaintances far away. Moreover, in chat rooms and bulletin boards focusing on political and social themes, users are able to circulate news and opinions, thereby generating nationwide discussions not previously possible. Some suggest that as a direct result of participation in these forums, the Chinese people will place demands for political liberalization on the state.[36]

In response to the potential challenges posed by the mass use of the Internet, Chinese authorities have forgone explicit control over every facet of Internet use in favor of seeking to shape what they term a "healthy and orderly" online environment.[37] To do this, they have adopted two main strategies: filtering material and the promotion of self-censorship through regulation, policing, and punitive action. Sites deemed politically sensitive, such as those of overseas human rights organizations and certain news organizations, are blocked by a nationwide firewall.[38] Regulations issued by the Ministry of Information Industry in October 2000 require ISPs to report on users and forbid politically sensitive information from being disseminated on the Internet. These and other regulations make clear that potentially "subversive" comments—including those promoting Taiwanese independence or highlighting Falun Gong practices—will not be tolerated.[39] Web site administrators are required to hire censors, known as "cleaning ladies" or "big mamas," to screen for and quickly remove offensive material from bulletin boards and chat rooms.

In 2001 a three-month police sweep of more than sixty thousand Internet cafés nationwide further encouraged café owners to keep a close eye on patrons and prompted users to patrol their own activities.[40] The official Chinese news agency Xinhua has reported that many cafés have installed a new type of security software that enables local public security bureaus to trace user surfing records as well as remotely monitor café web use, twenty-four hours a day (reportedly, the software is also available for use in homes and schools). Local public security bureaus have set up their own "Internet police" units, dealing specifically with cyberoffenses. Whether or not this comprehensive monitoring is implemented everywhere, the threat alone may be enough to deter users from visiting politically sensitive sites. The government is also actively seeking foreign help with its monitoring technology: fairs organized by the Ministry of State Security have attracted many large multinationals peddling such products as blocking and antihacking software.[41]

To reinforce its message, the government has arrested and detained several Internet users who have fallen afoul of the regulations or otherwise strayed into politically sensitive areas. Commonly, such detainees are not full-time dissidents or activists; many have merely voiced a politically sensitive opinion online. Middle-school teacher Jiang Shihua, for instance, was sentenced to two years in prison for posting the words, "We all think about one sentence that none of us will say: overthrow the Communist Party" while discussing government corruption on the Nanchong city web site. Others brought to trial include the operator of a Tiananmen-themed site, Huang Qi, and a distributor of the Chinese-language version of *The Tiananmen Papers,* Li Hongmin. While the government has traditionally clamped down on pro-democracy Internet users, it has also begun to apply pressure to hard-line communist critics, who feel that China's economic modernization has strayed from the path of pure Marxism.

By employing this mixture of regulation, policing, threats, and punitive action, the state hopes to contain and define new patterns of independent communication. It is also possible that the government is using the Internet as a form of "preemptive liberalization." In some authoritarian regimes, the state has responded to the challenge of economic liberalization by preemptively allowing forms of political liberalization—such as the broadening of acceptable discourse—to alleviate pressure while enjoying the boosted legitimacy that follows from such actions.[42] In this case, the Chinese government appears to be tacitly encouraging the public to air its views in the somewhat controlled environment of Internet chat rooms rather than in areas beyond state purview.

Yet this emerging public sphere is not easily categorized: while some users laud liberal democracy, others glorify China's Cultural Revolution and nihilistic Red Guards. As the volume and diversity of viewpoints grow, blunt state countermeasures are increasingly being tested. During several incidents Internet users engaged in politically volatile discussions that were both critical and supportive of the government. At times these discussions severely threatened the state's control of information. They also paint a complex picture of emerging trends in both online and offline Chinese public opinion.

For instance, following a Jiangxi province schoolhouse blast in February 2001, Chinese Internet users contradicted the government explanation that a sole madman was responsible for the explosion. They suggested instead that schoolchildren had been forced to construct firecrackers on the school grounds, which is illegal. Many abandoned self-censorship and harshly criticized government policies that failed to tackle such problems as child labor and underfunded schools. Although many of the controversial comments were deleted and chat rooms were shut down, enough posts remained to spark a wider debate, one that extended beyond Jiangxi to mesmerize much of the educated public. The ensuing groundswell of public outrage eventually led to a public apology by Zhu Rongji about the government's handling of the incident. The apology was an unprecedented act, one that underscored the growing importance to the Chinese leadership of both public

opinion and the medium through which it is voiced. For the first time officials were confronted with the Internet's potential to turn a small provincial
occurrence into an event of national importance.

China's leaders have proved equally, if not more, sensitive to nationalistic criticism. The U.S. spy plane incident on Hainan Island in 2001 also
touched off a flurry of online activity. The national mouthpiece newspaper, the *People's Daily,* has a "Strong Country" web forum, set up earlier
by the newspaper to stoke nationalism after the bombing of the Chinese
embassy in Belgrade. It witnessed an outpouring of vitriolic jingoism and
anti-Americanism. Similarly hued postings also rose in volume following
the September 11 terrorist attacks on the United States. On both occa-
sions, censors struggled to keep up with the scope and scale of comments,
often deleting the most extreme anti-American postings.

Such incidents illustrate how the Internet is increasingly crystallizing
public dissatisfaction with government while amplifying, however artificially, nationalistic sentiment. When dissatisfaction and nationalism over-
lap, they can place significant pressures on the regime. The government
has historically used nationalism to bolster its public support and divert
attention from domestic problems. Thus, during normal periods, much
official news on domestic web sites features a nationalistic tone or anti-
Taiwan or -American rhetoric. Yet during times of crisis, the government
is especially sensitive to nationalist critiques that question the regime's
legitimacy, particularly because such criticism has been used to overthrow
Chinese rulers in the past. In essence, the Chinese government is still trying to finesse the delicate line between massaging nationalism to boost
regime legitimacy and inadvertently encouraging overly militant public
opinion that questions the regime's qualifications and capacity to lead.
Although the opinions expressed online may not necessarily represent those
of the population at large, web forums have undoubtedly helped to mag-
nify this phenomenon, encouraging concrete state reactions.[43]

In sum, the public use of the Internet presents myriad challenges to
China's government. Many of these challenges are currently being coun-
tered within China's established framework of Internet control through a
combination of reactive and proactive government strategies. These actions can be seen in the fact that most users do practice some form of self-
censorship, generally avoiding politically sensitive web sites and the
expression of controversial opinions on politically sensitive topics. The
government can also rely on the natural predilection of many Chinese
Internet users: like Internet café patrons around the world, Chinese café-

goers more often than not spend their time playing games and e-mailing friends rather than attempting to contact overseas Falun Gong or Western news media sites. Surveys of Internet users find that most spend little time attempting to access proxy servers that allow access to forbidden sites.[44] Many users also favor some form of regulation of the Internet.[45] In many ways, there is an increasing convergence between current usage of the medium and the official vision for the Internet's development.

Yet, as users become more comfortable with the medium and the self-expression it enables, the government's existing strategies may be unable to circumscribe the growing online public sphere. For the state to realize its informatization goals fully, it has no choice but to continue its strategy of increasing mass access to the Internet, including the expansion of home access and the technological prowess of everyday users. The result is likely to be a population more difficult to monitor and potentially harder to restrain than the current generation of Internet users. Particularly in times of crisis, the government's efforts to control the online discourse may be overwhelmed, as in various incidents throughout 2001. As such, while the online population evolves, the government is likely to let its strategy evolve accordingly.

Development and Dissent in Civil Society

Internet use by domestic civil society organizations presents another, equally visible difficulty.[46] Recent reforms have led to changes in the relations between the Chinese state and society, creating space for rapidly forming and evolving groups that increasingly wield economic and political power.[47] Since the state views the emergence of large independent groups as a threat, it has attempted to disable quickly those it considers politically threatening. When these groups have used the Internet to organize and communicate, the state has responded with a series of technological measures, restrictive laws, and well-publicized crackdowns.

The Western media have chiefly focused on the case of the Falun Gong, the spiritual movement that has used the Internet to coordinate protests in China and spread information around the world. Although it has since evolved into a transnational movement, Falun Gong originally gained critical mass in China in the late 1990s, when followers started using the Internet to circulate the teachings of founder Li Hongzhi. The group soon established the Internet as the primary medium from which new and essential teachings could be downloaded and through which widely dispersed followers could establish local contacts. Falun Gong has also used the Internet to present a public face to the world and counter Chinese government claims about its practices.[48]

After an April 1999 protest that was in part organized over the Internet, authorities moved quickly to suppress the group's web use within China, shutting down its domestic web sites and blocking public access to those overseas. Subsequent Internet regulations included clauses forbidding the circulation of the "teachings of evil cults." Although the transnational group still relies on the Internet, mainland Chinese followers now find it difficult to communicate by e-mail with those overseas; increasingly, domestic adherents rely on pay phones and other low-end ICTs, which are less easy to trace.[49] While some mainland Chinese followers possess the technical prowess necessary to access overseas Falun Gong sites and evade identification, the government's campaign to eradicate the bulk of the domestic movement—in part by blocking their access to technology, in part through arrests and brainwashing—appears to be succeeding.

Other groups and individual dissidents who have sought to use the web to disseminate information have also met with arrest and imprisonment. Although it never attained the status of a formal opposition party, the now-dispersed China Democracy Party also claimed the Internet was critical to its formation and rapid early mobilization. In 1998 the group used e-mail to publicize its platform, growing from twelve to two hundred members and forming branches nationwide as a result, according to its founders.[50] The government halted the movement by arresting members and imprisoning them on charges of sending e-mails to exiled dissidents. Meanwhile, Shanghai software entrepreneur Lin Hai was arrested for providing a Washington, D.C.–based pro-democracy publication, *VIP Reference,* with domestic e-mail addresses.

On the other hand, state-connected CSOs not only have access to the Internet but are encouraged to use it in innovative ways to organize and disseminate information, in line with China's overarching plan for informatization. Organizations such as the All-China Women's Federation (ACWF) have made Internet use and skill acquisition a priority at all levels of the hierarchy. Originally a "mass organization" designed to act as a transmission belt from the party to the masses, the ACWF is changing and becoming modern, using e-mail and informative web pages to increase its contacts with overseas women's groups. The ACWF has also begun making extensive use of the web to disseminate health and domestic abuse information to rural Chinese women, although the success of such campaigns largely depends on the extent of Internet access in the countryside. Officials clearly see the Internet as increasingly crucial in augmenting their continuing work to educate rural women and to lift them out of poverty.

In essence, the government's unstated policy is to crack down harshly on a few key examples of politically sensitive Internet use while simultaneously increasing Internet access and usage in the rest of the public sphere. Since this policy, however, does not rely on carefully meting out access to the politically loyal, opponents of the regime will benefit from Internet use, at least until detected and identified as a threat, to the same extent as do sanctioned organizations. Government-connected CSOs such as professional associations, official trade unions, and other mass organizations may also leverage their increasing independence to use the Internet for nontraditional areas of development, perhaps posing conflicts with state goals.

Transforming Bureaucracy, Shaping Opinion

With no formal opposition parties, the Chinese government dominates the use of the Internet in the political sphere.[51] The successful use of the medium is seen as crucial to China's heralded reform and openness program, designed to bring administrative and political processes into step with the modern world. The state's Internet use in this area can be grouped into two main subdivisions, e-government and propaganda.[52]

A large part of China's informatization strategy is the implementation of e-government programs at various levels of bureaucracy. The Internet and related technologies are seen as helping to strengthen state capacity through administrative streamlining and automation, increasing citizen satisfaction with government by providing government services to the public online, and in some cases promoting increased bureaucratic transparency. In January 1999 China Telecom and the State Economic and Trade Commission launched the "Government Online" project, which is meant to bring all central government departments online within the next few years. Beginning with simple goals, such as the posting of government functions online, the project seeks to implement widespread online administration, using electronic databases and online document transfer to increase administrative efficiency. Although China's ambitions for e-government still outstrip its achievements, many departments and organizations have established rich web sites, while an increasing number are putting databases and archives on the web and using intranets to boost efficiency.

In fact, several departments, ministries, local governments, and other organizations have been making innovations on their own. The Ministry of Agriculture has quietly been implementing its own informatization process since 1997, which predates the central government's official program by two years. In 1998, when government organs were ordered to streamline operations, the ministry cut its staff by 45 percent, leaving it short of workers. It had no choice but to automate some of its systems; by January 2000 the entire ministry had undergone this process. Through the use of intranets, documents can now be reviewed and approved online; meanwhile, the intranet serves as an internal publishing platform, making department processes more transparent to managers. The ministry's Infocenter also provides managers with an internal network of agricultural information that aids in the construction of large-scale databases on farm statistics. Information is collected and disseminated through information kiosks at local levels of rural government.

In the cities, municipal governments are moving aggressively to provide citizen services online. The Beijing city government's web site is quite sophisticated, featuring professionally designed graphics and many helpful links. Visitor options include information about government services, new updates on laws and regulations, a local news center, and an e-mail section that allows visitors to e-mail Beijing's mayor with suggestions or criticisms of municipal government. A separate forum also gives visitors the opportunity to ask questions and have them answered on the site.[53] Beijing provides an example of the e-government direction other municipal governments may take.

Such moves are taking place amid a general movement toward greater accountability, transparency, and citizen interaction with government. An increasing number of official and academic studies in China are examining the link between the anticorruption movement and the Internet. A small but growing number of measures exist to increase transparency and accountability through the use of new ICTs. In 2000, the MII and the National Coal Bureau partnered with a private company, ECantata, to institute a system of online reverse auctions to replace the wheeling and dealing that typically characterize coal procurement in China. Such measures, which form part of the government's "sunshine purchasing" policy, use the Internet to help reduce graft in procurement and to boost efficiency.

Alongside its e-government program, the Chinese government is strengthening its uses of the Internet to distribute propaganda and engage in thought work. These practices, long crucial to the effective functioning of China's communist regime, have been adapted to the information age, primarily through use of web sites that present a new and often more subtle rendering of the government's perspective.

The government has set up specific web sites to publicize its perspective on current events. This is especially relevant when the government claims that "misinformation" is being disseminated by opposing groups, as in the case of the Falun Gong. Various reports in English and Chinese feature testimonials from "reeducated" Falun Gong practitioners and photographs of self-immolating protestors in Tiananmen Square. More subtly, the *People's Daily* maintains a strong web presence that is significantly livelier than its stodgy print counterpart. It offers an increasing mix of sports and lifestyle news, coupled with popular, nationalistically themed chat rooms that compete with those run by private companies.[54] The online English version of the *People's Daily*, designed to present a modern face to the rest of world, features news as well as links to government white papers, selected works of Deng Xiaoping, and the Chinese constitution. All these measures fit neatly into the government's plan to build a large, coordinated online propaganda system. The State Council Information Office has established an Internet Propaganda Administrative Bureau, responsible for "guiding and coordinating" web news content, while propaganda chief Ding Guangen has directed major state media organs to use the Internet fully.[55]

In addition to distributing propaganda on the global Internet, the government is reviving the idea of a national intranet, which is intended to substitute for the global Internet by providing online services paired with acceptable content (whose exact nature has yet to be detailed) for Chinese citizens.[56] Called CNet, the planned intranet is characterized as a proprietary communication and data network that will feature better security and "homegrown technology." Although such ideas have been discussed and deferred for a number of years, their perpetual revival as a national priority demonstrates the state's continued determination to address the infiltration of foreign ideas.

In general, Internet use in the political sphere has proved to be a net benefit for the Chinese government. Increasingly sophisticated e-government measures are geared toward service provision, which helps to increase citizen satisfaction with the government, and perhaps to provide a form of legitimacy that somewhat replaces the representative process. Reform-minded officials are pushing the use of the Government Online project as a tool to flatten and streamline China's government structure, as well as to reform governance itself. Such efforts, which mirror the plans for e-government programs in a variety of countries, will also help to strengthen state capacity from within. Meanwhile, propaganda organs are benefiting from Internet use, helping the government to reach a new, younger audience.

E-Commerce: A Bounded Frontier

Investors in China's Internet industry often liken their experience to prospecting in uncharted territory, with the possibility for untold riches or unexpected heartache always around the corner. It is true that the industry has generated a number of homegrown millionaires, many of whom highlight the pioneering aspects of capitalist freedom to be found in the Internet sector. Such romantic visions often belie the fact that the government has meticulously targeted China's ICT industry as a significant component of the country's economic development plan and has every intention of maintaining state control over what is admittedly a dynamic and unpredictable environment.

On a broad level, many believe that Internet-driven economic development may eventually help to create an entrepreneurial, market-oriented population that will push for political liberalization. Supporters of normal trade relations with China also assert that foreign investment in China's Internet sector will help open the country to more objective news and information, aid in the creation of a democracy-boosting domestic entrepreneurial class, and pressure the Chinese government to institute less restrictive policies on freedom of information. For now, however, the state (in the form of the MII, local government arms, or other bureaucratic organs) still retains great control over China's nascent private sector. It manifests influence in various ways, from domination of the country's ISP sector to the supervision of content provided by private ICPs.

Given the ICT industry's increasing relevance to the Chinese economy as a whole, such state influence is not insignificant. From 1996 to 2000, the ICT industry was the fastest-growing sector in the Chinese economy. Officials put the volume of e-commerce at $9.3 billion in 2000, which, though small by global standards, is high given China's still-developing financial markets. The electronic manufacturing industry has also grown substantially in recent years, with electronic products accounting for 23 percent of total imports and 21 percent of total exports in 2000.[57]

At the local level, the state has promoted high-technology industrial zones (as in Beijing's Zhongguancun district), which incubate domestic Internet start-ups and encourage homegrown talent.[58] It has also encouraged the graduates of China's top universities to stay at home and work in the technology sector rather than leave for lucrative positions abroad, a strategy that ties into the government's ambition to nurture a technologically savvy population that will power economic modernization.

Government influence is powerful, if subtle, in the realm of Internet service provision. The rapid proliferation of ISPs has led many observers to assume that private companies are driving expansion and collecting the bulk of profits. In fact, the sector has been dominated from the beginning first by the MPT and later by the MII through its high bandwidth ChinaNET backbone. ChinaNET–affiliated providers, which have leveraged their connections and financial resources to weather early fluctuations in the sector, are able to attract and keep the largest number of users. Independent ISPs struggle to cope with high MPT leasing fees and a lack of funding. Although leased line fees have been dramatically cut in the past few years at the behest of Zhu Rongji and other central leaders, cash-strapped independent ISPs have not been able to pass the reductions on to consumers. Many have given up trying to manage their own service, instead simply reselling regional ChinaNET–branded Internet connections. In late 2000, 90 percent of ISPs had a reselling arrangement.[59]

On the regulatory front, the government has taken a somewhat Janus-faced approach, attributable more to a lack of bureaucratic coordination than an overarching strategy. The result has thrown both domestic and foreign Internet entrepreneurs off balance. On the one hand, efforts are being made to safeguard intellectual property, pass investment legislation, and provide a fair investment environment in order to produce the type of stable e-commerce climate that attracts risk-averse foreign investors. On the other hand, the government continues to issue conflicting regulations, many of which have the effect of frightening or coopting the developing Internet entrepreneurial sector.

ISPs and ICPs have had to contend with new legislation that both mimics past media regulations and attempts to forge new ground. New decrees forbid ICPs from providing information that "undermines social stability," while requiring ISPs to tabulate users. Despite causing an outcry among human rights and free-press activists overseas, such regulations have been largely accepted by Internet companies, which have shown a propensity to self-regulate, self-censor, and determine for themselves which regulations are likely to be strictly enforced.[60] The largest portals feature a mix of sports, entertainment, and current events, and many have veered clear of politically sensitive areas, such as the provision of foreign affairs news that deviates from the party line. Since the state controls the broad regulatory environment as well as the minutiae of operating licenses, many take pains to cultivate good relations with the government at various levels.

In fact, many of China's up-and-coming Internet entrepreneurs see a substantial, if evolving, role for government in the Internet sector. Often heralded in the Western media as the future of a freer China, these businesspeople usually have visions for Chinese Internet development that are inherently pragmatic and complementary to state strategy. In early 2002, for instance, more than one hundred Internet industry entrepreneurs signed a pledge to promote self-discipline and encourage "the elimination of deleterious information [on] the Internet." Although this language may be viewed as merely rhetoric, many Chinese Internet companies seem to lack the desire to push for free expression, considering such activity to be a risky business proposition, if nothing else.[61]

Therefore, although Internet entrepreneurs note that their relations with the government are increasingly consultative, giving them some input into the policy-making process, few are willing to push the state on politically sensitive topics. On issues relating to the press and freedom of speech, many technology tycoons are conspicuously silent. This is hardly surprising, given that the companies were formed to make money and not to seek political change. Some Chinese Internet entrepreneurs note that Western observers often possess misguided expectations for the Internet's political impact in China because they fail to realize the realities of China's reform timetable and the government's proactive role in advancing it.[62]

Foreign media multinationals seem equally unlikely to push for a broadening of acceptable media parameters in China, having frequently toed the government line rather than challenge it.[63] In 2001 America Online signed a landmark deal with the Chinese government to broadcast a Mandarin-language cable channel into southern China; the channel features only politically and culturally inoffensive programming. AOL also recently unveiled a joint venture with Legend, the Chinese computer maker, but refused to specify whether any future Internet service run by the company would, if requested, provide officials with the names, e-mail, and other Internet records of political dissidents. Meanwhile, U.S. Internet corporations were silent when human rights organizations asked them to come to the defense of a Chinese businessman arrested for posting controversial articles on a web site.[64]

Such action (or lack of action) makes sense in the context of business practices that place great importance on good relations with government agencies. Although free-trade proponents suggest that foreign investment will help to reduce so-called crony capitalist practices, there is little evidence that foreign investors are inherently opposed to a reliance on guanxi. Like domestic entrepreneurs, many take pains to cultivate government relations and to adhere to what are often euphemistically termed local business practices. To what extent the post–WTO expansion of foreign ownership limits will affect issues of information freedom in China is therefore difficult to determine.

Another political side effect of foreign investment may be the enhancement, intended or otherwise, of the ability of the state to monitor and control Internet use. Through its Golden Shield project, the Ministry of State Security has courted the foreign makers of blocking and antihacking software. Overseas human rights groups have raised concerns about this and other projects designed to harness foreign technology for information control. Given the increased domestic acceptance of electronic surveillance tactics in the United States following the September 2001 terrorist attacks, such concerns are likely to find diminished purchase with both foreign investors and government policy makers.

In general, the demonstrated ability of the state to channel investment and to control the fortunes of domestic and foreign investors appears to have had the effect of keeping the emerging entrepreneurial class grounded in "a culture of dependence and anxiety," even as this class extols its newfound capacity to generate wealth.[65] As such, it remains to be seen if (1) an entrepreneurial class will emerge as an economically independent and powerful social force, and (2) it will take an active interest in politics, much less the politics of opposition. Foreign and domestic Internet companies seem likely to play a limited role in promoting political liberalization, especially if many choose to continue their policy of cooperation and consultation, rather than confrontation, with the state.

Cyberactivism and Cyberwar across Borders

As with other authoritarian regimes, dissidents and activists outside China have initiated some of the most large-scale and well-publicized web activity dealing with the country, from information gathering and dissemination to overt calls for political action. Such groups as Human Rights Watch, Human Rights in China, and the Committee to Protect Journalists post the news of arrests and human rights violations, circulate online petitions, and maintain e-mail databases of Chinese dissidents and other activists.[66] United States–based Chinese dissidents also maintain Chinese-language web sites and sometimes use e-mail to disseminate information within China.[67] The international arm of the Falun Gong has also used the Internet to influence international policy toward China, posting the details of Chinese government crackdowns on sites hosted by overseas servers.

Dissidents and other activists are growing increasingly sophisticated in their efforts to avoid Chinese censorship. Some, like the Washington, D.C., publisher of the *VIP Reference* e-mail newsletter, use tactics similar to those of spammers, changing headers to disguise e-mail origin and constantly shifting the e-mail addresses from which material is sent.[68] Others rely on software such as Peekabooty, which uses a combination of encryption and peer-to-peer software to make the sender anonymous.

Although such actions have primarily been the domain of transnational advocacy networks, the U.S. government has been increasingly involved in similar efforts (with a shift in focus, however, since the 2001 terrorist attacks). Voice of America's (VOA) new web site provides news and audio broadcasts in fifty-three languages. Meanwhile, California-based SafeWeb, already partially funded by the U.S. Central Intelligence Agency, has been seeking funding from VOA's parent agency to provide new computers that run software specifically for the Chinese audience.[69] Although it is unclear whether state-funded and transnational actions can affect internal Chinese politics, it has already begun to affect the country's foreign relations.[70]

For the most part, Internet use in the international sphere is out of China's direct control, so the government must respond by proactively disseminating its own point of view abroad. Its main strategy consists of posting counterinformation on government and government-sponsored web sites to influence both domestic and international opinion. Such efforts, while still rudimentary, are likely to become more sophisticated as propaganda workers use the full range of web resources.

Some international organizations claim that China is going beyond mere propaganda in countering politically sensitive Internet use in the international realm. The Falun Gong, for instance, contends that the Chinese government also uses information warfare techniques—hacking into web sites and spreading viruses—to disable and discredit its own organizations.[71] Reportedly, the government uses the same techniques in response to attacks by dissident hacker groups.

Such activities would be in line with the Chinese military's strategy to develop an information warfare capacity that will allow it to project sovereign power more effectively on an international scale.[72] The People's Liberation Army's (PLA) interest in telecommunication networks and their potential is not new. In the mid-1970s, the PLA was one of the first top-level organizations to press for its own alternative network, to bypass what it saw as the unreliable and slow public switched network of the MPT.[73] The development of dedicated PLA communication networks is now a top national priority, with the capacity of PLA communication networks having increased tenfold since the early 1990s. According to one estimate, dedicated PLA communication systems are thought to account for 20 percent of the central government's allocations for telecommunication budgets.[74]

Recent writings by Chinese military specialists show that China is increasingly focusing on "asymmetric warfare" options, including guerrilla war and cyberattacks against data networks.[75] In recent years, U.S. newspapers have reported suspected Chinese hacker attacks on U.S. weapons laboratories, and military experts believe that China is willing to reduce its standing army while increasing its reliance on a "multitude of information engineers and citizens with laptops instead of just soldiers."[76] Although Chinese hacker attacks on U.S. web sites in May 2001 did little more than deface home pages, the continuing study and development of information warfare can be seen as a top-priority government measure in line with a general strategy of informatization and the country's goal of modernizing and transforming its military establishment.

Finally, a significant political effect of international Internet use may lie in the expressions of nationalism by the overseas Chinese diaspora. Just as extreme expressions of domestic nationalism on the Internet are now posing a problem for Chinese leaders, their international counterparts present a more diffuse, and less easily addressed, challenge. During the May 1998 riots targeting ethnic Chinese in Indonesia, the Internet enabled the coherent expression of Chinese nationalism around the world, galvanizing widespread protests by overseas Chinese. Although the mainland Chinese press remained silent about the events in Jakarta, the Internet helped to inform and politicize Internet users in mainland China, culminating in a student-led demonstration in Beijing.[77] The transformation of overseas saber rattling online into concrete protest in the capital was no doubt one of the most worrying aspects of the phenomenon for Chinese leaders. In the future, the government may seek to block overseas sites that attempt to foment nationalist dissent, but since such sentiment can swiftly materialize on any number of Chinese-themed sites and bulletin boards, total blocking action would likely be futile. As such, the combination of domestic and transnational nationalist critiques during times of crisis may present the government with an even more severe challenge, one over which it has little direct influence.

It is possible that, as the Chinese user base grows, international advocacy campaigns may find a wider audience and greater leverage within China. As China increasingly opens its markets to the West and attempts to gain international legitimacy as both an economic and political world power, it may prove more susceptible to forms of Internet-based advocacy. Moreover, as Dai Xiudian points out, although dissidents based outside China currently reach only a small part of the total population, their target audience is intellectuals and students, a group strongly represented among the first wave of Internet users. Intellectuals and students have also been the community historically involved in organizing protests and pro-democracy movements.[78]

Conclusion: Change without Collapse

Through measures ranging from blunt punitive actions to the subtle manipulation of the private sector, the Chinese state has been largely successful to date in guiding the broad political impact of Internet use. This should not be confused with overt central control over every facet of the Internet. Many analysts accurately note that the Chinese state is increasingly fragmented and unable to monitor the Internet in its entirety; that bureaucratic battles plague the medium's development; and that access to forbidden information has become much easier as the technology has spread. While all these points are undoubtedly valid, they do not necessarily challenge the assertion that the state is effectively controlling the overarching political impact of the Internet. This political impact stems from several areas, including Internet use in the civil societal, political, economic, and international spheres. In all these areas, the reach of the state is still felt at a profound level, regardless of whether it has been achieved intentionally or by default.

In the realm of civil society, the central government has largely been able to shape the environment in which Internet use takes place, mainly by encouraging a level of self-censorship that still allows access to a plethora of information on the Internet. By offering some preemptive liberalization, the government may also head off more serious challenges in the future. In the economic arena, the government has shown that its ability to impose dictates on domestic and foreign companies extends well into the Internet sector, despite a proliferation of private companies that provide access and content to the public. At the same time, the government is harnessing the Internet to strengthen the state's institutional capacity through anticorruption and e-government measures. It is also countering the international use of the Internet with a heightened ability to influence global perceptions of China and its policies.

This is not to say that the government's ability to manipulate the political ramifications of Internet use is perfectly sustainable over the long term. The realm of public use, for instance, features a growing potential for political impact. One Internet entrepreneur has predicted that in five years China will have 300 million Internet devices, spanning cell phones and computers.[79] Although such estimates may be high, it is true that Internet access will continue to expand considerably, with the state's blessing, in the coming years. By wholeheartedly endorsing a market-led model of Internet development and by encouraging mass access, the state faces the increased probability of political challenges stemming from Internet use.

In fact, much of the Internet use most challenging to the state has taken place during times of crisis, such as during the U.S. spy plane incident. Heated anti-American sentiment, which reached a crescendo after the terrorist attacks on America, still simmers in many web forums and is likely to remain highly volatile in the post–September 11 environment. As Nina Hachigian argues, during a crisis, the Internet may refocus national discontent in unprecedented ways.[80] An unforeseen international incident, for instance, might precipitate a groundswell of public discontent that could mesh online with overseas Chinese nationalist sentiment, creating a potent challenge to the regime. In such an instance, the Chinese authorities appear to have two choices: responding harshly, setting off a chain of repercussions, or shifting to a more hard-line foreign policy in order to accommodate an increasingly agitated populace. Neither choice is likely to lay the groundwork for constructive liberalization, and both would at least temporarily enhance authoritarian tendencies.

The increasing openness and competition promoted by China's entry in the World Trade Organization may also shape the Internet's political impact, even if changes are incremental. As China's transition to a market economy encourages bureaucracies to fight for lucrative pieces of turf, the Internet has proved to be an irresistible lure. While such battles may speed infrastructure development, they do not facilitate effective centralized co-ordination and supervision. This presents one of the biggest challenges to the Chinese government: ensuring that future Internet development takes place according to centrally crafted timetables and blueprints. World Trade Organization entry is likely to cause further turbulence, if not substantial destabilization, in central steering. Given the high priority of informatization in the central government's design for economic and political reform, a further loss of control over the process would represent a genuine political setback for the regime.

In essence, the Internet's development in China is taking place against a highly fluid backdrop. Various forms of Internet use may erode authoritarian control in a number of ways. The public use of the medium, especially as it evolves, may prove to be, if not a catalyst, then a point of inflection along the road to concrete political change. Yet this change may not necessarily be of a democratic nature. Should popular nationalistic sentiment coalesce on the Internet into a significant opposition movement, the consequences may not bode well for stability or liberalization. The idea of a wired populace spontaneously pressing for democracy tends to appeal to Western policy makers. Yet Internet use that strengthens state capacity may be more conducive to long-term liberalization than Internet use that weakens the state in certain areas. Current e-government measures designed to boost transparency and promote efficiency may in fact gird the capacity of state institutions to weather a future political transition.

On its own, Internet use is unlikely to launch the dawning of a new political age in China. Concrete political change is likely to depend on several slow, incremental steps, many of which may have no connection to the Internet. At the same time, it is possible that Internet use may set the stage for gradual liberalization, facilitating a future transition from authoritarian rule. All told, the Internet is likely to contribute to change within China, without precipitating the state's collapse.

CHAPTER THREE

Channeling a "Limited" Resource in Cuba

And the Internet, you know, has done a lot to bring democratic capitalism to other parts of the world. It was instrumental . . . in bringing down the Berlin Wall. It was instrumental in having students protest the policies in East Berlin. . . . CNN, the networks, and the Internet were instrumental in the demise of the old Soviet Union. And we think the same thing should happen in Cuba.

—James Courter, former Republican member of Congress, June 5, 2000

More than a decade after Cuba first began to experiment with computer networking, the spotlight has begun to shine on the country's experience with the Internet. Internet-industry publications have highlighted the efforts of foreign entrepreneurs developing e-commerce applications for the country's tourist industry.[1] Newspapers and broadcast media from the *Washington Post* to the BBC have reported on the government's Internet access restrictions and on those enterprising Cubans who circumvent the rules to obtain unofficial connections.[2] Cuba has responded to less-than-favorable coverage of its Internet policies with scathing editorials in the state media while also publicizing its own efforts to extend public access to a national intranet.[3] As with almost every other aspect of the country's development, the issue of the Internet in Cuba has become intricately intertwined with Cuba's foreign relations (and U.S.–Cuban relations in general), and it has grown increasingly polemical over the years. The use of ICTs to promote political change is deeply rooted in the U.S. policy toward Cuba, and as Internet development has proceeded in the country, expectations about the medium's political effects have been greatly influenced by the conventional wisdom on the Internet's impact in authoritarian regimes.[4]

Unsurprisingly, Cuban authorities have not accepted the conventional wisdom that the growth of the Internet will inevitably bring political change to the country. On the contrary, they have attempted to steer the development of the medium along a course that will bring benefits in priority areas while avoiding potentially subversive or destabilizing effects. In choosing such a course, Cuba has much in common with other authoritarian regimes that are addressing the issue of Internet development, including each of the countries we examine in this book.

Still, Cuba is also distinctive among authoritarian regimes in the specific approach it has taken toward the development of the Internet. Most other authoritarian regimes have followed a market-led model of Internet development, allowing the proliferation of Internet access through cybercafés and residential dial-up accounts while blocking web sites, conducting surveillance, and promoting self-censorship. For its part, Cuba has eschewed such a rapid, market-led model of Internet diffusion. On the contrary, Cuban authorities have carefully planned out the diffusion of the Internet within their country, controlling the medium's pace of development and the sectors in which Internet access is granted. Cuban authorities seek control over the Internet not through a massive, centralized censorship mechanism but rather by denying Internet access where it could be potentially subversive.

Despite its atypical approach to Internet diffusion, Cuba resembles other authoritarian regimes in that it has proactively guided the development of the Internet to serve specific social, political, and economic goals. The government has long endeavored to harness computer networking for education and public health, and it is also rolling out a national intranet to bring the benefits of connectivity to the masses without granting full access to the Internet. Cuban authorities aggressively promote Cuban tourism on the Internet, and they are encouraging foreign investment in a growing number of e-commerce ventures. In charting its approach to Internet development, Cuba has looked to China as a model of state control over the medium, and it is actively seeking Chinese cooperation in that area. When forming a new Ministry of Computing and Communication, says its director, Cuba "took into account the experience of China, which is the other place where the state has played the role that it has played here."[5] Chinese investors have helped to modernize Cuba's aging national telephone system, and the head of China's Ministry of Information Industries has stated that "China will play a decisive role in the improvement of Cuban telecommunications."[6]

In this chapter we argue that Cuba's approach to the Internet has allowed its authoritarian regime to limit the medium's potentially threatening impacts while gaining tangible benefits from its diffusion. If the regime were to change its policy on Internet access, more challenging uses of the

Internet in Cuba might well emerge. It seems unlikely, however, that Cuba would abandon a successful policy of Internet control. For the near future, Cuba will probably continue to defy the conventional wisdom that the Internet poses an insurmountable threat to authoritarian rule.

Communism, Authoritarianism, and U.S. Policy

Cuba is a communist state that has been ruled by Fidel Castro since 1959, when the Cuban revolution toppled the government of Fulgencio Batista. The country is the largest island in the Caribbean, and with 11 million residents, it is also the most populous. Cuba registered a GDP per capita of $1,700 in the year 2000, placing it in the World Bank's category of a lower-middle-income country. Thanks to Cuba's emphasis on basic social development, its citizens are healthier and better educated than are those of most other developing countries. Cuba's infant mortality rate is among the twenty-five lowest in the world, and it has achieved 96 percent literacy.[7]

Cuba stands out among the countries in our study as one of the more economically isolated, partially as a product of its historical commitment to socialism and partially as a result of U.S. policy. Since 1962 the United States has imposed a general embargo on trade with Cuba, and while exceptions such as the provision of telecommunication services or the sale of food and medicines have been allowed in recent years, the general policy has remained solidly in place. During the 1990s two major pieces of legislation have strengthened the embargo: the Cuban Democracy Act of 1992, which extended the prohibitions on trade to foreign subsidiaries of U.S. companies, and the controversial Helms-Burton Act of 1996, which seeks to punish foreign firms doing business in Cuba.

Cuba's economy struggled greatly during the first half of the 1990s after the country lost its favorable terms of trade with the Soviet Union, and Cuban leaders were forced to undergo a limited amount of economic liberalization in response. Between 1989 and 1993, the country's GDP declined 35.9 percent, and petroleum imports dropped dramatically, resulting in severe shortages of electricity and gasoline.[8] Food imports also fell, causing a serious malnutrition problem for the first time since the 1959 revolution. To arrest the economy's downfall, Cuba's leadership initiated several economic reforms in 1993–1994: legalizing the U.S. dollar, permitting limited self-employment, reopening farmers' markets, and converting some state farms to agricultural cooperatives. The following year a new foreign investment law permitted the full foreign ownership of enterprises in most sectors of the economy, including telecommunications. The Cuban economy began to rebound in 1994, maintaining positive annual growth rates (as high as 7 percent) ever since.[9] Cuba's turnaround is due in part to liberalizing measures, though it has also been helped by the growth of its tourist industry and by remittances from exiles, which are the country's two largest sources of hard currency.

On the whole, however, Cuba has been quite ambivalent in its embrace of capitalism. With the exception of the domestic economic reforms passed in the early 1990s, Cuba has restricted all economic liberalization to its externally oriented, dollar-denominated economy. Authorities court foreign investment in such key industries as tourism, sugar, and mining, but they have taken pains to limit the influx of capitalism in the lives of ordinary Cubans. As we shall see, this pattern of economic bifurcation also holds true for Internet use in the Cuban economy. Certain domestic economic reforms have in fact been rolled back in recent years; for instance, since 1996 the regime has limited the growth of self-employment with tax increases and new regulations. Generally, Cuba's domestic private sector is small and subject to the whims of the regime. The informal sector, including black marketeers, tourist guides, and prostitutes, is the main area in which the state's control of the economy is challenged.

Cuba has been governed by a strict authoritarian regime since the 1959 revolution, and no significant measures of political liberalization have matched the limited economic reforms of the 1990s. The Cuban Communist Party is the only legal political party, and elections for both president and National Assembly delegates are run essentially as referenda, with only a single candidate allowed to stand for each seat. Municipal-level elections are somewhat more liberal, since multiple candidates can be nominated directly for each post. Cuba's authoritarian regime maintains political control through an extensive internal security apparatus under the Ministry of the Interior. Police surveillance is supplemented by the efforts of Committees for the Defense of the Revolution, which are block organizations that monitor "counterrevolutionary" behavior and can be mobilized to harass dissidents.

During the past decade Cuba has seen several periods of openness, such as the months surrounding Pope John Paul's visit to the island in 1998, but these have not led to any sustained political liberalization. Frequently, such periods of openness have given way to authoritarian backlashes, such as the passage of a draconian antisubversion law in 1999 and the imprisonment of four key dissidents who wrote a political manifesto. Hopes for reform within Cuba were again spurred in May 2002 by two significant events: the visit of former U.S. president Jimmy Carter, who was allowed to criticize the Cuban political system in a nationally televised address to the Cuban people, and a petition drive by Project Varela, a group of Cuban dissidents who gathered eleven thousand signatures calling for a national referendum on political and economic liberalization. While widely (and accurately) hailed as unprecedented occurrences in Cuba, it remains to be seen whether Carter's visit and Project Varela's petition will translate into meaningful policy reform.[10]

While the state dominates Cuba's economy and political scene, it (somewhat reluctantly) shares the stage with a small number of civil society organizations from across the political spectrum.[11] A handful of human rights activists, independent journalists, and dissident organizations have long existed (albeit illegally) within the country, tenuously clinging to life despite constant government repression. In addition to these openly critical organizations, a growing number of officially sanctioned CSOs have emerged, working in the areas of sustainable development, conservation, religious charity, or social, political, and economic research.[12] While official CSOs range in political orientation from mildly critical of the government to outspokenly supportive, all must gain approval from the Ministry of Justice to operate legally, so the true nature of their independence is constantly in debate. Nonetheless, many such CSOs favor the decentralization of political power and novel solutions to economic problems and have thus been considered potential initiators of reform. Still, even those that enjoy good relations with the regime have been subject to crackdowns if their activities run afoul of authorities.[13]

Cuban politics cannot be effectively understood outside the context of U.S.–Cuban relations, for much of the country's history during the past century has been intimately intertwined with that of the United States. Cuba gained independence in 1902 only after a four-year military occupation by the United States. As a condition of the military withdrawal, Cuba incorporated the Platt Amendment into its first constitution, giving the United States the right to intervene in the country's domestic affairs at will. Although this amendment was abrogated in 1934, the United States retained strong political and economic influence over the island until the revolution. During the U.S.–backed presidency of corrupt dictator Batista, American corporations such as International Telephone and Telegraph (ITT) and United Fruit dominated the Cuban economy, while the

American Mafia was heavily involved in Havana's lucrative nightlife and tourist industry. This history of American involvement in Cuba provided fertile grounds for resentment among Cuban nationalists long before the 1959 revolution, and it explains much of the fervor with which Cuba's present regime has confronted the United States.

Since Castro's 1959 victory, the United States has consistently sought the ouster of the regime by both overt and covert means. The most notable efforts include the 1963 Bay of Pigs invasion by U.S.–backed Cuban exiles and the CIA's numerous assassination attempts on Castro. Furthermore, ICTs have frequently been harnessed as a central component of this strategy. The CIA began clandestine radio broadcasting to Cuba as early as 1960, and congressionally funded Radio Martí has beamed anti-Castro programming at the island since 1985. TV Martí was added to the mix in 1990, though effective signal jamming and conflicts with Cuban programming on the same channel mean that few Cubans are able to view it.

In 1992 the United States passed the Cuban Democracy Act (CDA), bringing a new component into U.S. policy with its provisions of "support for the Cuban people." A major aim of this policy was to increase the flow of information between the two countries. In pursuit of that goal, telecommunication services were exempted from the embargo for the first time. The inspiration behind the CDA remains influential in U.S. policy, and policy makers are currently seeking ways to leverage ICTs to support internal opposition in Cuba. In February 2001, in his first public address as the new president of the Cuban American National Foundation, Jorge Mas Santos called for U.S. funding to provide cell phones, computer printers, fax machines, and Internet access for the Cuban opposition.[14] Three months later, these ideas were incorporated in the Helms-Lieberman bill in the U.S. Congress.[15]

An Information Revolution to Serve the Cuban Revolution

Owing in part to the prominent role of the media in its conflict-ridden relations with the United States, Cuba has long maintained firm state control over ICTs. Soon after coming to power, Fidel Castro quickly established control of the mass media and telecommunications through expropriation, intimidation, and economic sanctions. The Cuban telephone system was nationalized in August 1959, and by the end of 1960 the regime had effectively asserted control over print and broadcast media.[16]

Ever since, all ICTs in Cuba have been owned and operated by the state to serve the political goals of the Cuban revolution.[17] Internationally, the regime uses ICTs for propagandistic purposes through such vehicles as Radio Havana Cuba. Internally, Cuba has harnessed the mass media for extensive top-down political mobilization, an important function since the early days of the revolution. In addition, the Cuban leadership has long professed the belief that only the state-guided development of the media and ICTs can extend social benefits to the population as a whole. It has historically placed an emphasis, for example, on increasing rural telephone access. Finally, as the regime has faced mounting economic difficulties during the 1990s, economic concerns have increasingly come to play a role in its control of ICT development. Consequently, leaders have allocated scarce telecommunication resources in areas that can generate hard currency.

Cuba's control of ICTs implies the regulation of content, but its approach is somewhat different from that of many other authoritarian regimes. There is no central government agency charged with the censorship of the Cuban media. Rather, content control is exercised at the editorial level, where most editors have ties to the government power structure and share the perspective of regime elites.[18] The central government has taken a more active role in controlling unauthorized access to the means of information dissemination, reacting strongly against any attempts to communicate outside official channels. Cuba's handful of independent journalists are routinely harassed and frequently arrested, even though their stories rarely reach the Cuban people.[19] In 1999 the Cuban government passed a harsh antisubversion law, mandating long jail terms for independent journalists and others considered to be cooperating with U.S. attempts to undermine the regime.

Along with its legal prohibitions on independently disseminating information, Cuba has placed restrictions on obtaining mass communication and publishing equipment, from photocopiers and offset printers to fax machines, computers, and modems. Such equipment is legally available only in state-run dollar stores, which have traditionally sold only to such officially recognized institutions as Cuban firms and government ministries. Certain computer components not directly used for communication, such as keyboards and monitors, used to be available for sale to the general public, but a new resolution, passed in December 2001, has severely tightened these restrictions. There is now a blanket prohibition on the sale of mass printing media and computer equipment (including parts and accessories) to individuals and civil society organizations; exceptions require specific authorization from the Ministry of Internal Commerce.[20] Would-be computer users can circumvent such restrictions by purchasing equipment on the black market; often machines are cobbled together piece by piece from components acquired through different sources. Still, computers are extremely expensive to purchase, either legally or underground, and the difficulty and risk of acquiring a computer on the black market mean that only the dedicated are likely to pursue it.

Telecommunications: Stagnation and Recovery

Cuba was an early leader in Latin American telecommunications, with the first telephone company in the region and the first international connection to the United States.[21] Extensive U.S. investment in Cuba ensured a modern system through the time of the 1959 revolution. In the years since, Cuba's domestic telephone infrastructure and international links have not kept pace with the rest of the hemisphere. This lag is due largely to restrictions imposed by the U.S. embargo, which prevented Cuba from purchasing replacement parts and upgrades for a system that was initially based on U.S. technology. Lacking this option, Cuba built a domestic phone system based on a mix-and-match combination of 1940s equipment from the United States and 1970s technology from Eastern Europe, with significant compatibility problems between the two.[22]

The dismal state of Cuban telecommunications began to improve in the mid-1990s when the Cuban government partially privatized the country's telephone system. In June 1994 the Cuban Ministry of Communications sold a portion of the state telephone company, creating the new telecommunication monopoly ETECSA. Foreign ownership of the privatized portion of ETECSA changed hands over the years. Under the current configuration it is owned 51 percent by the Cuban government, 8 percent by the Cuban Central Bank, 29 percent by Telecom Italia, and 12 percent by a consortium of Panamanian investors.[23] Since its creation, ETECSA has steadily set about the task of modernizing the domestic telephone system in Cuba, with fairly impressive results. Half of the country's telephone exchanges were digitized by 2000, and ETECSA projects 84 percent digitalization by the year 2004.[24] ETECSA is also planning to install fiber-optic trunk lines throughout the country with the help of Chinese investors.[25] In addition to the landline system, Cuba has two cellular telephone networks—Cubacel, formed in 1992 with a Mexican partner, and the new C–COM, which caters largely to European tourists in Cuba.

Cuba's international capacity also improved in the mid-1990s, after the 1992 Cuban Democracy Act allowed U.S. investment in new telecommunication service to Cuba. Direct telephone service was established in 1994, and by 1998 at least seven U.S. carriers were offering long-distance service to Cuba, earning $250 million in revenues for ETECSA.[26] Nonetheless, strained relations between the United States and Cuba have disrupted international telephone service recently, and its future may be similarly problematic.[27]

Establishing State Control of the Internet

Although Cuba's quest for Internet connectivity has been limited by the state of its domestic telephone system and international telecommunication capacity, it has made some impressive gains. Cuba's first experiments with international computer networking came early for a developing country, and they were subject to only minimal oversight by the government. In the late 1980s a group of foreign activists and academics residing in Cuba proposed the establishment of an e-mail connection to the outside world that would be routed through the Canadian member network of the San Francisco–based Association for Progressive Communications. Negotiations over the e-mail link proceeded smoothly and without controversy, and a connection was established in April 1991 with the approval of a Communist Party official. Several times a day computers from Web Networks in Toronto placed a phone call to Cuba's National Center for Automated Data Exchange (CENIAI), transferring all e-mail traffic destined for or leaving Cuba. Over the next several years such connections proliferated, and by 1996 there were four Cuban computer networks that could exchange e-mail with the outside world. Each of these networks charted its own course of development, and network administrators established criteria as to who could gain access.[28]

The situation of laissez-faire networking in Cuba changed dramatically after CENIAI established a direct connection to the Internet in 1996. With this event all traffic passed through a single government-controlled gateway, and the state stepped up its efforts to regulate the Internet. In June of that year the Cuban Executive Council of Ministers passed Decree-Law 209 to govern access to the Internet in Cuba. Because the global diffusion of the Internet held important implications for Cuba, the law maintained, it was necessary to establish "regulations that would guarantee its adequate and harmonious development, as well as the interests of the country's defense and national security." To govern the various aspects of the Internet's development in Cuba, Decree-Law 209 created a regulatory commission with representatives from six ministries.[29] Such a diffuse structure may have been a concession to the multiple ministries that felt that some aspect of Internet development fell under their purview.

The major players in Cuba's Internet regulation were the Ministry of Steel, Mechanics, and Electronics Industries (SIME); the Ministry of Science, Technology, and the Environment (CITMA); and the Ministry of Communications. SIME, which presided over the interministerial commission, was given the task of establishing Internet security policy and connecting the central state administration to the Internet. CITMA was charged with the technical administration of the network, and its subsidiary CENIAI, a major player in the early days of Cuban networking, became the manager of domain names and addresses in Cuba. The Ministry of Communications, the Cuban parent of ETECSA, was charged with the administration of the underlying infrastructure for Cuban networking. The Ministries of Justice, Interior, and the Revolutionary Armed Forces were also represented to ensure the interests of the legal system, internal security, and defense.

In effect, the division of labor between multiple ministries may have proved too bureaucratically inefficient for Internet regulation in Cuba. In January 2000 a major consolidation of authority was undertaken with the creation of the Ministry of Computing and Communications (MIC).[30] Effectively, the MIC was created by removing the computing industry divisions of SIME and combining them with the tasks already handled by the old Ministry of Communications. With the merger, the MIC has now become the dominant player in Internet regulation in Cuba and is the agency in charge of charting the general development of ICTs in the country. The MIC licenses ISPs and all institutions operating private local area networks (LANs), and it also sets the prices that ETECSA can charge for access to the networking infrastructure.[31] ETECSA carries all international data traffic, though CENIAI still manages the technical side of the gateway as well as the assignment of domain names in Cuba. There are currently four commercial ISPs in Cuba that offer traditional Internet service: Infocom, Colombus, Teledatos, and CENIAI. Cuba's main cellular telephone company, Cubacel, has also been licensed as an ISP, though this appears to be only for the purpose of providing short message service (SMS).

In charting the number of Internet users in Cuba (and analyzing the impact of the Internet in general), one must be careful to distinguish between three levels of network access: access to national e-mail and the Cuban intranet (web pages hosted within the country); access to international e-mail with intranet access; and full access to the World Wide Web. These distinct levels of access are priced differently by Cuban ISPs and require different criteria for qualification, though such distinctions are often missed by outside analysts and may be deliberately blurred by government officials when reporting Cuban network statistics. Domestic-only access is generally priced in Cuban pesos, but access to international e-mail or the web requires the use of international bandwidth purchased in hard currency, and therefore the users of these services are charged in dollars as well. With the introduction of public access to international e-mail through the Cuban intranet, domestic-only access will probably become less relevant in the future, but it is still an option available to institutional customers with less hard currency or need to communicate abroad.

Given these levels of access, Internet diffusion in Cuba has continued fairly steadily since the medium's debut in 1996, though not as dramatically as in some other authoritarian regimes. Both international e-mail access and full Internet access approximately doubled between 1999 and 2001, compared with the doubling every six months that occurred in the early years of China's Internet development. According to government figures, there were one hundred thousand e-mail accounts in Cuba at the end of 2001, approximately one-half of which can send messages internationally. Of some 220,000 computers on the island, only 6,000 have been fully connected to the Internet.[32] It is common in Cuba to share accounts, so the number of users is much higher than the number of accounts; some roughly estimate ten users for every account.[33] In any case, full Internet users are a small proportion of the island's population of 11 million.

Access Restriction and Cautious Development

Since Cuba established its first Internet connection in 1996 it has taken a "slow but steady" approach to the medium, seeking to control carefully the pattern of Internet development within the country according to a centrally articulated plan. In part, this approach has been influenced by a fear of Internet use for political subversion, a concern exacerbated by the antagonistic context of U.S.–Cuban relations.[34] As Cuba's fledgling data connection developed in the early 1990s, some political actors in the United States began to consider how e-mail might be used to promote an open society in Cuba. In 1992, for instance, a RAND report to the undersecretary of defense for policy specifically mentioned the recently established e-mail connection and urged the United States to "build bridges across computer networks . . . in the expectation that freer information flows should foster pluralist tendencies."[35] The following year, the cultural attaché of the U.S. Interests Section in Havana obtained an e-mail account on a Cuban network and posted information on U.S. policy to an electronic bulletin board (the account was swiftly withdrawn in response). Members of Miami's Cuban exile community also discovered Cuba's e-mail connection and began spamming Cuban addresses with antiregime propaganda. In light of such incidents, and of the United States' history of using other media to challenge the Cuban regime, many Cuban officials considered the Internet "an influence coming from the North," the land of "the enemy."[36]

Security concerns have been important determinants of Cuba's cautious approach to the Internet, but the regime has long recognized that the Internet offers potential benefits as well. In their initial decision to connect to the Internet, Cuban authorities found that the medium's potential benefits outweighed the threat of political subversion. First, the Internet could be harnessed to address Cuba's social priorities. The country's international e-mail connection had already been used to improve the provision of public health services and to facilitate education and scientific research; the Internet could further those aims. Second, the Internet offered a potential economic benefit. Cuban enterprises and joint ventures stood to gain from improvements in international communication, and the Internet could provide a means for promoting foreign investment and Cuban tourism. Finally, the Internet was important for political reasons. It offered a vehicle through which Cuba could counter its negative image in the international media and share with the world its perspective on domestic and international events.

In an effort to address each of these priorities adequately while avoiding the potentially subversive impact of the Internet, Cuban authorities have chosen to control Internet development carefully within the country. Since 1997 they have guided the growth of the medium according to a "plan for the informatization of Cuban society" that seeks to achieve a harmonious balance in Internet use in the social, educational, political, and economic spheres. While other authoritarian regimes have encouraged the rapid commercial growth of the Internet, Cuba has eschewed a market-led model of Internet development out of a concern that it would lead to inequalities in access to the medium, a predominance of commercialism over social and political applications, and potentially subversive Internet use. In contrast to the abundant potential for growth that many developing countries see in the Internet, Cuban authorities view the medium as a limited resource, largely because the U.S. embargo makes it more difficult and expensive to acquire computer hardware, international bandwidth, and investment in telecommunications. As a consequence, they feel that the Internet must be properly channeled and controlled to have the most positive impact on society.

Cuba's approach implies the promotion of Internet development in certain priority areas, but it also means the restriction of Internet growth in areas that do not adhere to the general plan. The most notable implication of this strategy is that individual access to the Internet has been essentially prohibited. Since the Internet debuted in Cuba, access has been granted almost exclusively to institutions rather than to individuals. There is no true legal market for residential Internet access in Cuba; commercial ISPs are allowed to offer individual accounts only to those who have obtained sponsorship from a government agency, and such persons are rare.

There are also few opportunities for Cubans to purchase access to the Internet in public facilities such as cybercafés. Cuba's first cybercafé was established in 1999 in Havana's Capitolio building, which is the headquarters of the Ministry of Science, Technology, and the Environment. Internet access is available at an hourly rate in dollars, and tourists are the primary visitors; some reports suggest that Cubans need a letter of authorization from their employers or other sponsoring institution to gain access.[37] A second cybercafé, El Aleph, opened in Havana in November 2000, but it is restricted to members of the Cuban Union of Writers and Artists (UNEAC) and provides access only to select web pages.[38] Some tourist hotels in Cuba offer Internet access at dollar rates, but since Cubans are generally restricted from entering tourist hotels, few can gain access to the Internet in this manner.

Entities that do qualify for Internet access include government ministries, universities and schools, Cuban and foreign firms, professional organizations such as the official journalists' union, mass organizations such as the Federation of Cuban Women, and CSOs that are legally registered with the Ministry of Justice. Still, membership in one of the appropriate categories does not guarantee an institution access. The current regulations stipulate that any entity seeking to establish a local area network with a direct connection to the Internet must obtain a license from the MIC.[39] This rule apparently does not apply to dial-up accounts, but even those require approval, which can be denied. By controlling which institutions gain access to the Internet, the Cuban authorities seek to ensure that the development of the Internet proceeds according to their general plan.

Areas of Use

Informáticos *and the National Intranet*

Cuba's restriction of individual access to the Internet does not mean it has ignored the potential benefits that computers can bring to the public. For several years the regime has been enthusiastically pursuing a goal of "the propagation of computer culture," one that involves computer education and even computer networking, but not necessarily Internet access. Cuba has embarked upon a mass computer literacy program, making use of the post offices, the school system, and the youth computer clubs of the Union of Young Communists. These efforts are best understood as analogous to Cuba's massive literacy campaign in the 1960s in which thousands of volunteers fanned across the countryside to teach basic reading and writing skills to poor Cuban peasants. While the regime has consistently endeavored to increase literacy, it has also blocked the circulation of independent publications and used official newspapers and magazines to serve the political goals of the revolution. In a similar manner, Cuban authorities seek to provide the public with the benefits of computing while carefully controlling who has direct access to the Internet.

A major component of this strategy involves the construction of Cuba's national intranet. The intranet is accessible to the public through a network of post offices and through the youth computer clubs all around the island. Thirty facilities were in operation as of November 2001, and the Cuban government hopes to extend the network to more than two thousand locations. Intranet users can set up international e-mail accounts, but access to the web is limited to Cuban web sites. As with access to Internet cafés in Havana, use of the intranet must be paid for in dollars, but the internal network is cheaper than full Internet use, costing $4.50 for three hours of access.[40] This price is still high compared with the average state salary (equivalent to $10 a month), but it is more affordable for Cubans with direct access to dollars, such as those working in the tourist industry. Sending international e-mails through the intranet is significantly cheaper than placing international phone calls (costing \$2.30 a minute to the United States, for instance), and it is likely to be popular among those with family and friends abroad, particularly in light of the recent interruptions in telephone service to the United States.

While it is possible that Cuba may extend access to web sites hosted outside Cuba, its approach is likely to involve the selective white-listing of sites, as is the case with the Internet café El Aleph. Indeed, the head of Cuba's e-commerce commission has even suggested that selecting sites for inclusion on the national intranet might be a potential business opportunity for foreign investors.[41] Regardless of whether international web access is eventually introduced, the government control of network access points and the informal, nontechnological monitoring of users will be much easier in post offices and at youth computer clubs than in privately run cybercafés. Regulating and monitoring locations for public Internet access have been significant challenges for many other authoritarian regimes.

Beyond the continuing intranet project, the number of Cubans with full access to the Internet is too limited to constitute true mass access. In this context Cuba has not had to (or has chosen not to) develop the same sort of large-scale, centralized system for blocking web sites that many other authoritarian regimes employ. There have been reports that specific web pages are sometimes blocked, but Cuban officials claim (and most evidence confirms) that such censorship is carried out only at the institutional level, where an employer with Internet access, for instance, will limit employee access to certain sites.[42] This pattern fits Cuba's history of exercising control over the mass media at a local level rather than through a centralized government censorship agency. Furthermore, Cuba's selective granting of Internet access ensures a certain amount of trustworthiness among users.[43] While definitely not foolproof, this strategy means that those who have been privileged with Internet access are much more likely than the general population to share the regime's point of view and be unreceptive to critical or challenging information. However, if the regime ever does move toward widespread unrestricted public access to the Internet, it may choose to implement a centralized system of firewalls based on web site blacklisting or keyword analysis.

Admittedly, the Cuban government's access controls are not perfect. With a population famous for its resourcefulness and ability to circumvent official obstacles, there is a growing number of *informáticos* in Cuba, technologically savvy individuals who obtain underground access to the Internet.[44] Would-be Internet users with home computers have various options for obtaining unofficial access. Those with dial-up accounts at work may simply connect from a computer at home, and they may share that account with friends and neighbors, just as many Cubans who have telephones share them with those who do not. Similarly, one can purchase Internet access on the black market, usually to dial-up accounts that are legitimately used by approved institutions during the day. Various reports cite prices of $20–$40 a month for the service.[45] ETECSA has also started selling Internet access cards to foreigners ($15 for five hours), and some Cubans with computers have been able to obtain these cards illegally, using the card's temporary username and password to log on from home.

It is difficult to estimate the extent of underground Internet use in Cuba. Although it is undoubtedly limited by the considerable expense and difficulty of obtaining an Internet-capable computer, the potential exists for underground Internet access to grow and become more of a challenge to state control. In particular, Cuba may eventually choose to relax the restrictions on individual Internet access in order to capture some of the black-market revenue, just as it legalized the use and possession of dollars in 1993 to capitalize on the already widespread trade in the currency. The introduction of international e-mail through the national intranet may constitute a step in that direction. E-mail has always been one of the Internet's most attractive applications, especially for new users, and those who can legally and conveniently gain international e-mail access through a local post office may be dissuaded from purchasing full Internet access on the black market.

On the whole, use of the Internet by the Cuban public does not currently pose a great challenge to the regime. Admittedly, Cuban authorities have little control over underground Internet users and cannot assume they are as sympathetic to the government as those granted official access. Still, one can safely assume that only a minority of underground Internet users are actively seeking political information on the Internet. Many are likely to use the medium principally for entertainment, job-related research, or communication with relatives abroad, just as in the rest of the world. Cuba's continuing project to establish public access to a national intranet is also unlikely to pose a significant challenge to the regime, since the government will have oversight of all the domestic content that can be viewed. Indeed, the regime may benefit from the proactive use of the intranet for political mobilization and the dissemination of government information, just as it has with other media.

The main way in which public Internet use might challenge the regime is if the pattern of limited Internet access were to change, either through the extension of full Internet access to Cuba's post office network or with a relaxation of access restrictions to capture revenue being lost to the black market. The impact of public Internet use would then depend on how significantly access increases and how effectively the regime institutes a system of content control.

Civil Society Organizations: Access by Approval

While Internet use among the wider public has been limited in Cuba, civil society organizations in the country have long been important users of the Internet. Tinored, one of the four Cuban networks that established an international e-mail connection in the early 1990s, provided free e-mail access to a handful of officially registered CSOs (thirty-one by a 1996 count).[46] Tinored's connectivity for CSOs was discontinued in 1997 because of financial problems, but many of the organizations that were connected subsequently acquired accounts with commercial providers. Today, legally registered CSOs qualify as institutions that can apply for Internet access, and Internet use by such organizations figures into the government's vision for the informatization of Cuban society.

In practice, however, Cuba's policy of prioritizing Internet access has limited the number of CSOs that actually have use of the medium, and it has reduced the potential for politically challenging Internet use. A survey of sixteen organizations during the summer of 1998 found that the level of Internet access granted each was strongly correlated with its orientation toward the government.[47] CSOs operating in the areas of environmental conservation and sustainable development—both social priorities of the government—almost universally enjoyed access to international e-mail. Several think tanks, also pro-government in their orientation, received similar levels of e-mail access, and one was granted the privilege of full Internet access. In addition, two Protestant religious organizations favored by the government used e-mail for many years. Such CSOs shared macrolevel goals and priorities with the state, only rarely disagreeing with officials about the organization's specific approaches to projects or activities.

The picture was quite different for CSOs that emphasized their neutrality and for dissidents who were openly critical of the regime. While sympathetic religious organizations had long enjoyed access to e-mail, the famously neutral Catholic charity Caritas endured extensive delays in receiving an official ruling on its application for e-mail access. It had received no response at the time of the survey, although the government had rejected its request to connect directly to the network of Caritas International through a donated satellite system.[48] The situation was even more pronounced for three dissident groups that had been openly critical of the government and were unable to register their organizations legally. None had achieved access to computer communications of any sort, nor could they use fax machines or place international phone calls, and their local telephone communications were constantly monitored. Several had received donated computers from supporters abroad, which they used for such tasks as word processing and database management, but authorities eventually confiscated the machines under the guise of "registering" them.

Underground access is growing more common in Cuba, but the extensive surveillance of known dissidents makes it extremely difficult for them to gain access to the Internet. Even the introduction of international e-mail access through the Cuban intranet does not necessarily mean that dissidents will be able to get online, much less use the medium for political communication in an environment where use can be easily monitored. The one possible exception involves the Cuban Institute of Independent Economists (ICEI). In December 2001 ICEI established a web site that is hosted in the United States; it features the group's publications and other information related to its mission, including an extensive directory of other dissident groups and their contact details. The organization's director, Martha Beatriz Roque, claims that the site is the first run entirely by dissidents from within Cuba.[49] It is unclear, however, how much information these dissidents are able to send abroad by e-mail versus other, less high-tech means. The site itself implies that it is designed and managed by collaborators living abroad, contrary to Roque's statement.[50]

Pro-state organizations with access to e-mail have found it to be an effective tool for networking with foreign CSOs, forming alliances with organizations that provide funding and logistical assistance in carrying out their activities in Cuba. Several CSOs sympathetic to the regime use their international e-mailing capacity to help organize protests against U.S. policy toward Cuba, such as the Friendshipment Caravan, which circumvents the embargo to bring unlicensed aid donations to the island. All the surveyed CSOs with access to e-mail rated it their number one means of international communication, and many said that it had a significant impact on the functioning of the organization. It is clear that use of the Internet can support transnational networking efforts among organizations aligned with the regime. Cuba's controls on Internet access, however, have lessened the potential use of the medium by those who oppose the regime or who seek significant reform. In such an environment, the use of the Internet by Cuban CSOs poses little challenge to the regime and may work to its net benefit.

E-Health and State Propaganda on the Net

The provision of citizen services and the maintenance of the social safety net are important legitimating factors for Cuba's authoritarian regime. Its ability to successfully deliver its part of the social contract, however, has been challenged since the loss of Soviet subsidies in the early 1990s. In this context, e-government offers the possibility of better serving Cuban citizens while improving the regime's chances of survival. Although Cuba has not yet developed an extensive e-government plan, it hopes to expand its online citizen services in the future, especially as it develops the national intranet. According to its strategic objectives for 2003, the MIC hopes to introduce such services as online ticket sales, legal transactions, and housing exchanges through its wired post offices.[51] The Cuban government has operated an official web site for several years; at present it provides information but no interactive services.[52] The government's web site appears oriented more to foreign than domestic audiences, but that may change as the national intranet develops.

Cuba's most important and long-standing effort in the realm of e-government involves its medical information network Infomed, which is operated by the Ministry of Public Health. Because it involved connecting only medical personnel to the network, Infomed was established long before the implementation of other e-government programs involving the actual provision of public services online. Infomed was founded in the early 1990s as one of the first computer networks in Cuba and was one of four with access to international e-mail before a direct Internet connection was established. The network connects medical centers around the country and features such services as electronic journals, medical databases, and e-mail lists for disseminating health alerts. Infomed has been a boon to Cuba's otherwise struggling health system, which is plagued by difficulty in distributing information. The system has received support from foreign organizations, such as USA/Cuba Infomed, which delivers donations of used computers from the United States for use in the·network.

While e-government may be of growing importance to Cuba in the future, externally oriented propaganda currently constitutes the most extensive political use of the Internet. Countering Cuba's negative image in the international media was one of the original incentives for establishing Internet connectivity, and the regime has long made the use of the Internet for international propaganda a priority.[53] As the vice minister of the MIC stated in March 2001, "Our enemies are the ones who should be afraid, for the Internet is an ideal medium for disseminating the truth about Cuba."[54] Various government-affiliated portals in Cuba offer official perspectives on current events, with frequent criticism of the United States. The site <cubavsbloqueo.cu> (Cuba versus the blockade), for instance, rallies international opposition to the U.S. embargo of Cuba. Similarly, the site <elian.cu> was established to present Cuba's perspective of the 1999–2000 custody battle over Elián Gonzalez. Cuban officials have even used the Internet to communicate with members of the U.S. Congress opposed to the U.S. policy toward Cuba.

Cuba's state media have also made an adroit use of the Internet to increase their international projection. Radio Havana Cuba, the government's short-wave radio station, posts transcripts of its shows on the Internet. The international edition of the Communist Party's newspaper *Granma* established a web site in 1996, and its online edition can now be read daily in five languages.[55] Other important publications are also available on the web, such as the domestic edition of *Granma,* the national labor union's *Trabajadores,* and the Union of Young Communists' *Juventud Rebelde.*[56] The web sites of such international media as CNN often link to Cuba's online media when they wish to cite the Cuban perspective on a current issue. Such exposure can generate significant traffic. *Granma*'s site received more than 1 million hits in óne week at the height of the Elián Gonzalez crisis.[57] The Cuban government's various Internet portals and online publications are also extensively interlinked, and they form the dominant presence among web sites based in Cuba. Internet searches for general information on Cuba easily hit upon this externally oriented government information.

On the whole, the political use of the Internet has been beneficial to Cuba's authoritarian regime. E-government measures, although limited, work to strengthen the regime's legitimacy by facilitating the provision of public services. The Cuban government has also effectively used the Internet to share its perspective on international events and to improve the regime's image around the world. Without significant change in the Cuban political system, such as the legalization of opposition parties, it seems unlikely that any political use of the Internet could pose a challenge to the regime.

Venture Socialism? Online Tourism and E-Commerce

While Cuba has been careful to avoid the development of a primarily commercial Internet, it has enthusiastically pursued certain economic benefits that the medium has to offer. The economic use of the Internet in Cuba has generally followed the country's pattern of bifurcating its external and domestic economies. Hence, the great majority of Internet use has been concentrated in the export-oriented and tourist industries.

Among Cuba's small private sector of self-employed individuals, there has been only minimal use of the Internet, much of it involving underground access. Nonetheless, Internet use appears to be increasing among this domestic private sector. A handful of self-employed Cubans doing freelance web design or graphic design for international clients have been able to obtain legal Internet access and to market their services over the Internet.[58] Others have not received official permission for self-employment but use an underground Internet connection to provide web design and other Internet-related services on the black market. Often they create advertising web sites for Cubans who run private, home-based restaurants or who rent rooms in their homes to tourists; these are generally posted on free web servers outside the country.[59]

While Internet use in the Cuban private sector may be on the rise, it is still too limited to pose any real challenge to the regime. Cuban authorities are concerned with the social impact of growing class divisions and the emergence of a nouveau riche from gains made in tourism or the informal economy. Yet the regime has weathered this dynamic for a decade now, and while the emergence of class divisions remains a potential source of instability, the Internet has contributed only minimally to this trend. For the near future, many more Cubans will participate in the dollar-denominated economy as taxi drivers, tourist guides, and hotel employees and in any number of activities more accessible to them than profiting from underground Internet access.

As for legal Internet use by the self-employed, such as freelance web designers with officially sanctioned access, the government controls both Internet access and the legality of the activity itself, both of which it could cut off at any time. In fact, it is much more common for Cuban web designers to work directly for an employer rather than as freelancers and to do their work without being granted Internet access.[60] The government is promoting the study of web design to train workers for free trade zones, where they would work for foreign companies but be paid in local currency by the Cuban government. For all these reasons, it is unlikely that Internet entrepreneurship could emerge as a challenge to the regime under the current situation of controlled Internet access.

While the entrepreneurial use of the Internet has been limited in Cuba, the government has been actively promoting Internet use in the externally oriented economy. The Internet has long been an important vehicle for encouraging foreign investment in Cuba. When the country's first web site, <Cubaweb.cu>, was established in 1996, it secured financial backing from the Cuban magazine *Business Tips on Cuba,* and one of its important functions has been advertising Cuba as an investment destination.[61] Legislation relevant to investors, such as Cuba's foreign investment laws and customs regulations, is featured on the site in full text. In addition to Cubaweb, several other sites are specifically targeted to foreign investors. The web site of *Business Tips on Cuba* (which is separate from Cubaweb) touts the many opportunities for investment in Cuba, and the Cuban Chamber of Commerce runs a site providing information and advertising services for foreign investors already doing business in the country.[62]

In addition to encouraging foreign investment in general, the Cuban government has been enthusiastically promoting Internet development in key industries that can generate hard currency and stimulate the Cuban economy. Two of the most prominent are tourism and biotechnology. Many of Cuba's government-affiliated portals advertise Cuba as a travel destination and provide general information about attractions available to tourists who visit the country. Most of Cuba's state tourist firms operate web pages with extensive information on hotels, excursions, and car rentals, including some online reservations. Cuba's biotechnology industry has been an important area of computer networking since the days before the country's direct Internet connection. CIGBnet, a computer network linking biotechnology research centers, was one of the four Cuban networks with international e-mail access during the 1990s, and it has continued to grow in sophistication and services since Cuba's direct connection to the Internet. The network provides the biotechnology industry with e-mail and Internet connectivity, and its international web site markets Cuban biotechnological products.

E-commerce joint ventures constitute an increasingly important type of Internet use in the externally oriented economy. Some of Cuba's first forays into Internet development came in the area of e-commerce: a web-based music store was established in 1996, and a service for online remittances was set up in 1997, allowing foreigners to send money to Cuban residents by means of the Internet. Recently the Cuban government has become even more enthusiastic about e-commerce, in 1999 forming a commission to promote the activity.[63] Several e-commerce services have been established in the past several years, and more are likely to come online in the future. There are several Internet travel agencies specializing in travel to Cuba, most of which are run by foreign entrepreneurs in partnership with Cuba's state tourist firms.[64] Online stores selling Cuban merchandise abroad have multiplied, and many have moved beyond the traditional offering of Cuban music. The site <Latincuba.com>, for instance, offers multimedia CD–ROMs, photograph collections, books, videos, and Cuban artwork. Several web sites are geared to Cuban exiles, who may purchase consumer goods as gifts to be delivered to family and friends in Cuba.[65] Although most Cuban e-commerce ventures have been devised for foreign consumers, one business-to-business portal has been established for selling Cuban products to foreign firms.[66]

On the whole, the regime seems likely to benefit from the economic uses of the Internet in Cuba, since most serve to increase the government's intake of hard currency and move the Cuban economy further from the crisis years of the early 1990s. Cuba's economic division has insulated most of this Internet activity from the lives of everyday Cubans. They benefit from the state's increased economic solvency and improved capacity for social spending (which are important legitimating factors for the regime), but most Cubans are not directly exposed to the entrepreneurial culture of the Internet economy. As mentioned, a handful may be using the Internet to support self-employment or other private-sector activity (either legitimate or illegal), but the Internet's impact in this area is minimal and is unlikely to increase unless public access is widened. Even if the increasing inequality among Cubans poses a future challenge to the regime's stability, the Internet will not play a significant role in the process.

A final way that economic uses of the Internet in Cuba might challenge the regime is through the political preferences of foreign investors, either those that invest directly in Cuba's Internet ventures or those who are drawn to invest in other sectors through Cuba's online advertising. This possibility seems distant, however, given the current track record of most foreign investors, who tend to focus strictly on business and to maintain good political relations with the government. Among the foreign investors that have been involved in Cuba's e-commerce ventures, several have been explicitly supportive of the regime in their public statements. Renegade CIA agent Philip Agee, for instance, has boasted that his online travel agency, <Cubalinda.com>, represents "another concrete way to support the revolution."[67] Meanwhile, the web site for Tour and Marketing International (run by Stephen Marshall, another prominent Internet investor) states as part of its "corporate stance on Cuba" that it defends "Cuba's right to national sovereignty, independence and self-determination."[68]

Embargo on the Internet: Battles over Cuba Policy

The largest share of Cuba-related political information on the Internet emanates not from domestic sources but from foreign-based organizations trying to influence Cuban politics and U.S. policy toward Cuba. Groups from across the political spectrum use the Internet to organize campaigns and publicize their positions. Many organizations of similar ideological stance are linked online, creating pro- and anti-Castro online communities. Right-wing exile organizations such as the Cuban American National Foundation and Brothers to the Rescue maintain web sites that promote their activities while criticizing the regime. More moderate groups, such as the Cuban Committee for Democracy, criticize the U.S. stance toward Cuba and call for a peaceful transition on the island. Some web sites, including Cubanet and CubaFreePress, publish stories by independent Cuban journalists. Human rights and freedom-of-speech organizations such as Amnesty International, Human Rights Watch, and the Committee To Protect Journalists regularly post critical reports online. Several business associations, including the Cuba Trade and Economic Council and the American Chamber of Commerce of Cuba, call for an end to the U.S. embargo and offer information about Cuban trade on their web sites. Finally, Cuban solidarity organizations use the Internet in their efforts to denounce U.S. policy toward Cuba and to support the Cuban regime. These range from Global Exchange, which runs "reality tours" to the island, to Pastors for Peace, which organizes shipments of humanitarian aid in protest of the embargo.

It is difficult to say how much such international uses of the Internet ultimately matter for Cuban politics. While strong condemnations from Castro's critics abroad are unlikely to affect the regime's policies or political stability directly, organized interests do influence the policies of the United States and other countries toward Cuba. In turn, those policies affect the stability of Cuba's authoritarian regime, though the effectiveness of various policy options in promoting political change is a hotly debated issue. The Cuban American National Foundation has long been influential in the maintenance of a hard-line U.S. policy toward Cuba, while the farm lobby and pro-trade business interests have helped to soften the embargo in recent years. The positions of Cuban solidarity organizations may influence those governments inclined to take a more sympathetic view toward Cuba, while the reports of human rights groups provide fodder for those who openly criticize the regime. In the end, however, it is hard to identify an instance in which Internet use by such groups has had a major effect on the policy of foreign governments toward Cuba. The use of the Internet is likely to augment the visibility of organizations across the political spectrum that take a stance on policy toward Cuba, but their influence depends largely on relationships established and activities conducted offline.

Conclusion: Wishful Thinking Confronts Reality

As our analysis should demonstrate, much of the wishful thinking about the Internet's impact in Cuba is unfounded. Since the Internet first debuted in the country in 1996, Cuban authorities have guided its development according to a plan that prioritizes applications in specific areas while minimizing the potential for subversive or politically challenging uses. Unlike many other authoritarian regimes, Cuba has forgone a primarily market-led model of Internet development, choosing instead to implement a general moratorium on individual access and to control carefully which entities and institutions are granted connectivity. The inspiration for Cuba's efforts is broad, involving much more than simple political control. Cuba's leaders genuinely view the Internet as a limited resource whose development must be guided by the state to achieve the maximum social benefit. They have been enthusiastic about harnessing the Internet to improve public health services and to meet educational goals. National security concerns have also played a role in Cuba's approach to the medium, given the United States' history of using other ICTs to foment opposition in Cuba and its stated aim of using telecommunications to provide "support for the Cuban people."[69]

Certainly areas exist in which Internet use could provide a greater challenge to authoritarian rule in the future. Internet access among the general public is minimal and for the most part carefully controlled, but that pattern could change if black-market access expands significantly; if revenue lost to underground access encourages the state to relax restrictions on public use; or if the regime were ever to allow access to the Internet by means of the national intranet that it is building. The specific implications of more widespread Internet access in Cuba would depend on how the medium is being used by the public, for we cannot assume that public Internet use would be challenging to the regime. At the very least, however, such use would have the potential to pose a greater threat to authoritarian rule. Likewise, Internet use by Cuba's nascent domestic private sector, while minimal at the moment, would be likely to expand under a situation of increased Internet access. Again, such use would not necessarily challenge authoritarian rule in Cuba but would increase the probability of such a challenge.

These possibilities are highly speculative, however, and many are contingent upon marked changes in the regime's approach to regulating Internet access. It is much more likely that the development of the Internet in Cuba will continue with the state largely in control, allocating access to the medium only in priority areas. To date, this pattern of Internet development has largely proceeded beneficially for Cuba's authoritarian regime. As it continues to develop a national intranet accessible to the public through post offices and youth computer clubs, Cuba gains yet another mass medium over which it can exercise content control and which can be used for such goals as top-down political mobilization. The state's control of Internet access for Cuban CSOs means that sympathetic organizations can use the medium to support their activities, while those that are critical are denied the opportunity. The few existing e-government measures in Cuba work to the regime's benefit by facilitating the provision of public services, which is an important element of popular legitimacy. The most important political use of the Internet in Cuba involves the dissemination of international propaganda by the Cuban government, thus providing a soapbox for a regime that is oft-maligned in other international media. Cuba is also promoting Internet development in areas of the externally oriented economy, such as tourism, which serve to increase the regime's access to hard currency and to improve its financial solvency.

The belief that ICTs will promote political change in Cuba is certainly not a new one. A decade and a half of Radio Martí broadcasting attests to the U.S. government's great hopes for a technologically facilitated challenge to Fidel Castro's regime. A similar expectation is at work in the case of the Internet, as observers speculate about the Cuban revolution's supposed incompatibility with the information revolution. Yet Cuba's long history of exercising effective control over ICTs has carried through into the era of the Internet, and its strategy of restricting Internet development to priority areas has allowed the regime to reap benefits from the medium while avoiding potentially challenging impacts. Whatever the future holds for Cuba's authoritarian regime, it is unlikely that the Internet will play a significant role in its demise.

CHAPTER FOUR

Catching Up and Cracking Down in Singapore, Vietnam, and Burma

> The Net and related technologies are encouraging individuals to express their opinions more frequently, efficiently and vociferously. Asian governments that previously relied on control will be forced to concede a higher degree of freedom to their people. The Internet, inadvertently and indirectly, will soon be the foremost exponent of democracy.
>
> —Hong Kong–based businessman Yat Siu, as quoted in *Asiaweek*, November 24, 2000

As thousands of new Asian users log on every week, many predict that the region's authoritarian regimes will soon buckle under the weight of the Internet. Expectations about the Internet and political change in Southeast Asia stem from highly publicized anecdotes about the technology's use in places like Indonesia, Malaysia, and the Philippines, where such use did help to empower grassroots movements and in some cases to transform them into legitimate political opposition.[1] At the same time, high-profile arrests and draconian ICT laws contribute to the impression that governments in Southeast Asia are merely reacting to technology, not proactively engaging with it.

Yet authoritarian countries in the region have embarked on ambitious and successful ICT–promotion programs, attracting international investment and respect for their innovations. Malaysia has set up a censorship-free Multimedia Corridor to solicit investment in high-tech projects, with some success. Singapore has become the host to one of the world's foremost online governments, combining and streamlining government functions to enhance citizen services. Even Vietnam is ambitiously aiming to build a domestic software industry that will enable it to compete in the global economy. Clearly, the relationship between authoritarian rule in Southeast Asia and technology is more complex than has been commonly portrayed.

The authoritarian tendencies that characterize several Southeast Asian countries make the region particularly relevant for examining the Internet's political impact. Despite rapid economic development that has boosted regional standards of living, expectations for democratization following swift economic growth have not been borne out in most countries in Southeast Asia. While a few long-standing authoritarian regimes have collapsed (most notably in Indonesia), democratization elsewhere has stagnated. Some governments, such as Singapore's semi-authoritarian regime, have proved remarkably stable. As successive waves of democratization sweep the globe, authoritarianism in Southeast Asia endures, despite growing economic, social, and political pressures.

We examine three Southeast Asian cases in this chapter: Singapore, Vietnam, and Burma. Each exhibits different levels of authoritarianism and Internet diffusion, yet all three have devised strategies for managing the political impact of Internet use.

Regional Considerations: A Web of "Asian Values"

Internet growth in the region has been rapid. From nearly 49 million at the end of 2000, Asia's total number of Internet users is expected to grow to 173 million by 2004, increasing the region's share of the world's online population from 21 percent to 27 percent. Meanwhile, Asian e-commerce revenues of $39.4 billion in 2000 are projected to rise to $339 billion by 2004, which though a small part of total worldwide revenues is nonetheless a significant increase.[2] Expenditures on information and communication technology have been significant: Vietnam spent 6.5 percent of its GDP on ICT in 2000, which is less than the 9.7 percent spent by Singapore but more than that spent by countries such as Egypt, Russia, and Venezuela.[3] At the same time, differences between countries in Southeast Asia can be striking. Whereas Singapore boasts one of the highest levels of Internet penetration in the world, Burma allows virtually no domestic Internet access.

Drawing general conclusions about the Internet's political impact in Southeast Asia is difficult, particularly given different political systems and varying levels of Internet diffusion. Certain regional factors are nevertheless important. We find relevance in analyzing three of the region's authoritarian countries, not so much because of cultural similarities that may support authoritarian rule (which are often overstated and generalized) but because of shared regional and institutional pressures that affect Internet diffusion and use.

For instance, the debate over the existence of a shared regional political culture, or "Asian values," is significant for our purposes. The leaders of many Southeast Asian countries invoke these values, which supposedly encompass a respect for tradition and authority, a preference for consensus over confrontation, and a willingness to accept economic benefits in place of political rights, in justifying the maintenance of information controls and authoritarian rule.[4]

This view of Asian values subsequently influences powerful regional organizations such as the Association of Southeast Asian Nations,[5] whose membership includes the three countries we analyze here. ASEAN has been pushing its member states to promote the development of ICTs and the Internet to boost economic growth, all while ensuring an "Asian" environment on the Internet—that is, controlling for politically and culturally sensitive material. An ASEAN task force created in 1999 proposes to develop a comprehensive plan for an ASEAN e-community aimed at priming ASEAN's member nations to compete in the global information economy.[6] Regional encouragement, either specifically or by example, has been influential in convincing the governments of Burma and Vietnam to engage proactively in developing information technology.[7]

Another regional factor influencing the diffusion of the Internet in Southeast Asia is the pressure to adopt neoliberal economic reforms, many of which would require the deregulation of key sectors. Following the Asian economic crisis of the late 1990s, many countries in Asia adopted, voluntarily or otherwise, economic reform prescriptions from international financial institutions such as the International Monetary Fund (IMF). Such prescriptions often included the deregulation and opening of sectors such as telecommunications, which in turn has had an effect on Internet penetration in the region. Even in countries not subject to specific prescriptions, a regional perception that telecommunication reform is necessary to compete in the global economy has boosted a desire to incorporate Internet diffusion into economic growth plans.

Even while Southeast Asian countries are under pressure to deregulate their telecommunication sectors, many retain the ideal of the developmental state, in which economic progress is shaped by central planning.[8] The continuing diffusion of the Internet in the region thus has proceeded largely at the direction of individual central governments, which craft telecommunication policies and push other technology-related macroeconomic measures. State influence has been crucial in the diffusion of earlier ICTs, such as satellites and cable television.[9]

While these regional similarities and pressures exist, individual cases vary widely. Singapore, for instance, merits special consideration for its government's achievement of what many believed to be impossible: extensive ICT development with a negligible erosion of political control. The significance of this accomplishment is underscored by the fact that other authoritarian regimes, most notably China, have taken an active interest in learning from Singapore's example. As a leading force in ASEAN, Singapore influences its direction. The case of Singapore may therefore illuminate the strategies that other authoritarian and semi-authoritarian regimes will adopt in the future.

Vietnam features a much more authoritarian political system, one burdened by a creaky Leninist bureaucracy and ambivalent economic policies. The country's war-torn history, ambivalent relations with the West, and frequent zigzags on the path to economic development have left it struggling harder with the question of ICT control. The Communist Party sees the control of information as crucial in repressing dissent and in maintaining authority, but it has taken a more haphazard approach toward enforcement than has China. The government is simultaneously placing increased emphasis on the use of ICTs for development, in particular attempting to emulate India's example in creating a domestic software industry.

Military dominance and harsh authoritarian rule characterize Burma, a country largely isolated from the rest of the world.[10] Unlike the other authoritarian regimes we discuss here, the most salient political impact of the Internet in Burma concerns its use outside the country's borders. Given the harsh restrictions on public use of the Internet and other ICTs, the political impact of domestic Internet use in Burma is extremely limited. Yet overseas human rights activists and Burmese exiles have made effective use of the technology to pressure the regime, primarily through other governments and multinational corporations. Burma's military government is now responding with its own Internet information campaigns, although to date it has been unable to match the effectiveness of its transnational adversaries.

Taken together, Singapore, Vietnam, and Burma illustrate that Internet use does not currently pose a significant threat to the stability of authoritarian rule. It is possible that dissidents, exiles, and grassroots opposition groups may use the technology to challenge long-standing authoritarian governments, as they have in other countries in the region. Yet, given a trend toward proactive government ICT policies, increasing sophistication in repressing or coopting potential opposition, and the state's commitment to bolstering economic growth and political legitimacy through Internet use, it is unlikely that Internet use on the whole will pose a significant challenge to any of these governments.

Singapore: Mastering the Dictator's Dilemma

In contrast to the other cases that we examine in this chapter, Singapore is best classified as a semi-authoritarian regime where opposition parties regularly participate in legitimate parliamentary elections but are effectively prevented from competing meaningfully for power.[11] The ruling People's Action Party (PAP) dominates the elected legislature; in the November 2001 elections, opposition candidates won only two of the twenty-nine seats contested in the eighty-four-member parliament, despite rising dissatisfaction with a sluggish economy.[12]

Since Singapore's emergence as an independent republic in 1965 the PAP has dominated the government and come to be synonymous with the state. As Garry Rodan points out, Singapore's brand of authoritarianism features a system of legal limits on independent political activities.[13] Through regulations, legislation, litigation, and less coercive measures, the ruling party has effectively ruled out meaningful competition from potential and existing challengers. Subtler forms of political manipulation include the intimidation of the media and the channeling of popular dissent through the PAP's own civil society structures, created specifically to coopt public opinion. The government largely conflates independent organization with potential or concrete political opposition and acts to extinguish it. Hence, real contestation for political power is carefully limited. Several additional factors help the PAP maintain its hold on political power, including widespread voter support for the party's uncorrupted government policies, its historical legacy, and its consistent delivery of economic growth and high standards of living.

Extremely rich for its small size (it has a population of 3.9 million), Singapore has a GDP of $92 billion and a 1999 adult literacy rate of 92 percent.[14] Ethnic Chinese make up about 77 percent of Singapore's population, followed by Malay and Indian ethnic groups. This diverse ethnic mix is one reason the government extols stability and professes wariness of any activity that might inflame ethnic or group conflict. Mandarin Chinese, Malay, Tamil, and English are all official languages, but the use of English (Singapore's common language) in particular is widespread and has contributed to the Internet's rapid adoption.

Shaped largely by state planning, Singapore's ICT sector is one of the most dynamic in the world. Computer equipment manufacturing makes up a large portion of the economy; it is estimated that the ICT sector in Singapore currently employs about ninety-three thousand and grows 10–12 percent a year.[15] As of July 2000 Singapore's fixed-line telephone penetration stood at 48.4 percent, mobile phone penetration at 61.2 percent, and total Internet dial-up penetration at 57.4 percent.[16] According to some estimates, personal computer penetration stood at 44 percent in 1999, the second highest rate in Asia after Australia.[17]

The Singaporean government began promoting the widespread development of ICTs in the 1980s, having recognized early that technology would figure prominently in restructuring the economy toward higher value-added production.[18] The country's affluent population proved to be eager adopters of information technology. In the early 1980s, Singaporeans with new personal computers began to set up bulletin board systems with daily dial-up connections to the international FIDOnet for file exchanges with users in other countries.[19] In 1986 a national ICT plan recommended the implementation of a project that would integrate hardware manufacturing and telecommunication and software services. This effort involved the cooperation of several key organizations, including Singapore Telecom and the National Computer Board. By 1992 the National Computer Board had issued a plan to develop a comprehensive broadband computer network by the year 2000, a goal that has been largely fulfilled. In 1999 the National Computer Board and the Telecommunications Authority of Singapore merged, creating a new regulatory board called the Info-communications Development Authority (IDA), under the Ministry of Communications and Information Technology. The IDA continues to monitor the regulatory aspects of ISP licensing, although content falls under the jurisdiction of the Singapore Broadcasting Authority (SBA).

The National University of Singapore and the National Science and Technology Board jointly set up Singapore's first Internet service provider in 1991. Dubbed the Technet Unit, it provided Internet access to the local research and development community. While access was limited at first, by 1994 educational institutions, government organs, and commercial groups were also beginning to seek Internet connections. After a government study that year concluded that Internet access should be made available to the general public, Singapore's first three Internet service providers, Singnet, Pacific Internet, and Cyberway, were launched over the next few years.[20]

In April 2000 Singapore deregulated its telecommunication sector, opening the voice and data parts of its telecommunication industry to full competition and allowing full foreign ownership. Aided in part by this liberalization, the number of ISPs has expanded dramatically. Internet service providers are granted a three-year license by the IDA, renewable for another three. The SBA automatically grants licenses for ISPs, but they must register with the Authority within fourteen days of commencing service.[21] The government has promised a hands-off approach to telecommunication sector regulation and development, although a tradition of state-directed development means that government policy goals may continue to dictate how licenses and regulations are issued.

Currently, government ICT strategy comprises three major points. The first is the development of a broadband infrastructure, making it "a utility like water, gas, electricity and telephone connections."[22] The second is educating Singapore's population about the use of ICTs. Singapore's Education Ministry has implemented a program that aims to provide one computer for every two schoolchildren from the first grade onward. The third leg of the government strategy is to establish Singapore as a hub for electronic commerce, which will entail the further development of a legal framework for contracts, property protection, and privacy protection. The idea, according to a senior minister, is to transform Singapore into "a trusted electronic commerce hub working with other trusted hubs in the world."[23]

The development of this hub apparently does not depend on a more liberal information environment. Despite having a true enthusiasm for technology, Singapore has an extremely circumscribed media and press. Although Singapore's constitution guarantees a variety of freedoms, in practice the government strongly influences the media through both formal and informal channels. Pressure, intimidation, and litigation have worked to enshrine the practice of self-censorship among domestic and, some would argue, international media outlets.[24] Over the years, the PAP has developed a finely tuned media regulation mechanism, relying less on overt threats and more on a tacit understanding that the press will not publish stories that might upset the government. Since the markers delimiting politically sensitive territory can be vague, while punishment is often swift and harsh, self-censorship in the media is the norm rather than the exception, and it often exceeds that which even government officials deem necessary.[25] Although new media have experienced some freedom not found in traditional print and broadcast media, the government appears to be extending its information control methods to the Internet. This strategy relies less on technical censorship than on the underlying infrastructure of social control, one that has been progressively fine-tuned into a sophisticated mechanism.

The government also influences the media through ownership. Singapore Press Holdings Ltd. (SPH), which owns all the general circulation newspapers in Singapore's four official languages, is a private holding company with ties to the government. Every newspaper company must issue both ordinary shares and management shares. The government approves and can dismiss the holders of SPH management stock, who in turn appoint and dismiss board directors and staff.[26] In 2000 SPH also secured licenses to operate television and radio stations. The alternative to SPH is another government-owned company, Media Corp, which runs radio stations and television channels.[27] Given its legacy of media dominance, the government faces few obstacles in extending its influence to the Internet.

Innovation in a Sanitized Environment

Active government promotion has helped to achieve the widespread use of the Internet. As soon as officials decided Internet proficiency was crucial to Singapore's international economic competitiveness, they both facilitated and encouraged public access to the Internet. Computers with Internet access were set up at all national libraries by 1996. Cybercafés also sprung up in great numbers, although these have become much less popular now as more people access the Internet from their homes or offices. The rates for dial-up access were initially kept low to promote access, despite worries that this might cut into profits at the government-run telecommunication operator, Singapore Telecom.[28] As a result of telecommunication liberalization, the number of ISPs expanded from three in 2000 to thirty-six in July 2001.[29]

The Singapore Broadcasting Authority regulates content by granting licenses to web sites; ISPs must route all Internet connections through government proxy servers, which filter sites that the government considers objectionable. According to the government, the license system was adopted to encourage private-sector accountability for material made available to the public. In practice, this forces content providers to be extremely sensitive about what appears on their sites. In 1996 the SBA ordered ISPs to block access to certain sites it considered pornographic, although the exact number and nature of those sites are difficult to ascertain.[30] This was followed in 1997 by an Internet Code of Practice, which clarified the types of material forbidden. The SBA said it did not intend to monitor Internet or e-mail use, relying instead on blocking access through the proxy server system. It is unlikely that the SBA actively monitors Internet use in fine detail, although that option is technically and legally possible through the wide-ranging Internal Security Act. The government has at times taken unannounced strolls through several thousand personal computers with Internet connections, subsequently explaining such actions as sweeping for viruses or pornography.[31] While such intrusion does not appear to be the norm, these actions nonetheless reinforce the prevalent culture of self-censorship. They also diminish the need for the SBA to monitor Internet use continuously and actively.

The established media, which are connected to the government and generally espouse uncritical views, are more visible and widely accessed on the web than are the few independent sites that have sprung up. Almost all Singapore's newspapers, radio, and television stations have web sites; many have built portals, developed exclusive web content, or provided audio and video streaming.[32] AsiaOne, a portal owned by SPH, is an example of how Singapore's traditional media companies are using the Internet. AsiaOne hosts the online version of SPH's seven newspapers, and also contains content on various subjects such as health, sports, and computers. AsiaOne claims that it receives an average of 4.2 million page views a day, ranking second in time spent on Singaporean sites with an average of half an hour a session.[33]

Since most civil society groups tend to have some connection with the PAP, they generally use the Internet in government-approved ways. Nonetheless, a few independent groups have used the Internet to provide a platform for the independent criticism of the PAP. Sites such as Sintercom, Singapore Window, and Think Centre, which arose in the late 1990s, all presented independent news and public forums that gave Singaporean citizens a chance to read and express criticism of government policies and actions within a domestic online environment. Such sites took advantage of a gray area in the regulations, operating on the basis that such sites had not been specifically forbidden.

In the prelude to Singapore's 2001 general election, however, the PAP issued new rules requiring "political" sites to register with the government and making it an offense to publish any election advertising without identifying the publisher and the target of the information.[34] Seeing the rules as part of a general government attempt to stifle free debate through legislative measures, many independent sites quickly shuttered operations rather than risk the continual regulatory ire of the PAP.[35] In November 2001 a freelance journalist was the first person charged for violating the new regulations after he posted an article online that criticized PAP leaders for violating election laws.[36] There is now little room for strong criticism of the PAP on domestically run forums, apart from that permitted within such state-sanctioned arenas as the Straits Times online and its various affiliates.

In sum, although Internet use by the public and civil society organizations is substantial, it has not had much effect in either provoking or facilitating political change in Singapore. Through a long-standing policy of encouraging self-censorship, the government has effectively staunched much of the Internet's potential as a medium for political expression. Although the government often emphasizes the pornography-blocking aspects of its censorship scheme, the net effect appears to be one of generalized self-censorship, as users anticipate and avoid government backlash. Fledgling independent social organizations that attempt to use the Internet are generally stifled by legislative measures as well as less overt coercive means. Internet-enabled political discourse is not impossible in Singapore; through Usenet groups, e-mail lists, and internationally hosted web sites, Singaporeans can and do exchange views that politely debate the PAP's vision for society. Yet, by defining the parameters of discourse, the PAP has been able to ensure that such discourse remains unthreatening, perhaps even beneficial. Some have posited that Asian authoritarian regimes have in the past been able to preempt popular calls for political liberalization by allowing a modicum of breathing room in public discourse; this may be one convincing characterization of Singapore's online public sphere.[37]

It is in the realm of the state that Singapore's engagement with technology has had the most impact. Singapore's e-government strategy has proved to be not only immensely successful at home, but it is discussed and imitated by countries all over the world. The city-state has made it a matter of policy to incorporate the Internet and other ICTs into many aspects of government functions, facilitating the provision of efficient government services to most citizens. The government has also implemented ICT training and education programs for both civil servants and the public at large.

In April 1995 most government agencies in Singapore had little use for, or even knowledge of, the Internet. The government experimented with several network technologies, including teletext and interconnected public kiosks. Yet when the decision was reached to abandon an internal network system for the global Internet, the government moved with alacrity. Three months later, all thirty-six government agencies and ministries had been connected to the Internet. By August, the prime minister's office had launched an Internet recruitment system for government positions, and a few government web sites went online. Six hundred job applications were submitted over the Internet within three months.[38] Currently, Singapore's thirty thousand public servants use the government e-mail system, and the government intranet receives 50 million hits a year. Hundreds of public services are already available online, and more procedures are projected to be online soon. The government plans to spend S$1.5 billion (US$0.86 billion) on e-government programs over the next few years.[39]

Singapore's eCitizen project stands out among e-government projects, largely for its provision of several integrated services through a single portal. Service packages are organized according to life events rather than by government agency, which saves time for citizens. Each topic, such as "family" or "care for the elderly," smoothly integrates the services of various ministries, requiring substantial administrative coordination. As of June 2002 the portal allowed citizens to conduct hundreds of transactions—from paying parking fines to lodging formal corruption complaints—in areas such as business, education, employment, health, housing, and recreation.[40]

The PAP's vast resources also give it an edge over other political parties in using ICTs to promote its platform and agendas. Pop-up windows advertising web interviews with former prime minister Lee Kuan Yew enhance such features as party history, speeches, and information on how to join the party. Owing to uncertainties in legislation, opposition parties have been slow to use the Internet for campaigning. Some, such as the Singapore Democratic Party, have begun to host forums, post information on participation, and explicitly criticize the PAP. Government officials have explicitly noted, however, that "political advertisers" will not be able to circumvent the new rules against online political campaigning by sending mass e-mails disguised as private communications.[41]

All in all, the impact of Internet use in Singapore's political sphere has been significant. Since the PAP is best able to harness and deploy information resources, it appears that most of the political benefits of engaging with the Internet accrue to the ruling party rather than to a wider range of political actors. True, the citizenry at large benefits from the PAP's extensive and creative engagement with the technology, especially in its increasingly efficient and lifestyle-enriching provision of services. Yet, since citizen satisfaction with the state stabilizes the PAP's voter base, Singapore's e-government success appears to have been a net benefit for the PAP. It is possible that opposition parties might in the future make more extensive use of the Internet to reach potential supporters in the population or to rally support from abroad. This seems unlikely at present, however, with the PAP setting the rules, crafting the legislation, and controlling the political environment.

The government continues to drive the Internet agenda in the economic arena in accordance with its vision of state-led development. This agenda includes an ambitious plan to develop a knowledge-based economy, bolstering Singapore's potential to become an information hub for the region. Singapore's minister for Information and the Arts has said that "the lifeblood of Singapore has always been information."[42] In fact, over the past several years Singapore has made concerted efforts to promote itself as a base for international media companies seeking to do business in the region. Electronic business information services have been the most rapidly expanding area, perhaps because they are less troubling for authoritarian governments than is overtly political reporting.[43] Indeed, if Singapore's track record with investment by traditional media companies is anything to go by, it seems unlikely that investment in new media would lead to new pressures on the government to loosen controls on its media sector. The PAP has, through litigation and other measures, successfully pressured a number of international media companies to follow its dictates.[44]

With respect to e-commerce, the government introduced promotional programs as early as August 1996, already aiming to establish Singapore as an international e-commerce center. IDA has outlined a strategy to "Dotcom the Private Sector," involving the branding of Singapore as an "E-Business Thought Leadership Center." The government sees its role as crucial in laying a foundation for e-commerce, through the provision of a sophisticated infrastructure (such as broadband) and a pro-competitive policy and regulatory framework. The deregulation of certain sectors, such as telecommunications, has been undertaken to facilitate the growth of e-commerce.

As such, the largest political impact of Internet use in the economic sector may be that the government is forced to cede direct control of certain sectors more quickly than originally anticipated. To the extent that this mitigates the PAP's influence over those sectors—for example, government-linked corporations such as Singapore Telecom—Internet use and promotion in the economic sphere may undermine the PAP's capacity to direct economic development.

One might assume that further deregulation and economic liberalization in Singapore, which already boasts free and transparent markets, might naturally lead to genuine political contestation. Although modernization theories posit that an educated, entrepreneurial sector may push the government for politically liberalizing reforms, Singapore already has a well-educated, well-informed private sector that largely supports its semi-authoritarian government as long as it continues to provide material benefits. A transparent, corruption-free capitalist economy and the maintenance of a high quality of life have solidified rather than weakened the PAP's grip on power. Both domestic and foreign investors in new media companies seem likely to follow the practices of investors in the traditional media, inasmuch as they are more likely to submit to the Singaporean government's wishes than to lobby for greater media freedom. As such, further promotion of the Internet in the e-commerce or new media sectors seems unlikely to give rise to significant pressure on the state.

Internet use in the international sphere also appears to have little political impact. While a handful of web sites operating outside Singapore's borders criticize the PAP or, more broadly, Singapore's political system, they do not appear to have generated substantial support either inside or outside Singapore. Former opposition politicians such as Francis Seow or Tang Liang Hong, who now live outside Singapore, disseminate their criticisms through the Internet, but this has not led to any sort of transnational opposition campaign. International press freedom and human rights groups occasionally issue press releases condemning Singapore's restrictive media practices, but they appear to generate little pressure on the government from the outside. This compares starkly with Net-based campaigns against Burma, for example, where Internet use by transnational activists in the international sphere is leveraged to maximum effect against the military junta. This may be partially because Singapore has not produced a substantial exile community actively using the Internet to organize opposition within the country and partially because of Singapore's reputation as a modern, globalized, and corruption-free society, which bolsters its standing among governments and multinational corporations.

Ultimately, Internet use proves a net benefit for the PAP's stability. The PAP's long-standing grip on power has been aided by its active use of ICTs, helping it to modernize government operations and provide a level of citizen satisfaction that most democracies would envy. While some reports cite a level of progress toward greater openness, including increasing public debate in newspapers and Internet chat rooms, civil society organization uses of the Internet have not proved to be a potent challenge to the PAP's sophisticated matrix of official regulations and unspoken inducements to damp politically threatening speech. This same matrix also makes future civil society challenges unlikely. Further investment in e-commerce by either domestic or international companies seems unlikely to create the political opening envisioned by neoliberal optimists.

In short, the PAP appears to have come up with a strategy by which an authoritarian regime can successfully engage with technology without allowing itself to be overwhelmed politically. Future challenges to PAP rule are certainly possible, especially in the event of a prolonged economic downturn or regional instability. Under these circumstances, it seems more likely that Internet use will play a background, rather than a pivotal, role in those challenges.

Vietnam: The Bumpy Road to a Knowledge Economy

The Socialist Republic of Vietnam has been governed by a one-party communist regime since 1975, when North Vietnamese forces overran the formerly U.S.–backed south. With a population of approximately 79 million and GDP of $31 billion (in 2000), it is one of the poorest countries in Asia and is classified as a low-income country by the World Bank.[45] At the same time, Vietnam possesses a young, educated, and healthy population; it boasts an adult literacy rate of 93.1 percent, which is comparable with that of Singapore.[46] Government leaders, as well as aspiring entrepreneurs, dream of using this human capital to create a knowledge-based economy. It will not be a simple task. Organized around more starkly Leninist lines than even China, Vietnam's leaders are trying to promote economic modernization while still half-heartedly invoking communist ideals. Reform, known as *doi moi,* has progressed haltingly since its introduction in 1986. A large black-market economy has developed, and the country is frequently cited as being one of the most corrupt in Asia.[47] Some characterize the country as being in the middle of transitioning from a totalitarian communist regime to an authoritarian capitalist one.[48]

The Central Committee of the Communist Party has gradually reduced its involvement in the government yet still retains significant power and makes all major policy decisions. The elected National Assembly is essentially controlled by the party, which must approve both party and nonparty candidates. In recent years, the National Assembly has come under pressure to make itself more accountable to the electorate and independent from the party. The government has also pledged to expand "grassroots democracy" by giving local councils a greater role. Yet political organization still proceeds along orthodox communist lines. The government does not permit independent political or social organizations. Meanwhile, the Communist Party of Vietnam (CPV) continuously garners high membership, in part because it can provide better housing, jobs, and opportunities. In 2000 the CPV boasted 2.3 million members and gained 113,000 new recruits.[49]

In accordance with its state-led model of development, the government is officially focusing on the promotion of the ICT and software sectors as part of its 2000 Five-Year Plan. Vietnam is still primarily an agrarian society, with 70 percent of its labor force employed in agriculture and forestry.[50] The development of the country's software industry is seen as particularly crucial to establishing a knowledge-based economy. Although its targets are ambitious, the government has repeatedly declared that it is aiming for $500 million worth of software production by 2005. Hanoi is also trying to court high-tech overseas Vietnamese entrepreneurs, who are considered essential to duplicating the Indian model of soliciting investments from nonresident nationals.

At the same time, the government continues to exert strong control over the telecommunication sector, resisting global trends toward deregulation. The Vietnam Post and Telecommunications Corporation (VNPT) operates the telecommunication networks, while the Department General of Post and Telecommunications regulates them. Such close relations between operator and regulator, previously common worldwide, are now rare.[51] The party also keeps a firm grip on print and electronic media, exercising oversight through the Ministry of Culture and Information (MCI). Control is bolstered by security legislation designed to promote self-censorship. As a result, the domestic media rarely publish articles critical of the government. Press laws allow for media outlets to be sued for defamation regardless of the veracity of their information. New regulations have tripled (to 650) the number of press and Internet activities considered "offensive to Vietnamese culture."[52]

As in other countries, the academic and scientific research community pioneered access to the Internet in Vietnam. Yet the government quickly realized the economic and political benefits of a larger state role in the development and promotion of technology. In the early 1990s Hanoi's Institute of Information Technology, in cooperation with the Australian government and private firms, helped establish the first Vietnamese internal network with an international connection to Australia. Called VARENet, for Vietnam Academic Research and Educational Network, its reach was small. Infrastructure was so poor that at times e-mails sent from the Australian National University to Hanoi had to be hand-delivered, by motorbike, around the city.

Other networks subsequently began to proliferate in anticipation of imminent public access to the global Internet, although the government soon realized it would lose an important monopoly if each of those networks were allowed to connect independently to the Internet. It maintained control by issuing the sole Internet connection license to Vietnam Data Communications (VDC), a subsidiary of the monopoly telecommunication provider VNPT, which established a connection on December 1, 1997. VDC is still the only entity allowed to connect directly to the global Internet; all other Internet service providers lease access from VDC. By September 2001 Vietnam had five ISPs, four of them state-run and one a semistate firm. New regulations in August 2001 liberalized the conditions for establishing an ISP, theoretically allowing privately run businesses and foreign companies to establish and run ISPs.[53]

Statistics on Internet access in Vietnam vary widely. Different accounts cite anywhere from eighty-two thousand to two hundred thousand Internet subscribers. Many official subscribers have been reselling their access by establishing Internet cafés, allowing each account to be used by many people. A large percentage of official Internet accounts can also be ascribed to ministries and other government or party institutions. In a country where fixed-line telephone penetration stands at roughly thirty-two telephone mainlines for every one thousand people, most Internet users are concentrated in and around the big cities.[54]

Broadening Access, Blockading Exiles

The Vietnamese government's approach to controlling the political impact of Internet use in the public sphere is similar to that of China, where officials have attempted to promote Internet use while shaping the environment in which use takes place. Since Vietnam first connected to the Internet in 1997 the government has used a system of firewalls, top-down access controls, and encouragement of self-censorship to control the medium. At the same time, because the necessary economic and political infrastructure to achieve this strategy does not appear to be in place, Hanoi's strategy has been less successful in both promoting access and controlling content.

Broadly, Internet content is expected to follow the same rules as traditional media. Domestic content providers need a special license from the Ministry of Interior, and the Foreign Ministry has decreed that all Internet traffic accessible in Vietnam must comply with national security provisions in Vietnam's strict press laws and refrain from damaging the reputations of organizations and citizens. A 1997 interministerial circular requires certification for service and content providers as well as individual users. Since these regulations place the burden of censorship on ISPs and ICPs, many have taken it upon themselves to restrict content that could be construed as critical of the government, including information and databases that may be used by dissidents or NGOs pushing for political change.[55]

The firewall, formally installed in July 1998, prevents the public from accessing forbidden sites, largely comprised of politically themed web pages set up by Vietnamese exiles. VDC is authorized to monitor its subscribers' web usage. Some reports note that government organs selectively monitor e-mail by searching for key words. However, there are indications that Vietnam's firewall is not nearly as comprehensive as that of other authoritarian countries. A researcher for George Soros's Open Society who systematically investigated blocked sites in Southeast Asia in 1998 found that sites blocked in other countries, such as Singapore, were accessible in Vietnam.[56] Other users report few blockages, finding slow connections the main factor hindering access. Although the government has demonstrated its aversion to political speech on the Internet, the haphazard attitude toward enforcement and the tendency for enforcers to look the other way if monetary gain is possible mean that those dedicated to seeking browsers and proxy servers that render the user anonymous can likely circumvent the censorship system. Since web usage is still not particularly widespread, and since a minority of users are dedicated to such practices, many users are still inclined to self-censor when using the Internet.

Although wider Internet usage is in keeping with the government's economic reform goals, the government's pursuit of this policy appears to be ambivalent. Evidence exists that Hanoi is encouraging mass access by selectively granting several hours of free usage a day. Increased public usage of the Internet has also been facilitated by the proliferation of cybercafés in the larger cities, such as Hanoi and Ho Chi Minh City, which resell

Internet access at affordable prices. Yet without significant telecommunication reform it is unlikely that mass Internet use will grow significantly. Since ISPs must route traffic through monopoly provider VDC, its high costs are subsequently passed on to Vietnamese consumers. According to the Center for International Development, twenty hours of monthly Internet access in 2001 cost nearly 43 percent of GDP per capita.[57] Although costs are coming down gradually, the high cost of Internet use serves to discourage a broader segment of the population from accessing the Internet regularly. Moreover, although cheaper Internet cafés have been sprouting up in the large cities, new decrees in 2001 imposed stricter regulations, subjecting them to fines of up to 5 million dong, or US$330.[58]

With access to the global Internet expensive and delivery slow, many Vietnamese have continued to use the country's national intranets, which mirror select international sites and offer substantially lower fees than connecting to the global Internet.[59] These and newer intranets restrict subscribers to officially sanctioned web sites but do not require users to register with the government. The government is actively encouraging users to sign up for the national intranet service, which would provide a "safe" Internet environment for domestic users.

A few dissidents appear to be making increased use of the global Internet to publish their materials. In March 2002 the police arrested Pham Hong Son, a doctor who translated and posted online an article about democracy; in the previous month, another man, Le Chi Quang, was detained at an Internet café for writing an online essay criticizing bilateral negotiations between China and Vietnam.[60] In general, however, although public and civil societal use of the Internet is growing, it does not appear to have reached a state where such usage will pose a threat to the government. Many currently use it primarily for entertainment. Moreover, as domestic content grows, more and more Vietnamese users may be tempted to use government-sanctioned intranets as a way of bypassing exorbitantly high costs. In the future, should these intranets become popular, they would significantly limit the domestic population's access to information unfiltered by the government.

Apart from use by individual dissidents, there is little evidence of underground or potential domestic opposition organizations using the Internet to organize, solicit funds, or otherwise publicize their mission. Most CSOs are part of the Fatherland Front, a CPV–affiliated top-level grouping of organizations, and any Internet use by these organizations is likely to support the goals of the regime. Any group wishing to set up a domestic e-mail list must seek permission from VDC, and permission is rarely granted.

In conjunction with intranet promotion, the government is beginning to use the Internet to streamline its bureaucracy and disseminate propaganda. Even though data suggest that official publications are not widely popular, the official *Nhan Dan* newspaper, the voice of the Vietnamese Communist Party, was among the first to establish an online edition in 1999. The MCI, which regulates Internet content, was also one of the first ministries to set up its own internal information network, called the Culture and Information Network. Its early mission, as a program to "provide information on culture and market for domestic enterprises and introduce Vietnam to foreigners," was inspired by ASEAN meetings held to work toward an ASEAN information superhighway. Although instances of online propaganda are still few, they demonstrate the Vietnamese government's intention to use the Internet as a propaganda organ and a way to boost government efficiency.[61]

For now, the government accounts for the bulk of Internet use in the political sphere. There are no formal opposition parties to counter government claims on the web. At present, the system of user registration, coupled with the perception that the government monitors e-mail, is enough to deter potential opposition from relying extensively on newer ICTs to communicate.

With continuing pressure from ASEAN, the Vietnamese government is likely to further develop e-government service provision and potentially reap the tangible benefits of citizen satisfaction. In this area government officials are no doubt studying the positive effects of e-government in other ASEAN countries. Yet since the type of e-government environment espoused by ASEAN tends to place emphasis on service provision rather than participatory and transparency measures, it is unlikely that encouragement or concrete assistance from ASEAN will result in the increased accountability of elected officials or the oversight of government procedures in Vietnam.

In the economic realm, Internet use and promotion are growing rapidly. This follows Hanoi's plan, which is similar to that adopted by other authoritarian countries, to facilitate economic development by freeing up access to ICTs in the business sector while simultaneously maintaining stricter control over information flow in the political sphere.[62] Low tax rates and a reduction in Internet service costs for ICT businesses are intended to stimulate investment, while the regulation of contract disputes and online trading is intended to boost the development of e-commerce. There is evidence that the official encouragement is paying off: some Vietnamese businesses, particularly import-export operations, are now using the Internet to sell products directly to overseas consumers. Government efforts to use the Internet to increase foreign investment have also increased. The Finance Ministry recently launched a web site in Vietnamese and English featuring several hundred pages of information.

In 2001 Hanoi loosened its restrictions on private-sector involvement in Internet development, enabling any enterprise, state or private, to take part in Internet service provision. While significant, competition at this point is seen by many as simply superficial, since all ISPs must lease connections from the state-owned Vietnam Post and Telecommunications Corporation. Vietnamese businesses have complained over the years that restrictions on Internet use and access prevent them from using the technology to enhance their profits. Some have complained that firewalls make internal communication within companies impossible.[63] It is possible that such domestic pressures, as well as those arising from the U.S.–Vietnam bilateral trade agreement, may eventually help lift Internet restrictions, at least in the business sector.

As such, in the short term, combined domestic and international private-sector pressure may result in the further liberalization of the telecommunication regime and the state's retreat from various sectors. This, in turn, may give way to increased Internet entrepreneurship and the development of a wealthier, independently minded business class. Yet it is doubtful that Internet-driven entrepreneurship will lead to significant political change. Widespread corruption means a cozy relationship between business and government in Vietnam, one that will require significant time and political will to reduce. In the meantime, as is the case in other Asian authoritarian regimes, the business sector is unlikely to place heavy political demands on government.

In contrast to Singapore, significant Vietnam-related Internet use takes place among the nearly 3 million Vietnamese exiles who reside in Europe, North America, and elsewhere. Much of that Internet activity produces content critical of the Vietnamese government, whose reaction is informed in part by the leadership's suspicion of outsiders and mistrust of foreign, particularly "Western," values.[64] In 1997 the government reportedly compiled a list of 130 overseas groups that maintain web sites or e-mail weekly reports to journalists and other activists publicizing high-level corruption, media crackdowns, and action against dissidents. Since the list does not appear to have led to the active blocking of all transmissions from the overseas groups, some of the e-mail information reportedly reaches certain clandestine domestic student groups. Internationally based e-mail lists are easier for Vietnam residents to join—and more difficult for authorities to monitor—than those based within the country. In some cases, dissident publications are made available through overseas political web sites, which are haphazardly blocked.[65] Individual groups have successfully waged cybercampaigns, convincing the government to allow visits to imprisoned dissidents.[66] Meanwhile, organizations such as Amnesty International say that Internet use has made it easier to collect and redistribute information about human rights abuses within Vietnam.

In response to much of the internationally based Internet activity, the government relies on its commercial antispamming software and firewall system to filter out communications from overseas Vietnamese groups, not always successfully. While these controls can be circumvented, such activity is unlikely to provide the basis for major challenges to the regime, at least in the short term. Internet penetration in Vietnam is still sparse, and there are no opposition parties, so transnational Internet-based protests are likely to find scanty target audiences and domestic bases of support, even when their information gets through. While an Internet-enabled domestic base of support is not absolutely necessary for political impact (as the following discussion of Burma shows), the increase in friendly relations between Vietnam and Western countries may make it difficult to approximate the techniques used in the Burma campaign, including the "shaming" of multinational corporations that invest in the country. In the wake of the U.S.–Vietnam trade agreement, future transnational campaigns of this sort appear unlikely to be effective.

In the end, the political impact of Internet use is likely to depend on several supporting factors. Foremost among these is Vietnam's economic reform trajectory, which is far from predictable. The regime itself is in a period of transition and hence is less stable than other long-standing governments such as Singapore. As such, Internet use by the public may help to crystallize dissatisfaction with the government, especially if the state's attempts at controlling content remain as haphazard as they now are. Yet this type of expression depends on a significant broadening of access, which in turn hinges on telecommunication reform, itself linked to the broad apparatus of economic reform. In other words, as Andrew Pierre notes, "the Internet revolution appears a long way from opening Vietnamese society to the outside world."[67]

Burma: Nascent Networking in a Closed Society

A poor country of about 50 million people, Burma is governed by one of the most authoritarian regimes in Asia. Some form of military government has existed in most parts of central Burma since 1962, when the elected civilian government was overturned in a coup. The current government came to power in 1988 when the armed forces repressed a large pro-democracy movement, resulting in the deaths of thousands of students. In 1990 the ruling State Law and Order Restoration Council, now renamed the State Peace and Development Council (SPDC), allowed a somewhat free parliamentary election. The National League for Democracy (NLD) won more than 60 percent of the popular vote and 80 percent of the parliamentary seats, but the military junta refused to acknowledge the results. During the 1990s the SPDC prevented elected representatives from convening and strictly controlled their movements. In May 2002, however, the government released NLD leader Aung San Suu Kyi from house arrest, which was seen as a sign of improvement in the historically bad relations between the government and opposition leaders.

After several decades of economic stagnation, Burma remains poor, and its infrastructure is shoddy. Illiteracy runs at about 11 percent for males and 19 percent for females.[68] Burma's highly state-controlled economy is primarily agricultural, although sectors such as light industry and transport are also prominent. Tourism, strongly encouraged by the regime, is growing more important in the economy, although critics note that, as in other sectors, the tangible benefits of tourist dollars flow directly to the regime, not to the citizenry. Economic liberalization measures undertaken during the late 1980s and mid 1990s have aimed to stimulate the economy, but state enterprises remain inefficient and privatization is limited. Unlike other Southeast Asian states that have taken steps to incorporate ICTs in economic reform programs, the government of Burma has remained largely indifferent to such measures, at least until very recently. Meanwhile, the country remains a global center for the narcotics trade.[69]

Since it took power, the SPDC has instituted a highly centralized authoritarian regime that grants little power to individuals or the private sector. The telecommunication sector is under the direct control of the junta, and the government operates the country's only Internet server. The government has for the most part maintained total control over the Internet's use and diffusion in Burma since the technology's introduction.

The regime is clearly ambivalent about the benefits and dangers of ICT use. For instance, the same 1996 decree that forbids the unauthorized use of computers or computer networks contains language that promotes "the emergence of a modern developed state through computer science."[70] Despite this expressed enthusiasm for high-tech development, Burma's stance toward ICTs is one of the world's most restrictive. Security forces regularly screen correspondence and telephone calls. Ordinary citizens are barred from subscribing to foreign publications or satellite television. The government licenses, controls, and monitors all electronic communication devices. A 1996 decree makes the possession of an unregistered telephone, fax machine, or modem illegal and punishable by imprisonment of up to fifteen years. Indeed, individuals have been arrested for having installed unlicensed electronic communication devices.[71] In 1999 the government closed several unauthorized private e-mail services and decreed itself the country's sole Internet provider.

The regime severely restricts freedom of speech and of the press, exercising control over all domestic newspapers and radio and television. With the exception of one expensive English-language weekly, media organs serve primarily as propaganda vehicles and do not publish views critical of the government. In recent years weekly tabloids have also proliferated, but many are published by government departments and do not report on politics. A few foreign-language newspapers and magazines are available at hotels and bookstores.

There are signs that the regime is slowly introducing new elements into its scheme of media control, if not actually liberalizing its stance. The *Myanmar Times,* an English-language newspaper published by the government, has reported on topics such as government–opposition talks and the need to introduce the Internet.[72] Yet large-scale self-censorship is the norm, owing to the continual harassment of public dissidents and opposition figures, independent journalists, and underground critics of the regime.[73]

Even though Internet use in the country is minimal, older ICTs used by international actors remain important in information dissemination within Burma. In particular, short-wave radio has become a primary source of outside information. After the September 11 terrorist attacks on the United States, the state media provided no details, making only a brief mention the following day. Many people relied heavily on the U.S.–based Radio Free Asia and the BBC's Burmese language service, saying they would have known nothing about the attacks if they had depended on state media.[74]

Rattling the Regime, from Overseas

In early 2000 the SPDC issued updated guidelines for Internet users. Included in the new restrictions were bans on political commentary and multiple users of single e-mail accounts. The lengthy list of forbidden activities is somewhat unnecessary, given that the regime continues to prevent most of the public from accessing the Internet. The 1996 decree has largely done its job of discouraging the public from attempting to access the Internet illegally, and until recently, access has largely remained limited to a few hundred foreigners and elites with ties to the regime.

Only during the past year or so has the government of Burma, in an attempt to emulate the economic models of some of its ASEAN neighbors, allowed a wider group of people to access the Internet. According to local publications, the regime recently allowed the creation of four thousand e-mail accounts within the country. Tourists and business travelers can also access e-mail for a high fee from the more expensive hotels. In the past year, a few shops have offered e-mail illegally in downtown Rangoon. Customers reportedly have been able to send and receive e-mails but have not been able to access the World Wide Web. In July 2001 the government sanctioned an Internet joint venture with a private company, opening two Internet cafés that charge extremely high fees for access to approved web sites only. Since the fees effectively restrict access to elites only, many would-be Internet users have taken to gathering in tea shops and bookstores to debate the impact of being cut off from the information revolution.[75]

The government's 1996 decree mandated the implementation of measures necessary for the development of computer science and technology and the creation of opportunities for students to study computer science in a manner beneficial to the state. Furthermore, the decree provides the basis for the formation of a "nongovernmental" computer federation charged with research and development in computer science; supervising the instruction of computer science courses; "communicating with international computer organizations"; and implementing information technology–related projects at the behest of the government.[76] The Ministry of Education is encouraging wider public education in the use of computers and related technologies, although mass access to the Internet is still forbidden. Two universities are currently devoted to training information technology "professionals and entrepreneurs," according to an official government web site. Although the ministry boasts of multimedia classrooms and e-education programs, the programs are limited by the lack of access to the global Internet within these environments. In fact, instructors at Rangoon computer training schools have been detained in the past under the Official Secrets Act, presumably for circumventing government controls to download antigovernment material.[77]

Since the Burmese regime puts heavy restrictions on the capacity of domestic civil society actors to organize and communicate, it is doubtful that any can currently gain sufficient access to the Internet to use it for strategic purposes. Independent civil society organizations are forbidden, unions and human rights groups are banned, NLD members are heavily monitored, and trade associations and professional bodies must register with the government. Although the government is now permitting slightly wider access to the Internet, it is highly unlikely that access will be granted to any groups known to hold views critical of the regime. Consequently, Internet use by domestic civil society actors is unlikely to be politically significant in and of itself, although individual dissidents who do manage to use the Internet may be able to leverage their information with the help of transnational networks.

Should the government continue to liberalize its ICT policy and allow ordinary Burmese access to the Internet, the medium could be used by low-profile domestic actors to organize and establish linkages with transnational pro-democracy activists (whose activities are detailed in this chapter). The fact that the government is simultaneously loosening access restrictions and trying to implement ICT training and education makes it more likely that users will possess at least the technological skills, if not the will, to evade government Internet controls in the future. The spontaneous enthusiasm for the Internet in certain cities, despite the lack of the Internet, indicates a growing popular enthusiasm for the technology, which could exceed the government's capacity to control online activity. The Burmese regime, however, has much more leverage over domestic civil society actors than over transnational ones, which may significantly damp political use of the medium by the domestic public. Other regimes with much less surveillance capacity and punitive firepower have substantially cowed their populations into self-censorship. For the time being, Internet use by civil society and the public is so limited that it has no significant political impact on the regime.

Advancing Burma into the information age has hardly been a priority for the SPDC in the past. Yet the regime is now making a serious effort to improve the country's ICT infrastructure, to cooperate with other countries in developing information technology projects, and to use the Internet to disseminate propaganda and counter the claims of activists.

In late 2000, for instance, the government took the step of setting up a task force to help the country develop its ICT policies and infrastructure, in line with implementing provisions in the e–ASEAN framework agreement.[78] On the propaganda front, the junta has made extensive use of the web to disseminate its own point of view and counter arguments made by foreign activists. The SPDC's official web site, the government's only visible stab at e-government so far, reveals a concerted attempt to extol the virtues of visiting the country, solicit foreign direct investment, and volley information counteroffensives designed to refute, in a point-by-point manner, the claims of pro-democracy activists. Links to ministry home pages contain information, largely targeted at foreign investors, on laws and regulations. The government has also included a chat room for its visitors, although the space appears empty.

Given its lack of expertise in the field, the government is now actively courting international partners from whom it can learn how to construct both ICT policy and specific projects. The Burmese regime is seeking Malaysian assistance in ICT projects, and several ministers have toured Malaysia's Multimedia Super Corridor. Officials in both countries have signed agreements on boosting cooperation in information and tourism. The government has announced plans for cooperating with Japan to establish a software industry in Burma and has teamed up with India in a satellite communication venture. Meanwhile, the military also appears to have upgraded its technological capabilities with the help of friendly nations.[79]

While ten political parties technically exist in Burma, the regime restricts their freedom of assembly and speech, as well as their access to information technology. Although similarly subject to those restrictions, the large and well-organized NLD is best able to funnel information covertly, usually through nontechnological means, to supporters and transnational advocacy groups outside Burma. These groups then post NLD speeches, writings, and other news on international web sites. In 1996, for example, surreptitiously recorded images of large-scale student demonstrations were smuggled out of the country and posted on international web sites.[80] Speeches and footage of NLD leader Aung San Suu Kyi are widely available on the Internet, giving the NLD a global platform against which the SPDC is forced to respond.

Hence, in the political arena, the two main Internet-using actors appear to be the government and the NLD, although the latter's Internet activity occurs chiefly through the proxy of international actors. The SPDC's increasing use of the Internet is characterized more by its reactive nature—trying to counteract the claims of activists, for instance—than by any proactive efforts. Tentative steps in the direction of e-government are far from having any sort of effect that might engender wider citizen support. The NLD, while still physically constrained by the regime to an offline existence within Burma, has nonetheless managed to link itself into a global network of activists that do use the Internet to constrain the action of the SPDC on a global scale. As such, while domestic political use of the Internet is limited, the magnified international spotlight granted the NLD through international Internet use (discussed in more detail below) may help to weaken the SPDC's domestic bargaining position and power.

In the economic sphere, Internet use is circumscribed, although access is more widespread among businesspeople than among the general public. The regime is developing a more targeted program to encourage e-commerce development, although at the moment it consists largely of task forces. Many businesses maintain access to e-mail, and some have even set up overseas-based web sites to attract overseas customers. Business users of e-mail are clearly informed that the government regularly monitors the communications of those with Internet access, and those granted access tend to be sympathetic to the regime.

Given the low Internet penetration rate and insufficient telecommunication infrastructure, Internet-related economic activity is unlikely to have a major political impact on Burma in the short term. In the long term, the regime may find itself under increasing pressure to follow the ASEAN model and incorporate ICT use and promotion into long-term economic development plans, the beginnings of which now exist. Yet the future political impact of Internet use in this area depends on several other factors, including but not limited to telecommunication sector reform (which would increase access), financial sector reform (which would improve the prospects for e-commerce), and the rise of an independent business elite. At this stage of Burma's engagement with the Internet it is too early to make any strong prediction of outcomes. Moreover, nearly all foreign investment to date has benefited the SPDC.

Internet use by international actors has by far the most political significance for the Burmese regime. Beginning in the early 1990s with a Thailand-based newsgroup, use of the Internet became indispensable in connecting those opposed to Burma's regime and enabling them to take their message to a wider public. Although initially composed primarily of pro-democracy Burmese exiles, the movement has expanded to include people who have never been to the country, many of them foreign college students. While many transnational advocacy networks use the Internet to leverage connections based on face-to-face contact, the Burma campaign largely sprouted from the Internet and has relied on it since for both impetus and growth. Many Burma campaigners have never met personally. Yet through the use of e-mail lists, web pages, and e-mail petitions that augment traditional lobbying, various campaigns have linked together to form a transnational movement that has pressured the SPDC to an extent many assert would have been impossible without Internet use. Charismatic opposition leader Aung Sang Suu Kyi has also helped serve as an international rallying point, and her speeches and writings have been made widely available to non-Burmese supporters on the Internet.

Opposition groups based just outside Burma's borders with Thailand and India use the Internet to convey information on domestic conditions to transnational advocacy networks, which post the information on the web sites of human rights groups and other organizations. Such information has also been smuggled back into Burma on computer disks and in simple newsletters. International human rights groups and democracy-promoting organizations, such as the Open Society, have supplied some of these groups with laptops and Internet connections.[81] An umbrella group, the Free Burma Coalition, has chapters in several countries and hundreds of U.S. colleges. Through grassroots online organizing, the group has successfully pressured the U.S. government to impose sanctions on the SPDC and has convinced multinational corporations such as PepsiCo and Apple Computer to pull out of Burma.[82]

While Internet use in the international sphere has clearly played a role in changing the international perception of and behavior toward Burma, its precise political impact is hard to quantify. The campaign has affected the pattern of foreign investment in Burma, for instance, but the extent to which this is both detrimental to the SPDC and helpful to the NLD is perhaps a matter of perception. One could argue that, despite the best efforts of the transnational campaign, the SPDC retains power and the NLD remains constrained. On the other hand, any erosion of SPDC power—resulting, for instance, from a loss of foreign revenue—can be perceived as a victory for the opposition. Whatever the consensus, however, it is hard to deny that the transnational Internet campaign has placed a spotlight on SPDC actions and helped to create a more transparent environment in which the SPDC is likely to find its actions highly scrutinized by the international community and subject to reprisal.

In sum, Burma differs from the other cases we examine in this study mainly because it presents a strong example of how an authoritarian regime can be affected by Internet use outside its borders. Although the campaign has not resulted in large-scale political change in Burma to date, it has forced the SPDC to maneuver in an increasingly well-lighted space, one in which it could previously act with impunity. Increased Internet access within the country's borders is likely to increase the potential for politically challenging Internet use. While the regime appears to be taking a route similar to that of Cuba, selectively granting access to those unlikely to pose political challenges, it may find this strategy hard to sustain in the long term, particularly if ASEAN programs such as e–ASEAN continue to exert pressure to incorporate ICTs in modernization. However, since many ASEAN countries are rapidly becoming adept at balancing Internet promotion with political control, the SPDC may substantially benefit from ASEAN cooperation and investment. Moreover, although the transnational campaign against the SPDC has influenced the policies of large countries and corporations, its tactics seem less likely to succeed against ASEAN member states, which have welcomed Burma and are likely to continue to invest substantially in the country.

Conclusion: Joining the Global Information Economy, with Caveats

An examination of Internet use in Singapore, Vietnam, and Burma shows that, for the time being, authoritarian states can harness the Internet for economic growth while controlling political impact, even if increased Internet access raises the potential for challenging use. At the same time, Internet use will both shape and be shaped by other factors, including the strength of political institutions and party systems, the rise of civil society, the engagement of domestic populations with the outside world, and the influence of regional political institutions. Moreover, the political impact of the Internet will be constrained by individual approaches to economic reform as well as the importance officials place on Internet access as part of the reform process. Reductionist perspectives that emphasize firewalls and their cracks therefore prove to be of little tangible use in assessing the Internet's potential to facilitate political change.

Certainly, public use of the Internet in these countries is growing dramatically. Singapore's population, for instance, is one of the most wired and well educated in the world, and it takes for granted the incorporation of ICTs into every facet of daily life. Other Asian authoritarian regimes, sensing the importance of ICTs in Singapore's continued growth and prosperity, are likely to mimic the city-state's policies in an attempt to reap similar benefits. This is likely to increase the potential for politically challenging use of the Internet, despite extensive censorship schemes that incorporate web-site blocking, chat-room monitoring, and other measures. Human rights and democracy-promoting organizations are likely to intensify their efforts to provide censorship-breaking software to targeted populations, and it is probable that more and more users, especially in light of ICT training and education programs, will be able to evade government censorship mechanisms.

Yet government control of information in Southeast Asia incorporates more than the technical aspects of censorship. In Singapore, for instance, the belief that the government is able to monitor political web usage and content, combined with a history of successful PAP litigation against its critics, may be enough to discourage most users from voicing sensitive opinions in politically themed forums. This suggests that Singapore's system of media control has been effectively extended to the Internet. Even should viable independent web forums emerge, it is doubtful they would engender strong opposition to a party that maintains legitimacy through continued economic growth and a historical legacy based on liberating Singapore from colonial domination.

In extremely authoritarian countries such as Burma, where the regime does not boast historical legitimacy and has done little to improve tangibly the quality of life for its citizens, an international political or economic crisis combined with conditions of increased Internet access may spur the use of the technology as a catalyst for popular unrest. However, since the regime has shown little past compunction about retaliating against its citizens, an Internet-enabled protest might result in a harsh punitive backlash, setting back the timetable for political reform. Moreover, the emerging SPDC strategy of allocating Internet access only to politically approved individuals and organizations seems designed to protect against just such an eventuality. In short, elements such as historical party legitimacy, legislative measures for retaining control, citizen satisfaction with the regime, and other factors that shape the political environment must be taken into account when determining the political impact of mass usage.

Perhaps the most concrete example of the Internet's impact in the political sphere is that of e-government measures, designed primarily to improve citizen services while simultaneously strengthening bureaucratic cohesion and efficiency. Singapore's model, studied by many, has concentrated on streamlining administrative procedures to provide an optimal experience for consumers of government services. Yet government transparency does not automatically flow from this process. The PAP, for instance, has staunchly resisted calls for a freedom of information act for declassifying documents. E-government measures may therefore improve the quality of life for citizens but not necessarily provide societal oversight of government affairs. As suggested by the case of Singapore, their net effect may be to boost the popularity of the ruling political party.

Given Singapore's success, it is not unreasonable to expect that its model will find purchase in other authoritarian regimes around the world. Yet the extent to which such programs benefit authoritarian states also depends on the question of Internet access. In heavily wired Singapore, many are able to benefit. In Vietnam, where access is expensive and therefore the domain of elites, e-government measures may be perceived as disproportionately benefiting certain segments of the population, contributing to popular dissatisfaction with the government. The success of e-government strategies may thus depend in part on Internet access policies. On the whole, however, e-government measures are more likely than not to impart legitimacy and security to the authoritarian governments that implement them, particularly if those measures adroitly address basic public needs.

The Internet has not been widely used by opposition parties, such as they exist in these cases. In Singapore, legal deterrents have prevented the widespread use of the medium by opposition political parties, in contrast to sophisticated e-government programs. Even the PAP has proved slow to establish a presence on the Internet and to use fully its organizational and communicative capacities, although this situation is now changing. Interestingly, it is Burma's NLD, with its charismatic leader Aung San Suu Kyi, that has most tangibly benefited from Internet use (albeit in the international sphere). Internet use by a transnational advocacy network appears to have been key in increasing the NLD's bargaining power with the SPDC, partially by expanding international oversight of the country's internal political processes. The tangible results of this phenomenon may be difficult to quantify, but a heightened global awareness of the NLD's activities and leadership may increase its legitimacy on the international stage, should it successfully gain power through political means.

It is clear that Internet activity in the economic realm is of increasing importance to both the populations and leaders of authoritarian Southeast Asian regimes. Throughout Asia, economic development and Internet promotion are entwined in an increasingly symbiotic relationship. For many countries, an integral part of the reform process involves the creation of a broadly wired population that will provide the foundation for a knowledge-based economy. Expanded public access is likely to have political ramifications and may therefore be opposed by regime hard-liners. Yet hesitancy about economic reforms, particularly in the telecommunication sector, can also be important in determining the scale of Internet growth. In Vietnam, for example, the government has publicly committed itself to the development of a domestic software industry and the pursuit of an information economy. This contrasts sharply with its unwieldy telecommunication monopoly, which ensures that access remains too expensive for much of the poor country's population. To realize long-term economic development goals, the government must address these contradictions in its policy.

Consequently, the largest impact of Internet development in the economic realm may be a state retreat from strategic sectors such as telecommunications, with state-connected conglomerates and other large economic actors ceding resources to smaller independent players. To the extent that this decreases state control over lucrative and politically important economic functions, Internet-based activity can be seen as undermining the capacity of authoritarian states to direct the scope of development or reform. Yet even significant economic and financial liberalization does not necessarily lead to political transformation. As Garry Rodan asserts, the expansion of media markets in Southeast Asia has encouraged self-censorship as foreign media corporations attempt to avoid costly legal battles with authoritarian regimes.[83] Many regimes, such as Singapore's, have demonstrated their prowess in coercing international media and other companies to play by their rules. It is likely that that success will be replicated with Internet investors, many of which have already established working relationships with the governments in question.

Internationally, Internet use has had varied effects upon authoritarian regimes in the region. Even in cases where a substantial diaspora exists, the success of a transnational advocacy network pushing for political change is not guaranteed. Although a large network of activists and exiles is pressing for political change in Vietnam, it has had less tangible impact than the Free Burma Coalition has, for instance. This may be partially owing to Vietnam's complete prohibition of opposition politics, giving the transnational network little leverage on the ground. In contrast, Burma's charismatic opposition leader, who heads the remnants of a legitimate political party, has lent international credibility to the network's pro-democracy efforts. Meanwhile, there has been little international use of the Internet to pressure the Singaporean government and those who do business with it, despite widespread acknowledgment of the PAP's semi-authoritarian practices.

Some types of Internet use, such as the transnational campaign for democracy in Burma, might appear overwhelming when taken out of context. The equally striking absence of Internet access in Burma, however, is itself an important counterbalance, one that should be considered when assessing political impact. The same can be said of the other cases we have examined, underlining the importance of weighing various spheres of Internet use against one another.

In the long term, it is conceivable that the desire of these countries to compete in a global information-based economy may contribute to the erosion of authoritarianism in Asia. Should broader access policies enable wider public discussions, existing political weak points—such as the Burmese government's lack of popular support, or Vietnam's troubles in implementing economic reforms—may become magnified online and overwhelm the state's capacity to contain dissent. It is more likely, however, that the larger political impact of the Internet will be felt not in one highly public event but through a variety of accumulated effects over time.

CHAPTER FIVE

Technology and Tradition in the United Arab Emirates, Saudi Arabia, and Egypt

> The Internet and globalization are acting like nutcrackers to open
> societies and empower Arab democrats with new tools.
> —Thomas Friedman, "Censors Beware,"
> *New York Times*, July 25, 2000

As the Internet diffuses throughout the countries of the Middle East, observers have begun to speculate that this technology will spread democracy in a region where authoritarian rule has long been predominant.[1] Optimistic sentiment of this sort builds upon a long-standing belief that new ICTs will encourage political change in the Middle East. Daniel Lerner's classic, *The Passing of Traditional Society,* considered the role of newspapers and the mass media as drivers of political modernization in the region. More recent studies have looked at the challenges that videocassettes and satellite television pose to existing political dynamics.[2] With the Internet taking its place alongside other technologies that frustrate the centralized control of information, there is an expectation that the medium will pose a threat to many authoritarian regimes in the Middle East.

The use of the Internet may indeed pose challenges to information control in much of the Middle East, but most of the region's governments are actively seeking to ensure that Internet use does not threaten the political status quo. Several countries (including Saudi Arabia and the United Arab Emirates) feature elaborate censorship schemes for the Internet, employing advanced technology to block public access to pornography or political web sites. Others, like Egypt and Turkey, promote self-censorship in the population, making well-publicized crackdowns against uses of the Internet that are considered politically or socially inappropriate. Many leaders are encouraging the growth of e-commerce and (to a lesser extent) e-government. The development of these online services may boost popular satisfaction with existing political regimes. In short, the impact of the Internet on authoritarian regimes of the Middle East is an open question, one that must be subject to systematic empirical analysis on a case-by-case basis.

In this chapter we examine the political consequences of Internet use in three countries of the Middle East: the United Arab Emirates (UAE), Saudi Arabia, and Egypt. As in our analysis of other cases, we argue for a nuanced conclusion about the impact of Internet use on these authoritarian and semi-authoritarian regimes.

Regional Considerations: Geopolitics and the Mid-Tech Revolution

While Internet penetration in the Middle East is limited when compared with much of the rest of the world, it has been growing rapidly in recent years. A March 2001 study found 3.5 million Internet users in the Arab countries of the Middle East (that is, excluding Iran, Israel, and Turkey). During the previous year the number had increased by more than 1.5 million. By the end of 2002 there were expected to be 10–12 million Internet users in these same countries, about 4 percent of their total population.[3]

Within these numbers there is much variation. At one end of the spectrum, the UAE has seen spectacular Internet growth, with a full quarter of its population now classified as Internet users. At the other end, Iraq achieved an Internet connection only in 1999; it is estimated to have 12,500 users and a mere five hundred separate accounts. Many countries in the Middle East, from Morocco to Yemen, have Internet penetration rates of under 1 percent.[4] There are also significant variations in the many determinants of Internet diffusion, including a country's literacy, wealth, size, and engagement with the outside world.

As a consequence of this variation among countries, generalization about the region as a whole is a difficult task, one that we do not presume to undertake in this study. Nonetheless, much of the existing literature on the information revolution in the UAE, Saudi Arabia, and Egypt has been framed in a regional context, and several regional considerations are relevant to the analysis of Internet use in these three cases.

First, other ICTs are currently much more influential than the Internet in most of the Middle East. Jon Alterman argues that the Middle East's "mid-tech" revolution—the widespread diffusion of 1970s technologies, like videocassettes, photocopiers, and satellite television—will be more socially and politically consequential than the Internet in the short to me-dium term.[5] Arguably, these ICTs are breaking state information monopo-lies and undermining mass media censorship throughout the region. The Qatar-based regional news network al-Jazeera, for instance, regularly airs frank reporting and spirited political debates, and its content has elicited criticism from the leaders of several Middle Eastern countries.[6] Public ac-cess to satellite television is widespread in much of the region; some gov-ernments have sought to ban it, but such regulations are rarely enforced. By comparison, low literacy rates and levels of Internet penetration limit the medium's impact in many countries, as does the region's dominant oral culture and a general reluctance to put ideas into writing.[7] This ca-veat applies more to Saudi Arabia and Egypt than to the UAE (where literacy and Internet penetration rates are high), but it is worth keeping in mind throughout our analysis.

Second, geopolitical concerns and regional political dynamics condi-tion the Internet's impact in the Middle East and the manner in which different governments have responded to it. Many states in the Middle East face both the perceived threat of Israel and frequently violent politi-cal opposition from Islamist groups that may operate across borders and challenge multiple governments in the region.[8] Such concerns are often invoked as a justification for continued authoritarian rule as well as for authoritarian control of the Internet. Still, growing public access to the Internet and other ICTs also complicates the manner in which govern-ments can respond to security issues. In particular, the events and after-math of September 11, 2001, have raised the stakes for regimes in the Middle East, which have been pressured to side with the United States in the war against terrorism but must also make foreign policy decisions with an eye toward public opinion. As the diffusion of the Internet and other ICTs provides alternative channels of information (including ex-treme Islamist information) that the state cannot easily control, many au-thoritarian regimes in the region will find it increasingly difficult to balance geostrategic concerns against popular demands.

Although one should bear in mind the salience of both mid-tech media and geopolitical concerns, there are many unique features about each of our cases. The United Arab Emirates, for instance, is substantially more wired than other countries in the region. The Emirate of Dubai has made particularly impressive gains in promoting e-commerce, luring foreign in-vestment in the Internet industry, and implementing e-government pro-grams to facilitate the provision of citizen services. Access to the Internet is censored in the UAE, though the main concern seems to be pornography; there is little dissent in the country in general and virtually none that finds its way onto the Internet.

Saudi Arabia has expressed more visible concern over the Internet than has the UAE, and it has taken a more cautious approach to the medium. Public Internet access was introduced only in 1999, and the medium is filtered through one of the most extensive mechanisms for content censorship in the world. In addition to pornography, Saudi Arabia is concerned with political information on the Internet, including criticism of the royal family by Islamist opposition groups both within the country and abroad. There have been some initial stirrings of e-commerce in Saudi Arabia, though it is unclear whether this sector will exhibit much independence from a state that largely dominates the economy.

Egypt is distinctive among the cases examined in this volume in that it has taken no concrete measures to censor content or restrict public access to the Internet. The country has been enthusiastic about the medium's prospects for economic development, implementing programs to encourage the rural diffusion of the Internet and bridge the digital divide. President Hosni Mubarak has also sought to attract Internet investors from wealthy countries such as the United States. Yet Egypt's semi-authoritarian political regime is well supported by a system of patronage and the marginalizing of political opposition, and its leaders have not shied away from repressing criticism of the government. While Egypt does not censor the Internet, it has made a few well-publicized crackdowns against what it considers socially and politically inappropriate Internet use.

In each of these cases we do see some ways in which Internet use can challenge authoritarian rule. In the event of a political crisis brought about by nontechnological means, for instance, the Internet could provide a forum for the expression and escalation of popular unrest. The use of the Internet by diaspora groups promoting extreme Islamist sentiment may also challenge governments that take more moderate stances in foreign policy issues. Yet the UAE, Saudi Arabia, and Egypt are all stable authoritarian regimes that have weathered many political challenges in the past, and they may prove similarly capable of meeting the challenges posed by the Internet.

United Arab Emirates: Stable, Wealthy, and Wired

The United Arab Emirates is a federation of seven emirates established in 1971. Each emirate is governed by its own royal family, but Sheik Zayid bin Sultan al-Nahyan (the ruler of Abu Dhabi) has been the president of the entire federation since its founding. The country is small, with only 2.4 million residents, at least 66 percent of whom are foreign nationals who have come to the UAE solely for work. The UAE's population is comparatively well educated and has achieved a literacy rate of 79.2 percent.[9]

As a result of its oil wealth, small population, and generally sound economic management, the UAE is one of the wealthiest countries in the region, with a GDP per capita (purchasing power parity) of $22,800. Although oil is the centerpiece of the UAE economy, mineral wealth is unequally distributed among the emirates: Abu Dhabi holds substantial reserves, Dubai's are much smaller, and the holdings of other emirates are negligible. While each emirate maintains separate economic and financial systems, the poorer ones receive subsidies from Abu Dhabi and Dubai. In recent years, the UAE has sought to diversify its economy. Dubai has been leading this trend by aggressively promoting technological development and seeking to establish itself as the business and free trade hub of the Middle East.

While comparatively liberal in its economic policies, the UAE has maintained an authoritarian political system since its founding. Ruling sheiks of the seven emirates appoint the country's president, vice president, and members of the Federal National Council, a consultative body that offers policy recommendations but has no legislative authority. There are no elections for any public office in the UAE, and other than the traditional majlis (where citizens gather to voice concerns to their rulers), there is no popular input to the political process.

The rentier dynamics of an oil-exporting state are key to understanding the stability of the UAE's authoritarian political system.[10] Oil revenues have allowed the state to bring in a large expatriate labor force to sustain the country's economy, massively supplementing the work that can be done by the small population of native-born Emiratis. The government collects no taxes, and it provides nearly free social services to both citizens and noncitizens. As a result, there is little basis for political unrest and scarce incentive for political participation. All expatriates in the UAE reside there by choice and are generously compensated; those who voice criticism of the government are simply deported. Emirati citizens do not suffer the threat of deportation, but their material well-being provides little basis for popular unrest. Furthermore, political Islam is not a major factor in the UAE and does not provide a rallying point for criticism of the government, largely because of the country's widespread wealth, prevailing culture of tolerance, corruption-free bureaucracy, and the absence of conflict between different Islamic sects.[11]

With the state playing an extensive role in almost all aspects of economic and political life, independent civil society in the UAE is extremely weak. There are few independent CSOs within the country; those that do exist must be licensed by the government and are dependent on it for financial support.[12] In contrast to many other Arab countries, there are no particularly strong professional guilds or advocacy groups articulating the interests of their constituencies. Neither are there any politically significant dissident organizations within the country or abroad, which is a testament to the people's general satisfaction with the regime.

The government of the UAE has sought to maintain control over ICTs for both censorship and financial gain, though it is more open to information than are many of its neighbors. The state owns virtually all broadcast media and applies guidelines for reporting, but satellite dishes (which are legal and widespread) can receive uncensored content from abroad. Local print journalists routinely avoid lists of proscribed topics, and foreign publications are subject to censorship, though they are not censored extensively.[13] Telecommunications in the UAE is the province of Etisalat, a 60 percent government-owned monopoly provider that operates the only ISP in the country, Emirates Internet and Multimedia.[14]

In recent years the UAE (and Dubai in particular) has emerged as the undisputed Internet star of the Middle East, with the highest penetration of all countries in the region. From March 2000 to March 2001, the number of Internet subscribers grew by 57 percent. With an estimated three users for each account, there were 660,000 people online in the UAE. Beyond its leadership status in the Middle East, the country ranks impressively on an international scale. The March 2001 figures placed it twenty-second in the world in the percentage of the population as Internet users, ahead of Italy, France, and Spain.[15]

Building a High-Tech Oasis, with Islamic Values

As these numbers suggest, public use of the Internet is common in the UAE. The government has played an important role in encouraging public Internet use; it was the first in the region to allow cybercafés, and it is planning to introduce public Internet kiosks to facilitate access further. As in many countries in the region, the rulers of the UAE (as well as the conservative elements in the society) voiced concerns early on about the impact of public access to sexually explicit material on the Internet. When the Internet was introduced in 1995, Internet content was totally unrestricted, but soon afterward the UAE government decided to implement a technological censorship scheme for the web, filtering Internet content through a proxy server that can block sites based on blacklisting or active content analysis. The censorship mechanism applies only to Internet café users and those who dial up from home; leased-line customers (the majority of which are businesses) are exempt.[16]

Officials claim that their sole desire is to censor socially inappropriate material, primarily pornography, although there is some evidence that political sites are also blocked. In particular, the UAE has sought to block a foreign-based web site and chat room called the UAE Democratic Discussion Group, which was established in 1999 and hosted some political criticism of the government.[17] Human Rights Watch found that the UAE blocks a gay and lesbian political advocacy site, and the U.S. Department of State reported that the regime blocks radical Islamist material from other countries.[18] In general, however, there is not much UAE–relevant political information on the Internet that the government might want to block. With no real domestic opposition (Islamist or otherwise) and little international criticism of the UAE's political system or human rights record, there are few sources generating online material that the regime might find threatening.

All in all, public Internet use in the UAE poses little threat to the regime's stability. Although the censorship scheme is imperfect and users can get around some restrictions by using a foreign-based proxy server to relay prohibited content, Internet censorship in the UAE seems to be a cat-and-mouse game of only moderate intensity.[19] As opposed to Saudi Arabia, the UAE does not threaten to punish those who access forbidden material, and the country's information minister has admitted that the government cannot really control material accessed by citizens.[20] The regime finds little information on the Internet that it considers politically threatening; the UAE Democratic Discussion Group is about the only instance of online dissent, and it is safe to assume that this site has effectively no impact on UAE politics. As long as the government continues to make an effort to block pornography, it is likely to satisfy the more conservative elements in society that support content restrictions. The Internet may not have much marginal impact on people's access to information in any case, since access to satellite television is widespread and unrestricted, while the majority of the population consists of expatriate workers with extensive knowledge of the outside world. In general, information control is not a pillar of the regime's stability.

With a small country to manage and a capable bureaucracy to do the job, the UAE is well positioned for establishing e-government to enhance the provision of its extensive citizen services. Because of the highly decentralized nature of government in the UAE, e-government has been more a collection of initiatives by individual emirates than the product of a single cohesive plan at the national level. The national government runs a web site (www.uae.gov.ae) with general information on the country and links to individual ministries. As of May 2002 much of the site was still under construction. Only half of the ministry links were operational, and the e-government services listed did not yet seem to be available. Internet-related education projects at the national level have been more notable. The IT Education Project, introduced in the 2000 academic year, incorporates computer and Internet use into the curriculum of the country's primary and secondary schools.[21] The UAE also features the region's first online degree program at al-Lootah International University.[22]

National-level initiatives are greatly overshadowed, however, by the e-government efforts of Dubai. Sheik Mohammed, the Crown Prince of Dubai, released an e-government plan for the emirate in the spring of 2000, calling for the establishment of e-government services in every department to eliminate red tape and long lines in government offices.[23] After a year and a half of preparation, Dubai's integrated e-government portal debuted at the end of 2001.[24] The site, www.dubai.ae, allows for access to a wide variety of government services, including automobile registration, the payment of fines and utility bills, business registration and licensing, and visa services.

For the most part, other emirates have failed to match Dubai's stellar progress. E-government in Abu Dhabi and Sharjah, for instance, is limited to the web sites run by each emirate's Chamber of Commerce and Industry, which provide information (and a few online services) for the private sector. However, none of the emirates besides Dubai has implemented (or even announced) an e-government initiative that would provide a comprehensive range of services for both citizens and businesses.

The effective provision of government services is a key component of the UAE's political stability. To the extent that e-government improves its service provision, it is likely to increase citizen satisfaction and further solidify the political regime. The only downside for the UAE's rulers is the potential perception that e-government benefits are distributed unequally. With a large and growing percentage of the UAE population online, it is unlikely that access to e-government will be viewed as an elite privilege, but Dubai's significant head start may lead residents of other emirates to feel that their local governments are not measuring up. It remains to be seen how rapidly Dubai's neighbors will follow its example and what the impact of the disparities will be.

Perhaps the most significant Internet developments in the UAE have been economic. The country's principal motive for promoting Internet development has been to advance its already strong position as the business and technology center of the Middle East. Consequently, businesses are the most important users of the Internet in the UAE, and those that have leased-line access to the Internet enjoy the special privilege of being exempt from the country's censorship mechanism. An Emirates Bank Group survey of one hundred UAE firms in the year 2000 found that 14 percent had e-commerce operations, 42 percent had transacted business over the Internet, 60 percent had their own web sites, and 88 percent had Internet access.[25]

The government of Dubai has been particularly active in promoting Internet development for its economic benefits, encouraging e-commerce and high-tech investment as a part of the UAE's general strategy of diversifying its economy and reducing its dependence on petroleum exports. Dubai's efforts have centered on the Dubai Internet City, an Internet-related free trade zone modeled after the Singapore Science Park. Like the country's other free trade zones, the Internet City permits tax-free investment, 100 percent foreign ownership, and the full repatriation of profits, plus a couple of special perks: a single window for government transactions and "more bandwidth than any tenant will know what to do with."[26] The Dubai Internet City opened in November of 2000 and has attracted such prominent investors as Hewlett-Packard, Microsoft, and Oracle. It has also been the site of regional e-commerce events, including the Organisation for Economic Co-operation and Development's Emerging Market Economy Forum on Electronic Commerce held in January 2001.

As with e-government services, most of the UAE's Internet-related economic activity is likely to enhance the stability of the regime. While the country as a whole has extensive oil reserves, Dubai's will last only another ten years, so its promotion of trade and high-tech investment is geared toward maintaining the prosperity of its residents and their satisfaction with the government.[27] In general, the UAE is exceedingly friendly to foreign investors, so they would have little incentive to oppose the policies of the regime and almost no reason to do so openly. The only way in which Internet-related economic activity might (in the long term) increase political demands on the regime is in promoting the growth of an independent business sector. There is essentially no independent private sector at present, since almost all businesspeople and professionals in the country are either employed by the government or depend on the government for contracts. The Internet, however, may eventually emerge as an economic sphere in which UAE citizens can pursue more independent business ventures. Whether such a group will emerge and whether it would have any negative implications for the government remain to be seen.

In sum, it appears that the UAE may be one of the best examples of an authoritarian regime where the Internet can be introduced without any serious negative political ramifications. There are few preexisting weak points in the political regime where use of the Internet could threaten the government. Dissent is minimal, e-government improves the regime's provision of citizen services, and economic uses of the Internet increase material well-being. The possibilities for Internet use posing challenges to the regime remain a matter of long-term speculation. If the stability of the UAE's political system is altered by other factors, such as an economic decline, a succession crisis, or problematic relations with other countries in the region, widespread popular access to the Internet could provide a venue for the expression and escalation of discontent, forcing a political concession. For the near future, however, the UAE's authoritarian regime stands on solid political ground, and the development of the Internet is most likely to solidify this base further.

Saudi Arabia: The Measured Steps of a Conservative Kingdom

The Kingdom of Saudi Arabia, a monarchy established in 1932, is ruled by King Fahd, with day-to-day affairs managed by Crown Prince Abdallah. Saudi Arabia is governed according to Islamic law, and it has few civil and political liberties. There are no political parties or elections for any public office. Saudi Arabia has the largest land area of any country in the Gulf, but it is sparsely populated for its size, with only 23 million people. Oil is the centerpiece of Saudi Arabia's economy, accounting for 40 percent of the GDP and 75 percent of the government's budget revenues. The country is the largest oil producer in the world and has the largest verified reserves. The kingdom has garnered significant wealth as a result of the oil industry, though its GDP per capita (purchasing power parity) of $10,500 is lower than that of the smaller Gulf kingdoms. Saudi Arabia's population is fairly well educated with a literacy rate of 62.8 percent.[28]

Modern Saudi Arabia was founded as an Islamic state. The al-Saud regime claims explicit religious justification for rule, based on its enforcement of the strict Wahhabi interpretation of Islam and its stewardship of the Islamic holy cities of Mecca and Medina. The country's influential religious scholars, the 'ulama, have been fully incorporated into the state bureaucracy and function as civil servants. Islamic politics are central to political life in Saudi Arabia, and Islam forms the basis for the most significant dissent against the Saudi regime, both within the country and abroad.[29]

In addition to Islam, the rentier dynamics of the oil-producing state are central to understanding the Saudi political system.[30] Like the UAE, the Saudi government levies no taxes but rather funds itself through oil revenues. It distributes the gains from this state-controlled industry in the form of social services; subsidies for food, utilities, and basic goods; and employment in the extensive government bureaucracy. This distribution of benefits is important in maintaining popular loyalty to the Saudi regime. The state dominates the country's economy, the private sector is small and dependent on government contracts and subsidies, and an independent middle class does not truly exist. However, rising unemployment (the result of a rapidly growing population) has forced the regime to pursue privatization, seek foreign investment, and begin to diversify its economy. The oil-based state dominance of the economy may therefore be on a gradual decline.

Civil society is weak in Saudi Arabia, and the government must license all associations that are active in the country.[31] Few CSOs are openly critical of the regime. Religion provides the largest space for civil society in Saudi Arabia, and some Islamic humanitarian organizations are active in the country. Professional societies and chambers of commerce also give their members an important arena for networking, communicating with the government, and (sometimes) articulating policy positions.[32]

Saudi Arabia exerts substantial control over the media through legal measures, patronage, and censorship. Domestic newspapers are privately owned but rely on government subsidies. The government appoints the editors of print publications and issues guidelines for reporting on sensitive issues; many newspapers avoid covering such topics until they have been reported on by the government-owned Saudi Press Agency. Several laws explicitly prohibit publicizing criticism of the government, although there has been tolerance of newspapers that criticize specific policies or individual government bodies. The government allows the distribution of foreign publications, but they are routinely censored when they contain offending material. Foreign newspapers that are read widely within the country, such as several Saudi-owned Arabic-language newspapers published in London, typically engage in self-censorship to comply with government regulations.[33]

Saudi Arabia established its first connection to the Internet in 1994, but it was the last country in the Arabian peninsula to permit public access, which came five years later. Before that time, access was limited to a few research institutions. The possibility of dialing into neighboring Bahrain for Internet access existed since the mid 1990s and was a popular option for wealthy Saudis before the country allowed public access.[34] While many of its neighbors quickly established public Internet access after it became technologically feasible, Saudi Arabia took a notably cautious approach, studying the idea for several years before approving it in principle in 1997. Access was further delayed for two years while the government perfected its technological and institutional mechanism for censoring Internet content.[35]

Public access to the Internet was finally established in 1999 and has expanded steadily since then. As of April 2001 the country had 570,000 users, constituting 2.6 percent of the population.[36] These figures place Saudi Arabia second in the region in Internet users. The country permits multiple privately owned ISPs (twenty-eight were active as of March 2002), but all international traffic passes through a gateway managed by the Internet Services Unit (ISU) of the King Abdulaziz City for Science and Technology. Currently, all ISPs connect to a national backbone controlled by Saudi Telecom, the government telecommunication provider. In May 2001 the government approved a bill to end Saudi Telecom's monopoly and to open the sector to foreign capital, though the major investment to date has involved a partnership between Saudi Telecom and Compaq rather than the establishment of independent competition.[37] In any case, it is almost certain that the ISU will maintain its control over international Internet traffic for the near future.

Cultivating E-Commerce, Guarding against Dissent

In light of the country's strongly conservative social traditions, the government of Saudi Arabia gave great consideration to the potential impact of Internet use before authorizing public access. Since the Internet came to the country, the government has filtered all Internet traffic through a system of firewalls that "is likely the most extensive attempt at Internet content access control in the world."[38] While other regimes often maintain that their sole motivation for censorship is the blocking of pornography, Saudi Arabia's stated concerns are broader. It openly endeavors to block information it considers both socially and politically inappropriate, including pornography, criticism of the royal family, and material considered offensive to Islam.[39] Attempts to access a forbidden site are greeted with a message that all access attempts are logged, which is certain to encourage self-censorship among more risk-averse users, although there is no evidence that anyone has been prosecuted for such transgressions.

In recent years the government has expanded its censorship mechanism to keep pace with the burgeoning sources of objectionable content. Saudi Arabia made headlines in 2000 when it blocked access to Yahoo! clubs that contained sexual information, and in April 2001 it announced plans to double the number of forbidden sites (to a total of four hundred thousand) using new, advanced equipment.[40] Foreign firms (including many from the United States) have been eagerly competing to provide hardware and software for Saudi Arabia's censorship efforts, so the country is likely to stay up to date with the latest filtering technology.[41] In an innovative move to incorporate popular participation into the censorship regime, the ISU has included forms on its web site with which Internet users can request that sites be blocked or unblocked. Cynics might label the move a palliative measure, but it is more likely an indication of how seriously the government takes popular concerns over Internet content. Requests to block sites are much more common than requests to unblock sites: an ISU director has stated that the organization receives five hundred of the former and one hundred of the latter each day.[42]

As with all forms of Internet censorship, Saudi Arabia's measures are far from foolproof. A supervisor at the ISU said in April 2001 that 44 percent of users are currently accessing blocked sites through the use of overseas proxy servers.[43] The previous year a government official admitted that many Saudis with Internet access are visiting sites that detail corruption in the royal family or that belong to overseas opposition groups.[44] Despite these difficulties, the government still seems as committed to maintaining its Internet content controls as it is to expanding Internet access within the country.

As access increases, Internet usage among the Saudi public has the potential to exert a more significant political impact. In some ways, the Saudi regime appears to be in a difficult political position with regard to the mass public's Internet use. On the one hand, the current generation of Saudi youth (which is large and growing rapidly) is better educated, more literate, and more aware of the outside world than ever before and is likely to want increased access to information on the Internet.[45] On the other hand, if the regime imposes too little control over Internet content or moves too quickly in scaling back restrictions, it could provide another serious grievance for Islamist criticism. Ironically, while conservative Islamists support the censorship of what they consider socially inappropriate material, censoring Islamists' own political material on the Internet is probably the regime's greatest concern. Though the country's dominant oral culture and a reluctance to trust online material may limit the impact of Islamist material online, its mere presence means that the Saudi public's Internet use will be more of a political phenomenon than in countries such as the UAE.

While public use of the Internet poses some potential challenge to the Saudi regime, Internet use by civil society organizations and dissident groups constitutes much less of a threat. There is evidence that a few domestic CSOs use the Internet, at least by maintaining web pages, and more may come online in the future. Still, CSOs do not figure prominently in Saudi politics, and their use of the Internet is unlikely to have strong implications for regime stability. Among dissident groups, those based abroad have been avid Internet users, but those within the country traditionally rely on cassette tapes, a medium that can reach many more people and may resonate more firmly in Saudi Arabia's oral culture.[46]

With a state that dominates Saudi society and the economy, the government's use of the Internet has been more significant than Internet use by civil society actors. The principal state use of the Internet has involved putting religious information online. Before the establishment of public Internet access, several religiously oriented state media were set up to be broadcast on the web, including Saudi Arabia's Channel 1 and an Islamic radio server that carries prayers from Mecca and Medina. The government's Ministry of Islamic Affairs, Endowments, Call, and Guidance has in the past operated a web site at www.islam.org.sa, though the site now links only to an Islamic-oriented portal that is run by a private software company. After the death of former religious official Abd al-Aziz bin Abdallah Bin Baz, the government established the site www.binbaz.org.sa, with details on his devotion to both Islam and the Saudi regime. State efforts such as these can be seen as attempts to counter and preempt the influence of overseas dissidents who use the Internet to criticize the regime on religious grounds.[47] In addition to posting religious information online, Saudi officials have implemented a religiously oriented government service on the Internet, establishing a web portal that speeds the processing of paperwork for foreigners visiting Islamic holy sites.[48]

Saudi Arabia's record with secular e-government follows the pattern of its religious efforts: much online information combined with a few initial moves toward providing government services on the Internet. Some government ministries have established Internet homepages, mostly describing their responsibilities and accomplishments.[49] In addition, Saudi authorities have begun to make plans for a much broader e-government initiative involving online services. The conference E-Commerce Saudi Arabia 2002 (held in April) focused specifically on e-government services, including international case studies and a showcase of e-government hardware and software.[50] The Saudi government will certainly implement many of the plans for online services that it is currently developing.

The political impact of increased Internet use by the Saudi government is likely to be mixed. Religious information and services on the Internet work to the regime's advantage by helping it to counter the influence of overseas Islamist critics. Effective e-government services would likely increase satisfaction with the regime if they improve the state's ability to deliver benefits. However, more extensive e-government in Saudi Arabia might also increase transparency and expose government corruption, which is a potential development whose political impact is more uncertain. Corruption in the royal family is a rallying point for critics of the regime and one of the major grievances of Saudi Arabia's most influential dissident groups. The greater exposure of such corruption might provide further grounds for opposition, but it could also give the appearance that the government is effectively addressing the problem.

There are no political parties in Saudi Arabia, and there has been no use of the Internet for political participation, although a limited potential may exist for this pattern to change. In the early 1990s both liberal and Islamist intellectuals generated petitions to the king calling for political reforms, and the regime responded by creating a constitution-like document, a consultative council, and regional governments. As in other countries, the Internet might facilitate the circulation of such petitions, but the Saudi regime is unlikely to be pressured into any reforms that it sees as threats to its stability.[51]

In contrast to the limited political uses of the Internet, the use of the medium in the economic sphere is both significant and growing. The Saudi government appears to be turning serious attention to encouraging Internet-related investment and e-commerce. In May 2001 Saudi Arabia hosted the Saudi International Conference on E-Commerce, the country's first such event. The conference produced a series of announcements about new government policies as well as other ventures designed to encourage the growth of Internet business. The government set up an advisory panel of fifteen businesspeople to coordinate e-commerce and announced that e-commerce regulations would soon be released, including guidelines on security and digital signatures. It also announced plans to build an IT investment park in Riyadh, although it is unclear when these plans will be implemented.

A few Saudi firms have taken the lead in e-commerce. Saudi Aramco (the government oil monopoly) has spearheaded a push for online procurement, requiring all local suppliers to deal with it electronically. OgerTel, one of Saudi Arabia's ISPs, is implementing business-to-business e-commerce strategies for Saudi Aramco, among others. The Saudi firm Integrated Visions has signed a contract with Microsoft to be the first application service provider (ASP) in Saudi Arabia, offering services to other firms that seek to develop e-commerce operations. The members of the Saudi royal family, increasingly involved in Saudi business ventures, have also been active in the country's Internet economy. Prince Alwaleed Bin Talal, one of the world's leading technology investors, has backed an Arab web portal, a Saudi ISP, and a satellite wireless network.[52]

It is possible, though unlikely, that the beginnings of Internet-related activity in the Saudi economy will pose political challenges to the regime. The Saudi government is by far the most important presence in the country's economy. Businesspeople have traditionally cooperated with the regime, which is responsible for awarding contracts, distributing subsidies, and otherwise supporting the private sector. While firms or business associations might be opposed to particular policies, it is extremely unlikely that they would openly oppose the regime.[53] Yet a growing population has brought rising unemployment, and the government has been seeking to enlarge the size of the private sector since it can no longer meet all the demand for public-sector jobs. An emerging Internet industry might help to employ some of the excess labor force and to relieve popular pressure on the government, but it could also have a role in increasing the private sector's independence from the state. Whether this will happen, and how much it matters politically, remains to be seen. The state will almost certainly dominate the economy well into the future even as the private sector grows.

In contrast to many other regimes in the Middle East, some of the most significant Saudi-related Internet use occurs overseas among Saudi dissident groups whose leaders have left the country and are based abroad. Most of these groups criticize the Saudi royal family for its corruption and betrayal of Islamic ideals. The two external dissident groups most relevant to Saudi domestic politics are the Committee for the Defense of Legitimate Rights (CDLR) and the CDLR splinter group, the Movement for Islamic Reform in Arabia (MIRA).[54] Both operate web sites in Arabic and English, but the sites are blocked in Saudi Arabia and are primarily geared to an international audience. Still, some Internet users within the country can circumvent those controls, and the dissident web sites do include information specifically for users in Saudi Arabia. CDLR's site, for instance, has featured detailed instructions on using toll-free numbers to call the group's London headquarters from Saudi Arabia.[55] In addition to the web, CDLR and MIRA use e-mail (as well as faxes) to communicate with followers at home.

While the dissidents' use of the Internet has received much international attention, the ultimate political effect of the activity is questionable. It is unlikely that the groups' online information reaches enough Saudis to influence domestic sentiment concretely. Even if such information were more widely accessible within the country, there is reason to doubt its resonance among the Saudi public. Mamoun Fandy argues that the Internet-based efforts of CDLR and MIRA have had little impact within Saudi Arabia because of the limited literacy of the Saudi public, the Saudi oral culture, and the tendency to trust information from close confidants much more than information on a computer screen.[56] Whatever the reason, none of the externally based Saudi dissident groups has emerged as a real threat to the regime. It is possible that these organizations (especially CDLR, which frames its message in the context of human rights) might have an indirect impact on the Saudi regime by convincing foreign governments and international organizations to pressure Saudi Arabia to be more tolerant of dissent. The international criticism of Saudi Arabia, however, has resonated little among Western governments to date, most likely because the regime is stable, strategically important, and a key supplier of oil.

In general, Internet usage itself is unlikely to strongly affect Saudi Arabia's stability. The country's authoritarian regime is stable and has successfully weathered multiple shocks in the past several decades: the mid 1980s collapse in oil prices, the Gulf War, and the multiple calls for political reform that followed. While some forms of Internet usage pose potential challenges to the regime, each of them pales in comparison with the political challenges that the Saudi monarchy has previously withstood. As Gregory Gause argues, the most likely threat to the regime would involve the combination of several potential areas of weakness—generational change, an economic shock, and the rise of Islamist opposition.[57] The Internet could play a role in augmenting the impact of several such occurrences, and in the event of a serious political crisis the medium could provide a forum for the expression and escalation of discontent, posing a more serious threat to the regime. In the absence of such an occurrence, the al-Saud regime will probably continue to develop the Internet within its borders, incurring some challenges but on the whole benefiting from the technology.

Egypt: A Censorship-free Zone

The Arab Republic of Egypt stands out among the cases examined here as the only one that is not a monarchy, not a strict authoritarian regime, and not a significant exporter of petroleum. Egypt's political system has its origins in the 1952 revolution, which saw the rise of a socialist regime, though President Mubarak has steadily moved the country away from its Arab socialist roots. In the 1990s Egypt emerged as one of the economic reform success stories of the International Monetary Fund, as extensive privatization and a burgeoning private sector led to increased foreign investment and steady growth (although growth has stagnated more recently). With the largest population in the Arab world at 70 million and only modest oil reserves, Egypt is the poorest of our three cases, although its GDP per capita (purchasing power parity) of $3,600 compares with that of other middle-income countries in the region. Its literacy rate is also the lowest of the three at 51.4 percent.[58]

Egypt is a semi-authoritarian regime with a multiparty system and an elected legislature but no real possibility of a change in power through elections.[59] The president is nominated by the legislature and confirmed as the single candidate in a national referendum. Every Egyptian president has transferred power to a hand-picked successor upon death. President

Mubarak has held office since 1981, longer than any other leader. The ruling National Democratic Party currently holds an 85 percent majority in the parliament. Previous elections (particularly those in 1995) were marred by excessive fraud. As May Kassem argues, Egypt's political system is deeply personalized and based upon government patronage.[60] Real power is concentrated in the president, and candidates for legislative office, from the ruling party and opposition parties alike, are generally elected not on an ideological basis but rather on the belief that they will be able to channel state-controlled resources to their constituents. Egypt is a secular state with no legal religion-based parties, though the outlawed Muslim Brotherhood is the government's most significant opposition. The country has repeatedly been plagued by Islamic terrorism, and the government has cracked down harshly on Islamist dissent, supported by a long-standing emergency law.

Civil society is stronger in Egypt than in many neighboring countries. Because Egypt's semi-authoritarian political system precludes the possibility of meaningful change through elections, many CSOs constitute an alternative channel for attempts at political change and are thus drawn into political advocacy. Still, there is a fair amount of government control of these organizations. Egyptian authorities must approve the formation of new organizations, and the government has sought even greater control: in 1997 it passed a law (overturned by the judiciary in 1999) that gave it the right to veto and replace candidates for CSO board membership.[61] The government has also disciplined overly critical CSOs, often through questionable legal proceedings. In a trial that was widely condemned by international observers, for instance, much of the staff of the Ibn Khaldun Center for Development Studies were convicted in 2001 for tarnishing Egypt's image abroad and for misusing foreign funding.[62] As in Saudi Arabia, professional associations (such as the Engineers' Syndicate and Bar Association) are also an important part of Egyptian civil society. Here too, the government has sought to exercise control, restricting the election of officers in order to limit Islamist influence.

The Egyptian government has concerns about the content of information available through the mass media, including extremist and opposition political information, criticism of the government, and material considered to be inappropriate or offensive to Islam. Foreign publications are subject to censorship, and English-language newspapers like the *Cairo Times* and the *Middle East Times* have had stories cut from the print editions sold in the country.[63] The domestic press is not subject to direct censorship, but it widely engages in self-censorship to remain in the good graces of authorities.

Egypt achieved an Internet connection in 1993, which is early by comparison with its neighbors, and commercial service has been available ever since.[64] Unlike many other countries in the region, Egypt has promoted Internet expansion with little visible concern for the possible political impacts of that expansion. One year after connecting to the Internet, the Egyptian cabinet's Information Decision Support Center (IDSC) and the Regional Information Technology and Software Engineering Center (RITSEC) implemented a program to provide free Internet access for various corporations, government agencies, CSOs, and professionals. Egypt also stands out in terms of its policy toward competition and the private ownership of ISPs. Basic telecommunications remains the province of government-monopoly provider Telecom Egypt, but the ISP market is one of the most vibrant in the Middle East, with some fifty private ISPs (even though the majority of these serve only Cairo).[65] As early as 1997 the government permitted multiple international gateways to the Internet, including one operated by a private ISP.[66] Egypt's Internet users constitute a smaller percentage of the total population than do their counterparts in the UAE and Saudi Arabia, but their total numbers are still comparable. As of March 2001 the country had 560,000 users, constituting 0.8 percent of the population.[67]

Promoting the Internet, Targeting Immorality

Compared with other countries in the region, Egypt is unusual in the enthusiasm with which it has actively extended Internet connectivity without overt efforts at Internet censorship. The country may face greater obstacles in poverty and illiteracy, but it has attempted to overcome them with projects to expand Internet access and training in rural areas. The IDSC has taken the lead in this activity. Along with its efforts to offer free access in the mid 1990s, it has begun a program to introduce the Internet on a temporary basis to more than three hundred villages around the country. Free connections are established for several weeks in community centers, and training staff are on hand to introduce the Internet to local residents, with the expectation that they will pursue connectivity in the future after learning of the Internet's potential benefits.[68] Another project, sponsored by the United Nations Development Program, seeks to establish technology access community centers with free Internet access, training, and education.[69] The United States Agency for International Development has also stepped in to support the diffusion of the Internet in Egypt with a five-year, $39.1 million ICT assistance program to target Egypt's legal and regulatory environment; promote e-government, e-commerce, and ICT diffusion; and provide grants to U.S. and Egyptian CSOs that will help to develop ICT use.[70]

The Egyptian government is notable in that it has taken no concrete measures to control Internet content available to the mass public, even though it is concerned over the political content of other media. It has imposed no censorship on the Internet, and the kind of information it prohibits elsewhere is widely available online. Both the *Cyprus Times* and the *Middle East Times* publish their full, uncensored content on the web, even allowing users to search for specific stories that were banned in the print edition.[71] Likewise, the Islamist-influenced Labour Party newspaper *El-Shaab* was banned from print publication in 2000, but it reported no interference with its Internet edition.[72]

Although there is no overt censorship of public Internet use in Egypt, the government has cracked down on some individuals who posted controversial material online. In several recent cases, Internet users have been prosecuted and jailed for advertising or soliciting gay sex on the Internet, and the web masters of one gay site claim that security forces have been tracking Internet users who visit it.[73] In November 2001 the web master of the newspaper *al-Ahram Weekly* was arrested for posting on the Internet a poem expressing frustration with the government; authorities charged him with "distributing immoral materials."[74] Since then, there has been speculation that the government is stepping up its monitoring of Internet use and preparing to prosecute others who engage in controversial activity online. Targeting "immoral" material on the Internet may constitute a partial concession to extreme Islamists, the same political forces that have generally supported overt Internet censorship in other countries.[75] If such arrests and questionable prosecutions continue, they are certain to encourage self-censorship among Internet users in Egypt.

Given the country's limited Internet penetration, one could argue that the government can afford to leave the medium uncensored. As access increases, however, the mass public's Internet use may become more politically relevant. It seems unlikely that the regime will be able to implement a massive censorship mechanism in the future once the technological and institutional infrastructure of unrestricted access is in place. Jon Alterman argues that the government's support base has narrowed as it attempts to contain Islamist political sentiment, and he notes that the Egyptian public is more knowledgeable and "wired" than ever before.[76] In such an environment, increasing Internet access could provide a vehicle for the expression and escalation of dissatisfaction with the regime.

Internet use by Egyptian CSOs is another factor that might be expected to pose a challenge to the regime, since civil society is stronger in Egypt and CSOs are not prevented from using the Internet. The crackdown on the Ibn Khaldun Center, for instance, was vehemently protested on the group's web site and through an e-mail list (both based abroad), and that may have figured in drawing international attention to the case.[77] Apart from this example, however, there have been no high-profile examples of Internet use in campaigns to place pressure on the government. Several Egyptian CSOs that maintain ties to the international human rights community operate web sites based abroad, but it is unclear how this affects their activities.[78] None of Egypt's professional associations appears to be a major user of the Internet. In the future, the use of the Internet by Egyptian CSOs is likely to increase, though the government's nontechnological measures of control will probably continue to be the major determinant of CSOs' political impact.

In the Egyptian political sphere, the most significant use of the Internet has been for e-government measures. After the UAE, Egypt appears to have implemented the most advanced e-government initiatives in the region. Efforts to promote ICT use within the government began early. A program to computerize regional governorates was instituted in 1987, and after 1992 an effort was made to connect them through a national network.[79] Egypt currently has a central government web site, www.alhokoma.gov.eg, which provides information but does not yet allow for interactive services. Some five hundred other government sites are online, including those of various ministries. Most provide information only, though citizens can pay their phone bills online through a partnership with Egypt Telecom.[80] In April 2001 Egypt announced an e-government initiative to provide citizen services and promote intragovernmental collaboration; Microsoft is supplying the technical infrastructure for this effort.[81]

As in other cases, e-government measures are likely to work to the benefit of the regime in that they improve citizen satisfaction with the government. Yet this effect may be less politically relevant than in Saudi Arabia and the UAE, where the provision of services is more essential to the social contract that underlies support for the regime. More relevant for Egypt is e-government's potential impact on bureaucratic efficiency. A more efficient bureaucracy could better equip the state to pursue economic development projects in the future, something that is likely to benefit the Egyptian people as well as the regime. Increases in government efficiency, however, could lead to job elimination, and government jobs are an important means of buying political support in the current system. Greater transparency through e-government is likely to have similarly mixed effects.

Egypt's political parties have not been particularly active users of the Internet to date. The ruling National Democratic Party does not have its own web site, although as the party synonymous with the government it may feel no need to establish an independent web presence. Several opposition parties maintain online editions of their newspapers but do not have specific party web sites.[82] The most notable use of the Internet by an Egyptian political party involves the Muslim Brotherhood, which is technically illegal and prohibited from openly campaigning or participating in elections under its own banner. Before the 2000 parliamentary elections, the Muslim Brotherhood established an election web site with photographs and biographies of members who were running for office as independents.[83] The Muslim Brotherhood did well in the elections, winning seventeen seats and emerging as the largest opposition block in parliament, though it is difficult to specify how much its online campaign strategy assisted in the election.

As Internet access expands in Egypt, other opposition parties may seek to make greater use of the medium, which could help them to compete more equitably, given that under its emergency laws the government currently restricts group gatherings and the distribution of printed material. It is conceivable, however, that the government would extend such restrictions to cover the Internet if the medium ever becomes a serious tool for opposition politics. Furthermore, the regime's marginalization of opposition parties in Egypt is deeply imbedded in the political system and depends on many factors beyond the restrictions on campaigning. The patterns of patronage that render opposition parties politically unthreatening are unlikely to be affected by their increased access to the Internet.

As in the UAE and Saudi Arabia, the economic sphere is an important area of Internet use in Egypt. Economic development is a strong incentive for the government to promote Internet growth. Like the UAE, Egypt is pushing to become a regional technology center (often in competition with nearby Jordan), though the size and relative inefficiency of its bureaucracy have not permitted the same kind of swift and effective actions that Sheik Mohammed has undertaken in Dubai.[84] Still, the country has undertaken notable steps. Its "smart villages" initiative seeks to build several ICT business parks, which would offer a ten-year tax holiday to foreign investors; a $40 million investment in the project was planned as of June 2000.[85] The first of the parks, the Pyramids Smart Village, was scheduled to open in mid 2002. In March 2000 President Mubarak made a much-publicized visit to the Dulles technology corridor in northern Virginia, including stops at the headquarters of AOL and PSINet, where he promoted Internet-related investment in Egypt.

Mubarak's efforts have yet to fully bear fruit, but to date there have been several significant Internet initiatives in the Egyptian private sector. CareerEgypt.com, for instance, is a job-matching web site started by students at the American University of Cairo. It has excelled locally and recently expanded to CareerMideast.com, with portals for twelve countries in the region. CarOnNile.com is an innovative portal that brings together buyers and sellers of used cars; to boost sales it has set up an electronic showroom and payment center at a physical car dealership. Egyptian ISP LINKdotNET has been successful in partnering with foreign Internet investors: together with Microsoft it manages MSN Arabia, the first international portal in the Arab world and a source for business news, online games, and Internet-based e-mail. In addition to these ventures, the Egyptian government and several Egyptian firms are using the Internet to promote tourism, one of the country's major sources of hard currency.[86]

Economic uses of the Internet may pose more of a challenge for the Egyptian government than in Saudi Arabia or the UAE. In Egypt, the state is less of a dominant force in the economy, and as the private sector has grown larger it has sought more political representation. The development of an Internet industry might contribute to the emergence of more politically active business interests, but the growth of the private sector will not necessarily pose a political challenge to the regime. To counter the influence of Islamist opposition, the Mubarak government has been actively seeking to strengthen ties with the private sector for some time now, and it has rewarded those businesses that support the regime with access to policy makers in Egypt and the United States.[87] In addition, Egypt has been pursuing economic liberalization for many years now. It has seen steady growth rates since the early 1990s without any visible threat to the political regime. Indeed, the country has been held up as an example of why economic growth and liberalization in semi-authoritarian regimes do not necessarily spell democratization.[88] Future growth may continue to reinforce the regime's patronage-based system of allocating resources and power.

Internationally, there is a small amount of Internet activity with relevance for Egypt. One example is the transnational campaign in support of the country's Coptic Christian minority, which uses the Internet and other technologies to denounce its persecution in Egypt and to call for equal treatment.[89] Another is the Muslim Brotherhood Movement homepage in the United Kingdom, which lists information on the group's political stance and its operations in Egypt and other countries.[90] In addition, international organizations like Amnesty International and Human Rights Watch have used the Internet to publicize criticism of Egypt's human rights practices, particularly with respect to the crackdown on the Ibn Khaldun Center. These international uses of the Internet may help to increase international attention to the plight of various persecuted groups in Egypt, tempering the severity of government crackdowns, even though there is no solid evidence of such an effect. To the extent that these campaigns seek to influence the stance of foreign governments toward Egypt, they are probably even less effective. As in the cases of Saudi Arabia and the UAE, human rights and domestic politics take a back seat to trade and security concerns in relations between Western governments and their allies in the Middle East.

In general, Egypt is distinct in that it has taken no concrete steps to control the Internet, either through censorship or through restrictions on access. Consequently, the country features prominent examples of Internet use that would be impossible in the other cases examined here—newspapers publishing banned content on the Internet, an illegal opposition party openly campaigning online, and domestic CSOs posting criticism of the government's human rights record. From an examination of those incidents alone, one might assume that Internet use in Egypt poses more serious challenges to the country's government than it actually does.

A more complete picture of Internet use in the Egyptian political context calls for more carefully shaded conclusions. Given its long-standing pattern of coopting secular opposition parties and managing the expansion of the private sector through political patronage, Egypt's semi-authoritarian regime is stable. A potential weak point is the regime's low tolerance of legitimate outlets for Islamist political sentiment. As Internet use among the mass public becomes more common, such sentiment could find an outlet on the Internet and galvanize concrete action. The Muslim Brotherhood has already taken initial steps toward Internet-based campaigning, and it may develop other ways to use the medium for political purposes in the future. Still, the country's semi-authoritarian regime may benefit from other uses of the Internet in Egypt, namely, the country's e-government initiatives and Internet-related economic activity. The ultimate political impact of Internet use in Egypt is therefore uncertain. Until access to the medium becomes more widespread, a series of nontechnological factors will weigh much more heavily in the course of Egyptian politics.

Conclusion: Persistent Stability, Few Tangible Threats

As the Internet diffuses throughout the UAE, Saudi Arabia, and Egypt, it will likely grow in political significance, and the liberalizing tendencies of certain types of Internet use will become increasingly influential factors in national politics. As such, they will complement many other, more long-standing potential forces for liberalization: greater contact with the outside world through tourism and travel, more integration with the global economy, and the increasingly modern outlook of a youthful population.

Yet the impact of these factors to date should lead one to sobering conclusions about the influence of the Internet. Authoritarian political systems are generally stable in the UAE, Saudi Arabia, and Egypt, and potentially liberalizing forces have had only a minimal, piecemeal impact to date. Factors such as the political economy of rentierism and the influence of political Islam still provide a solid bulwark against political liberalization. Challenging uses of the Internet in the three countries must also be weighed against those likely to reinforce the current political order. In each case, e-government works largely to this end, and many economic uses of the Internet could do so as well.

Much of the expected impact of the Internet in the Middle East involves use by the public. On the surface, it appears that this is the area where states are most concerned, given the massive censorship efforts that some have undertaken. Both Saudi Arabia and the UAE have poured extensive resources into censorship in an effort to block unwelcome social and political content. In the case of Saudi Arabia, the regime was willing to delay the introduction of public Internet access for several years so that it could perfect its mechanism for content control. In both countries there is evidence that determined users can access blocked sites using foreign-based proxy servers and avoid detection through the use of new services like Triangle Boy and Peekabooty. These services facilitate anonymous access to the web and will give additional tools to those who seek to view forbidden sites. It is safe to say that as long as countries like Saudi Arabia and the UAE continue to enforce their censorship regimes, some users will be able to get around the restrictions they impose.

Evaluating the political impact of public Internet use, however, requires moving beyond questions of censorship and evasion. In each case (including Egypt, which does not censor the Internet) there are reasons to doubt that public use of the medium will seriously threaten authoritarian regimes. Several analysts have noted that throughout the Middle East, those with Internet access tend to be the elite, who have a vested interest in the status quo and are less likely to risk their position in society through political activity.[91] Efforts to bridge the digital divide may alter that dynamic, but the political effects will be seen only in the long term. In countries like the UAE, where there is little dissent and the control of political information is not crucial to regime stability, there may not be much information on the Internet that is politically threatening to the status quo. In all the countries that we have examined, the most significant impact of public Internet use is likely to be social rather than strictly political, in that it challenges conservative Islamic traditions. In Saudi Arabia, where political Islam is a significant factor, moving too quickly with Internet development or imposing too few controls could increase the likelihood of an authoritarian backlash.

Yet it would also be wrong to discount completely the politically challenging potential of public Internet use. Both Egypt and Saudi Arabia feature much online information that is critical of the government. In the event of a crisis brought about by factors such as succession, international disputes, or economic shock, Internet usage could provide an outlet for the expression and escalation of popular unrest, with possible political consequences.

While Internet use by the mass public has the potential to become politically significant, Internet use by CSOs seems less likely to do so. In other parts of the world, Internet use by these organizations has been heralded as a major force for democracy, and some have suggested that similar dynamics may occur in the Middle East.[92] The cases we have examined suggest otherwise. In rentier states like the UAE and Saudi Arabia, the state dominates the economy and can afford to buy off independent CSOs.[93] Even in Egypt, where CSOs are more widespread and influential, not many have engaged in politically relevant uses of the Internet. While such activity could increase as the Internet diffuses, the regime's extensive legal mechanisms for controlling CSOs are likely to limit their impact well into the future.

In the political realm, the most notable use of the Internet in our three cases has been for e-government measures. While Dubai's stellar progress is clearly unrepresentative, Saudi Arabia and Egypt are both turning attention to the matter as well, and Egypt has made some notable steps in getting government services online. Particularly in the rentier states of Saudi Arabia and the UAE, the effective provision of social services is central to the political stability of authoritarianism. Consequently, e-government measures should reinforce citizen satisfaction with their governments as it more effectively distributes the benefits of oil wealth. Even nonrentier states like Egypt will benefit from better serving their citizens through e-government. E-government may also lead to increased bureaucratic efficiency and a greater capacity to promote economic development, something that is clearly in the interest of both states and their citizens.

The development of e-government may pose several potential challenges to the authoritarian regimes we examined. Government jobs are an important form of patronage, and increases in bureaucratic efficiency through e-government measures might lead to job losses for many. Increased transparency through e-government may lend support to authoritarian regimes if they are seen as rooting out endemic corruption, but the exposure of existing corruption could contribute to political crisis. In addition, disparities in Internet access (and in the UAE, disparities among the e-government progress of different emirates) may create political tensions as to who is better served by e-government. It remains to be seen how well those countries pursuing e-government will manage those challenges. In general, however, the development of e-government seems a positive factor for the stability of political regimes in the UAE, Saudi Arabia, and Egypt.

There has not yet been an extensive use of the Internet for opposition politics within the countries we have examined (although in Saudi Arabia, there is significant Internet use by dissidents based abroad). This may be obvious given the lack of political parties in the UAE and Saudi Arabia, but even in Egypt, political parties (including the ruling party) have not made extensive use of the Internet. The illegal Muslim Brotherhood has gone furthest in Internet-based campaigning, and it did do well in the 2000 parliamentary elections, though we cannot be certain how much online campaigning contributed to the group's success. In general, opposition parties in Egypt still face serious legal and institutional obstacles to effective competition, and Internet use would give them only marginal help in overcoming these barriers. In the more closed political systems of Saudi Arabia and the UAE, democratic movements (to the extent they exist) may shy away from the open defiance that Internet use implies, opting instead to seek influence through inside channels.[94]

While most speculation about the political impact of the Internet in the Middle East has focused on its use by the mass public, the economic sphere is the most significant area of Internet activity in the cases we have examined. As the Mosaic Group notes, the impetus to develop the Internet in most countries of the Middle East has been largely commercial. In contrast to the common pattern in many other parts of the world, there were no strong academic, CSO, or other noncommercial interests to shape the early growth of the medium.[95] Among our cases, the UAE (specifically Dubai) has been the leader in promoting Internet-related foreign investment. Egypt is following its lead with its smart villages initiative, and Saudi Arabia is exploring the idea of an Internet-focused high-tech development zone. In each of the countries, domestic firms (often in partnership with foreign investors) have launched initial e-commerce ventures. The UAE, Saudi Arabia, and Egypt will be certain to see much more significant Internet-related economic activity in the future. The Arab world's common language will facilitate regional ventures, especially as the technology for dealing with Arabic text on the Internet is improved and more widely disseminated.

A rise in Internet-related economic activity seems unlikely to have major political effects in the short term. Economic uses of the Internet will mean more investment by Western partners, but neither the technology nor the involvement of foreign firms will necessarily change the nature of business in the UAE, Saudi Arabia, and Egypt. As Jon Anderson argues, local businesspeople will "Arabize" the Internet; it will be adapted to Arab business culture, and its growth in the economic sphere will be shaped by Arab commerce and development policies.[96] In each of our three cases, the state plays a strong role in the economy, and government contracts and contacts are important to both local businesspeople and foreign investors. The private sector knows the political rules of the game, which change only gradually (if at all). Furthermore, economic diversification through Internet development may help oil states like Saudi Arabia and the UAE to weather fluctuations in petroleum prices with less chance of political instability.

On the other hand, the long-term growth of Internet-related economic activity might cause shifts in the nature of economic power and political influence in the Middle East. As Jon Alterman notes, the Internet could empower small businesses and shift power away from large family conglomerates, which have traditionally enjoyed strong political ties to the regime.[97] In the rentier states of the UAE and Saudi Arabia, economic diversification and an increase in Internet-related economic activity could contribute to the growth of a private sector that would be less dependent on government favors. Either of those developments might increase the political demands on authoritarian regimes, but as the example of Egypt demonstrates, authoritarian rulers may be able to accommodate a larger and more influential private sector with greater patronage in return for political support.

Internationally, the most visible uses of the Internet we have examined involve the efforts of organized overseas dissidents to criticize national governments, especially in Saudi Arabia. The domestic impact of these organizations' Internet use may increase as access to the medium becomes more widespread, although in Saudi Arabia the blocking of political sites will limit the distribution of material critical of the government. In addition, as Mamoun Fandy argues, local residents may be reluctant to trust the antigovernment discourse that they read on a computer screen.[98] To the extent that foreign-based organizations shift their discourse to appeal to liberal values with greater resonance in the West, they may lose some credibility within their target countries, as has happened with the CDLR. And while such organizations may pressure Western governments to demand political reform in the offending country, the democratic and human rights credentials of regimes in the Middle East have had little real impact on whether the United States and others choose to lend them support. Security concerns easily outweigh the promotion of democracy in the formulation of policy toward the region, especially at a time of increased global terrorism.

Besides the explicit political criticism of foreign-based organizations, there is another, less trumpeted use of the Internet in the international sphere that may have political implications in the countries we have examined. The Internet (including chat rooms and e-mail) has been widely used by Middle Easterners living or working abroad, including for discussions of political issues in their home countries. As these expatriates return home, or as local users participate in the same online forums, the use of the Internet for political discourse in a more liberal environment could have an effect on the way the medium is used at home. A similar dynamic has already taken place with other ICTs, where Arabic-language satellite television stations based in London and elsewhere have helped to craft a more open environment for political discussions in the Middle East.[99]

Osama Online? Islamic Fundamentalists on the Net

The events of September 11, 2001, have focused a global spotlight on Osama bin Laden and his al-Qaeda terrorist network, including its use of ICTs. Al-Qaeda's most important use of the Internet is for the coordination of logistics among operatives, and the main impact of this activity is on international security, issues that are of great importance but outside the scope of this study. However, international uses of the Internet in relation to the events of September 11 do have more direct implications for the stability of political regimes in the Middle East, including those that govern the UAE, Saudi Arabia, and Egypt.

To some extent, Bin Laden and his followers are relevant to the politics of the Middle East where they specifically target such regimes as Saudi Arabia. Bin Laden got his start as a critic of the Saudi monarchy, shifting his primary focus to the United States only after U.S. troops were stationed on Saudi soil during the Gulf War. While Bin Laden does not use the Internet against the Saudi regime to the same extent as CDLR and MIRA do, he has proved to be savvy in using other international media to shape public opinion. Through his al-Qaeda network he could easily begin to disseminate critiques of the Saudi government (or others) on the Internet. Bin Laden's domestic following in Saudi Arabia, however, is less salient than his international impact, and his group is less influential within the country than is either CDLR or MIRA.

More significant than the resonance of Bin Laden's critiques against the Saudi regime is the potential for Internet use after September 11, 2001, to stir extreme Islamist and anti-Western sentiments that could ultimately pose a threat to regimes in the Middle East. Many governments in the region have carefully nurtured such sentiments in the past, but in the future they may find them difficult to control, especially if they choose to ally with the United States while their publics sympathize with Bin Laden's international agenda. In Pakistan, Musharraf's government appeared to be on shakier ground after siding with the United States over substantial public opposition. Such public opposition is informed by the use of ICTs, primarily satellite television networks such as al-Jazeera, though the Internet is also important for shaping opinion in the Middle East. Chat rooms and web pages, many based in the United States, provide a forum for the airing of views on Bin Laden's activities and the United States' military response. Such online expression can tend toward extremism; a number of ISPs in the United States spent the weeks after September 11 shutting down offending web sites and censoring chat-room postings.

If extremism of this sort, expressed by diaspora groups and other sympathizers around the world, is able to reach and influence domestic populations in the Middle East, it could have an impact on political regimes in the region. In the UAE, of course, there is not much public opposition to the government's foreign policy stance. In Saudi Arabia and Egypt, Internet access is too limited at present for online extremism to have much of an impact on public opinion. As access expands, however, online extremism does have the potential to exert a greater influence, especially in Egypt, where a firm censorship scheme is not currently in place.

In spite of the potential for online extremism, we should still conclude that Internet use in the United Arab Emirates, Saudi Arabia, and Egypt does not yet pose a significant threat to the stability of those countries' authoritarian regimes. In each case, authoritarian rule has enough nontechnological bases of support that use of the Internet in its current nascent form is unlikely to affect them very much. As access to and use of the Internet become more widespread, the dynamics we have identified in this chapter are likely to become more politically relevant. Some of them may pose challenges to existing authoritarian regimes, such as use of the Internet by dissident organizations or increased access to information that turns public sentiment against the government. In the event of a political crisis, the Internet could provide a forum for the expression and escalation of dissent, leading to a greater impact than would be possible without the technology. It is conceivable that at some point Internet use might play a role in the downfall of one of these regimes. It seems equally possible, however, that the authoritarian states of the region will successfully manage the introduction of the Internet in their societies, just as they have weathered manifold potential challenges in the past.

CHAPTER SIX

Beyond Blind Optimism

The information revolution is exerting both a push and a pull toward
greater openness in Communist-controlled countries. Whatever the
ultimate fate of communism as a system of rule, there is an absorbing
challenge for the West to maintain policies and programs which will
encourage a more open flow of information within these societies and
thus contribute to modifying the very nature of these regimes.

—Walter R. Roberts and Harold Engle,
"The Global Information Revolution and the Communist World,"
Washington Quarterly, Spring 1986

Throughout history, every form of technological advance has provoked
a maelstrom of speculation about its societal impacts. Modern information and communication technologies are no exception. Long before the
Internet became a global phenomenon, innovations in ICTs were expected
to bring myriad social, economic, and political changes. During the 1980s,
for instance, Western analysts pondered the ways in which ICTs could be
employed to break the Soviet Union's stranglehold on information. The
subsequent fall of communism at the end of the decade helped to cement
enthusiasm about the technology's promise and policy uses, particularly
in regard to toppling authoritarian regimes.

This enthusiasm builds on the idea that globalization and the information revolution are eroding the importance of the state in the modern world.
Tightly integrated markets, connected by a web of electronic transactions,
have constrained central banks in charting macroeconomic policy.[1] New
security threats have emerged in the form of amorphous, wired terrorist
networks, leading some to suggest that warfare will increasingly involve
conflicts with nonstate combatants.[2] Globally connected activists and civil
society organizations play an increasingly important role in the management of transnational issues and the negotiation of multilateral treaties.[3]
Amid changes that challenge even the most capable of governments, it is
easy to imagine the Internet as a menace to the creaky bureaucracies
and aging dictators of authoritarian regimes. Hence, policy makers and

activists have been seeking to harness what is now widely perceived as the Internet's innate power to bring about the collapse of authoritarian rule.

Undoubtedly there are many ways in which Internet use may pose challenges to authoritarian regimes. Publics in closed societies can now access information unavailable through censored print and broadcast media. Independent Internet entrepreneurs may crop up in countries where economic resources have long been controlled by the state and a coterie of wealthy elites. Dissidents gain a new and potentially empowering tool, one susceptible to monitoring by authorities, but nonetheless able to facilitate organization and communication. As Catharin Dalpino notes, demonstrations of "people power" carry great resonance with the American public, and the view of civil society as a catalyst for change permeates much of U.S. policy toward authoritarian regimes.[4] It is therefore no surprise that American policy makers tend to fixate on such images when speaking of the Internet's impact on authoritarian rule.

Yet the authoritarian state is hardly obsolete in the era of the Internet. In fact, the state plays a crucial role in charting the development of the Internet in authoritarian regimes and in conditioning the ways it is used by societal, economic, and political actors. Through proactive policies such as instituting e-government and wiring key industries, authoritarian regimes can guide the development of the Internet so that it serves state-defined goals and priorities. This may extend the reach of the state in significant ways, even as other types of Internet usage challenge state authority. Furthermore, by laying out the broad framework of the Internet's physical and policy architecture, the state is able to shape much of the environment in which Internet use occurs. Because of these efforts, Internet use by nonstate actors may exert less of a political impact than is typically envisioned. Public Internet users may back away from politically sensitive material on the web, for instance, and entrepreneurs may find it more profitable to cooperate with authorities than to challenge their censorship policies.

While the Internet has certainly disrupted the status quo in many authoritarian countries, its ripple effects do not travel in a straight line. In this final chapter, we outline those effects and present the major findings drawn from our eight case studies. On the whole, we argue that the Internet is not inherently a threat to authoritarian rule. Rather than sounding the death knell for authoritarianism, the global diffusion of the Internet presents both opportunity and challenge for authoritarian regimes. For U.S. policy makers, this means discarding simplified notions about the Internet's impact in favor of supporting specific actions and policies that are likely to promote openness in authoritarian countries.

The State Still Calls the Shots

- **Governments build on a legacy of ICT control.**

In most authoritarian regimes, the state has historically played a strong role in the development and control of ICTs and the mass media. This legacy usually translates into a dominant role in Internet development. While the academic or scientific community often takes the lead in early experimentation with Internet technology, state authorities are almost always responsible for guiding the broader diffusion of the Internet within national borders. In the course of doing so, they typically devise both technological and policy architectures that facilitate state control over the Internet.[5]

For instance, all the states in this study (with the exception of Egypt) control much of the physical network infrastructure within their borders, including national backbones (high-speed paths used for long-distance traffic) and gateways to the global Internet. Theoretically, this would allow governments to pull the plug on domestic Internet access. The likelihood of such an occurrence is remote, since the economic costs would probably outweigh any potential political gain. Yet control of national network architecture has other concrete benefits for authoritarian regimes. In particular, it provides an important form of state revenue and also facilitates the monitoring of online traffic.

- **National ICT plans shape the environment for Internet use.**

In addition to controlling the physical architecture of the Internet, many authoritarian governments have devised national ICT plans that set out a strategic vision of how Internet development will serve state-defined social, political, and economic goals. Cuba, for instance, is concentrating on harnessing computer networking for education and public health, while simultaneously restricting mass Internet access. China's strategy aims at the complete informatization of Chinese society, which will fuel and complement the country's wide-ranging modernization plans. Others, such as Burma, appear to be in the midst of constructing national ICT plans, even though their official policies toward Internet development remain highly restrictive.

In developing Internet policy, many of the authoritarian regimes in our study have looked to one another for "best practices," from promoting e-commerce to controlling public Internet use. Cuba is both studying and receiving assistance from China in its ICT development plans. For its part, China has long looked to Singapore to understand how it has balanced a modern, corruption-free, and technology-friendly society with political and social controls. Other authoritarian countries outside the region, such as the UAE, have also been inspired by Singapore's example.

- **State capacity matters.**

While authoritarian regimes are influenced by one another's efforts, implementation of ICT policies depends heavily on individual state capacity. A large, inefficient bureaucracy with many competing divisions can hamper the effective execution of an ICT strategy. This is particularly true in the case of China, where Internet development is seen as a lucrative activity for power-hungry government organs. Leadership that is divided or ambivalent about the benefits of Internet promotion, as in the case of Vietnam, can also contribute to contradictory policies.

On the other hand, a small, efficient authoritarian state benefits greatly from focused leadership and few checks on policy implementation.[6] Singapore was rapidly wired, largely due to PAP's ability to implement its ICT vision quickly, without the hindrance of a confrontational political opposition. The country's small size has also helped officials to execute their vision of an "intelligent island" rapidly. In the UAE, Sheik Mohammed has made a push for rapid and effective Internet development in Dubai, though other emirates have pursued individual policies.

- **Efficient states make for effective e-government.**

In addition to pursuing macrolevel ICT policies more effectively, small authoritarian states with enlightened leaderships have generally been able to implement specific e-government policies more efficiently than larger ones have. Singapore and the UAE, both unencumbered by a nettlesome bureaucracy or political opposition, have proved to be particularly quick in developing e-government services. Singapore especially has led the world in revamping its bureaucracy and rethinking the way that government provides services to its citizens. Many countries around the world, both democratic and authoritarian, now seek to follow Singapore's example. Meanwhile, larger and more inefficient states, such as China and Egypt, view e-government as the solution to some of their problems, but they are not as able to reorient their bureaucracies quickly to accommodate new solutions. Essentially, in smaller states with ICT–friendly leaders, efficiency leads to good e-government, while in larger states, good e-government is seen as leading to better efficiency.

- **Responsive e-government boosts perceived legitimacy.**

On the whole, e-government programs that effectively provide citizen services are likely to boost regime legitimacy, particularly in countries where the state has traditionally offered extensive services in exchange for political support. In the UAE, for instance, effective government services are an important source of regime stability, so any e-government programs that enhance service provision will probably prove to be of benefit to the regime generally. In Singapore, where the ruling party derives much support from its ability to maintain a high standard of living for the public, the implementation of innovative e-government services is likely to consolidate the PAP's support base further. Yet disparities in access may lead those excluded to perceive e-government services as an elite privilege. In this regard it is useful to observe the future of e-government in countries such as the UAE, where its promotion in Dubai has been ambitious, even though access to online services is uneven across the country as a whole.

- **E-government provides citizens with important benefits.**

Effective e-government certainly has the potential to strengthen authoritarian states, particularly if it streamlines government bureaucracies through networked information management or allows large states to consolidate central authority through more efficient communication with provincial governments. Cynical power calculations, however, are not the only motivation for pursuing e-government. Officials in many authoritarian regimes are genuinely attempting to increase transparency, reduce corruption, and address the concerns of their citizens with government performance. Hence, even if these goals are not "democratic" per se, they still constitute developments that provide important benefits to local populations and may prove to be the basis for political liberalization.

- **State propaganda grows sophisticated.**

In addition to putting government services online, several authoritarian regimes have made extensive use of the Internet for propaganda. Many state-run newspapers are now entirely online, and additional features, such as web forums, are occasionally introduced to make use of the interactivity of the Internet. In some countries the state has used these new features to fine-tune its ideological message, crafting a political environment that sets the tone for online behavior. In China, the government has used the online versions of its official newspapers to project a more engaged, inviting image than it does in print publications. Chat rooms featured on the web site of the official *People's Daily,* for instance, allow users to vent nationalistic feelings that support the regime's position on a number of international issues. Essentially, the state can provide these forums for Internet users to support its positions, which is a subtler means of influencing the ideological environment than the blunt instrument of official rhetoric.

- **Authorities learn to constrain politically threatening use.**

Governments possess many tools for limiting politically challenging Internet use by the public. The most common method is to filter Internet traffic through a national system of firewalls and proxy servers, blocking access to material that is considered politically or morally inappropriate. When outright censorship of the Internet does occur, blocking pornography is the most commonly stated motivation, although that may be only part of the real reason for the government's blocking efforts. Substantial public support for such censorship may exist, however, particularly in the Middle East. In countries such as the UAE and Saudi Arabia, significant public constituencies support blocking pornography and would probably express dissatisfaction if the practice were discontinued. Elsewhere, blocking pornography may be largely an excuse for more extensive censorship. The Vietnamese government, for instance, does block pornographic sites, but its primary concern is walling off antigovernment web sites run and hosted abroad by Vietnamese exiles.

Censorship, of course, is never totally effective. Many web-savvy surfers find ways around the system in order to access pornography, antigovernment web sites, and other politically or culturally sensitive material. Yet most authoritarian states realize that their censorship efforts need not be totally comprehensive, and they rarely aim for a foolproof firewall.

Countries that are more wary of users circumventing censorship controls sometimes opt for a simpler and cruder method: restricting public access to the Internet. Regimes that rely wholly on access restriction do not have the same need for a massive, centralized censorship system involving firewalls and proxy servers. Cuba and Burma currently control Internet access without filtering all traffic through a proxy-server system (although some web-site blocking may occur at the institutional level). Saudi Arabia restricted Internet access for several years, but it abandoned its scheme in 1999, implementing a complex censorship mechanism and allowing widespread public access to this filtered version of the Internet. Saudi Arabia's example may highlight the direction that other access-restricting countries are likely to take in the future.

In countries that engage (or have recently engaged) in access restriction, national intranets are frequently deployed as a substitute for the global Internet. Since users cannot step outside these politically "safe" networks to access the global Internet, the prospect of mass intranet use poses little political threat. In Cuba, the state has deployed an intranet in the belief that it can bring the benefits of computing to the masses without actually giving them Internet access. In Vietnam, where intranets became popular during the Internet's infancy, they remain an inexpensive alternative to pricier, and riskier, global Internet access. Intranets, however, are not a fail-safe solution for all authoritarian governments; they are extremely difficult to put in place once public access to the full Internet has become common. Hence, in China, where government officials have long been speaking wistfully of intranet implementation, rapidly increasing mass access to the global Internet renders the plan much less feasible.

- "Soft" control proves effective.

In addition to censorship, access restriction, and other overt forms of Internet control, authorities often employ "soft" measures when addressing potentially challenging Internet use. These include promoting self-censorship among the population (often accomplished through a few high-profile arrests) and encouraging private-sector Internet companies to filter content or police their own users. Such measures reduce the need for authoritarian governments to explicitly control the Internet with firewalls and other measures. Many casual web surfers in authoritarian countries understand the boundaries of politically acceptable Internet use, and authorities exploit this understanding to create an environment where comprehensive censorship is not necessary. Singapore's government employs this tactic frequently with the traditional media and has successfully applied it to the Internet. China also increasingly relies on shaping the environment in which Internet use takes place, rather than attempting to control it at the individual level.

- Opposition parties are mostly offline.

Opposition parties, where they exist, have not made extensive use of the Internet. In many authoritarian regimes, official opposition parties are either prohibited or rendered ineffective through mechanisms of political

control. Only in Egypt and Singapore has there been any attempt by opposition parties to use the Internet, and even in those two cases use has
been minimal. The methods of cooptation that limit political competition
in Singapore and Egypt generally extend to the Internet, preventing opposition politicians from campaigning online. In Egypt, for instance, many
opposition parties maintain online editions of their newspapers but have
not set up specific party web sites. One exception has been the illegal
Muslim Brotherhood, which established an election web site for the parliamentary elections in 2000. Meanwhile, Singapore's ruling party has
effectively prevented the rise of any viable opposition, either online or off.
Regulations and legislation ensure that its critics cannot use the Internet
for political communication.

As access to the Internet increases in the future, more opposition movements may try to use the medium to organize and communicate directly
with the public. There is a distinct possibility that a political or economic
crisis could precipitate more extensive use of the Internet by existing or
potential opposition parties.[7] It is extremely difficult, however, to predict
the circumstances in which an economic crisis might spur political change,
much less the possibility that Internet use would contribute to these events.

Civil Society and the Public:
People Power or Government Support?

- **Access is still mainly for elites.**

Conventional wisdom presumes that a large proportion of the population
can gain access to the Internet and that the information it seeks will be
politically significant. At present, however, those with Internet access in
authoritarian regimes are chiefly the elite, who are more vested in the
status quo. In Burma, for instance, Internet access is restricted to a very
small number of business and political elites who are highly unlikely to
use the medium for politically sensitive activity. Cuban authorities have
also sought to limit Internet access to politically trustworthy individuals
and organizations. This pattern of elite access holds true even in countries
that do not practice access restriction, such as Saudi Arabia and Egypt.

- **Risk-averse usage predominates.**

While most prevalent among elites, Internet use by the mass public in
authoritarian regimes is steadily increasing. Undoubtedly, some will gain

exposure to ideas and images that the authorities would prefer to block. Yet many citizens of authoritarian regimes use the Internet in much the same way as do citizens of democracies: they communicate with friends and family, consult easily accessible news sources, browse entertainment and sports sites, and look for information specifically relevant to their lives. Although some may wish to access uncensored news or politically sensitive web sites, average users are too risk-averse to do so. Moreover, a lifetime of exposure to propaganda has taught citizens of many authoritarian regimes to be skeptical of all media, international as well as domestic. It is therefore questionable whether mere exposure to outside news is enough to sway popular opinion in authoritarian regimes.

- **Internet use does not occur in an information vacuum.**

The marginal impact of public Internet use is likely to be less significant where there are other forms of access to outside information. Many authoritarian regimes allow (or are unable to prevent) access to many ICTs besides the Internet, whether mobile text messaging or satellite television. Local and Western-based satellite television is widespread in most Middle Eastern countries, for instance, and regulations banning the medium often go ignored. Citizens can also gain information about the world from other sources, such as through contact with tourists or news from relatives abroad. In Cuba, both of these conduits of information are particularly prevalent and play a much greater role than the Internet in informing public opinion. Where the public is already fairly informed about the outside world, broader Internet access might not have much of an additional effect.

- **A handful of dissidents have access.**

Any authoritarian country without stringent restrictions on Internet access usually has political dissidents who use the Internet to inform the public and communicate with one another. Such dissidents, however, are usually few in number and disproportionately well known internationally. Domestically, they may generate little interest, either because they possess little name recognition or because some may be well known enough that anyone associating with or receiving communications from them may be endangered. Furthermore, the political impact of Internet use by dissidents is still contingent on their ability to communicate with others who also have Internet access.

- **Opposition CSOs are a minority on the Internet.**

Internet use is more common among civil society organizations that are not necessarily opposed to the regime that governs their country. In the cases we examined in this study, the most common uses of the Internet by domestic CSOs are either nonpolitical or likely to support state policies. In places such as Cuba, where the government limits public Internet access, only CSOs thought to be neutral or politically supportive are allowed to connect to the Internet. Many Cuban CSOs work with the state to achieve such goals as sustainable development, environmental conservation, and poverty eradication. Those fortunate enough to be permitted Internet access are careful not to jeopardize their special status.

Moreover, civil society is weak in many of the cases in this study, the result of state efforts to dominate political space within society and to coopt potential opposition. In Singapore, for instance, CSOs can use the Internet freely, but few are likely to use it to challenge the government. Groups that have tried to establish independent web sites that facilitate independent organization have been warned off through threats of legal action and subtle intimidation. Sites such as Sintercom and Think Centre, which gave Singaporean citizens a chance to read and express criticism of the government, closed operations when it appeared that new regulations would soon render their activities illegal.

New Economies: Mostly Business as Usual

- **Economic development is a powerful incentive for Internet development.**

Delivering economic development is an important legitimating factor for most authoritarian regimes. In many cases, there is a strong historical legacy of the state providing economic benefits and stability in return for the right to rule. The Internet is attractive to authoritarian rulers because it can be harnessed as a powerful tool for promoting social and economic development. In China, for instance, authorities are studying how to use the Internet to improve standards of living, particularly in the poverty-ridden western provinces. In Cuba, the pursuit of social development has been a central component of the revolution, and authorities have sought to leverage Internet technology for such purposes as online health. For its part, Egypt is attempting to bridge the digital divide and promote rural education by developing technology access community centers.

In addition to using the Internet for state-run development projects, governments have taken a lead role in promoting private-sector economic activity on the Internet, from Sheik Mohammed's development of the Dubai Internet City in the UAE to the efforts of Singapore's Infocomm Development Authority to "Dotcom the Private Sector." Some authoritarian regimes focus their efforts on key industries that generate hard currency or are otherwise central to the economy. In Burma and Cuba, for example, the state has placed strong emphasis on tourism promotion online, reflecting the importance of this industry to the economy as a whole.

- **Internet policies mirror global economic engagement.**

Countries that strive to be full participants in the international economic system are under increased pressure to adhere to the norms set by advanced industrialized countries through such bodies as the World Trade Organization. Consequently, authoritarian regimes that seek global economic engagement generally permit more private-sector investment and market-led development within their Internet sectors. Those that seek and receive aid from international financial institutions such as the World Bank and International Monetary Fund are also encouraged (and sometimes required) to undertake certain types of reforms, such as deregulating their telecommunication sectors and inviting foreign investment. In turn, this can lead to a reduction in state influence in key areas of the economy. It can also pave the way for local entrepreneurial growth in the domestic ICT industry.

China, for instance, has initiated sweeping telecommunication reforms, driven primarily by its desire to join the WTO. In addition to carving up its government-owned monopoly telecommunication provider to allow for greater competition, China will soon allow more extensive foreign investment directly in its Internet sector. Private-sector use of the Internet is widespread and encouraged by the government, even when the private sector directly competes with former state monopolies. Egypt, which has adopted an economic reform model prescribed by the IMF, also features a lively private sector and a competitive ISP market, characteristics that are lacking in many other authoritarian countries.

In wealthier countries a strong incentive for Internet development is the desire to achieve regional status, usually as a technology and services hub. This is true of both Singapore and the UAE, which have adopted policies promoting mass Internet use. Singapore has strongly encouraged the wiring of all its citizens in order to nurture an educated, technologically literate population and to cement its status as Asia's foremost knowledge and service center. The UAE, particularly Dubai, has also sought to promote technological development aggressively and to brand itself the information-age star of the Middle East.

Countries that are less engaged with the global economy have fewer incentives to promote Internet access for e-commerce and other private-sector uses. As an isolated economy, Cuba has been under much less pressure from international organizations and foreign investors to adopt policies that would facilitate entrepreneurship or greater competition in the Internet industry. Cuba has encouraged Internet development in export-oriented sectors of its economy, but it has been wary of introducing market mechanisms into the domestic economy, including a market for individual access to the Internet. Burma has also been isolated from the international economy, although this situation is changing with its induction into ASEAN. Combined with the preferences of regional investors, ASEAN's policy emphasis on regional ICT development is beginning to pressure Burma to lessen its restrictions on ICT policies.

- **Internet development weakens economic centralization . . .**

In many authoritarian regimes the development of an Internet private sector may play a role in dispersing economic resources and diffusing the concentration of state economic power, particularly if this process is initiated by smaller entrepreneurs. In Egypt and Saudi Arabia, the rise of independent Internet entrepreneurs could challenge the hegemony of the large family conglomerates that help to sustain authoritarian rule. In China and Vietnam, independent Internet entrepreneurs are sprouting in formerly state-dominated sectors. The Chinese state, for instance, has traditionally controlled all information industries but must now share space with privately held Internet companies.

Yet, in some economies, economic decentralization may also be a positive development for a regime. For countries that are natural resource exporters, such as Saudi Arabia and the UAE, the development of an Internet industry can serve the important purpose of economic diversification. Policy makers may be anticipating a time when natural resource depletion will challenge the state's traditional ability to distribute wealth. Consequently, economic diversification into a high-growth industry may prove important for the stability of the regime. In practice, this type of diversification strategy is just beginning to take shape; only the UAE (particularly Dubai) has pursued it with any seriousness.

- **. . . but Internet investment need not prove to be a political challenge.**

Even though Internet entrepreneurs may play a role in dispersing economic resources and fragmenting state economic authority, they do not necessarily assume an independent or challenging role vis-à-vis the state. Many domestic entrepreneurs are willing to work with the regime and are under pressure to abide by the state's rules of the game. Authorities can reach a tacit understanding with the private sector about what sort of behavior is and is not acceptable, as part of a general strategy of soft control. In China, where Internet entrepreneurs have taken a voluntary pledge of self-discipline, many private-sector companies are far from being trailblazers of free speech. Rather, they understand when it is necessary to cooperate with the state, and many may support the state's policy goals. Meanwhile, the UAE and Singapore are confident enough in the political trustworthiness of the private sector to allow more ICT privileges, such as uncensored Internet access for leased-line customers (mostly businesses) in the UAE.

Foreign investors also tend to cooperate with authoritarian regimes, even if it means contravening the principles of online privacy and freedom of expression that they ordinarily support in their home countries. Although foreign Internet investors are under much less of a threat of direct retaliation from the state than are domestic entrepreneurs, they are nonetheless sensitive about protecting their assets and investments. Consequently, they are unlikely to take a stand on sensitive issues, such as freedom of information. Moreover, some foreign investors may aid state control of the Internet in authoritarian regimes by providing software for filtering web content and monitoring Internet traffic. This has already been the case in countries such as China and Saudi Arabia.

A country's attractiveness as an investment destination often determines the extent to which foreign investors are willing to comply with a government's wishes. China's 1.3 billion potential consumers, for instance, mean that the country is perceived as an essential market for many foreign companies. This desire to invest in China may well override whatever political or policy-related disagreements foreign investors might have with the government. Many information industry companies feel compelled to establish relations with the Chinese government in order to have the freedom to invest and expand later. Singapore and the UAE are attractive for a similar reason: they are important regional economic hubs, with sophisticated communication and service industry infrastructure.

Countries like Burma and Cuba are less obvious investment destinations; therefore companies that invest in those countries are often somewhat self-selecting, possessing few qualms about investing in a pariah state or an embargoed economy. Since the ICT sector is so politically sensitive, Internet investors in such countries may be particularly sympathetic to the ruling government. Foreign investors in Cuba's Internet sector, for instance, often express solidarity with the Cuban government. Similarly, investors in Burma's ICT industry are often fellow ASEAN members and are unlikely to voice overt dissatisfaction with the regime.

Beyond Borders: Transnational Activism and Agitation

- **The Internet is important but not sufficient for successful activism.**

The Internet can be an important tool for transnational activism, and certain well-publicized examples have served to solidify the conventional wisdom about the Internet's impact on authoritarian regimes. For instance, the Internet was crucial during the early mobilization period of the international campaign for regime change in Burma and continues to be a key instrument during the campaign's mature phase. Few other transnational networks against authoritarian regimes have benefited so extensively, or so publicly, from Internet use.

The size and success of the Free Burma campaign have led to common assumptions that similar campaigns will be as effective everywhere. However, although nearly all transnational activist campaigns now use the Internet, there are reasons to question their ultimate impact on authoritarian rule. Although the Free Burma campaign did achieve a heightened global awareness of the Burmese government's abuses and a reduction in foreign trade with the country, it has not resulted in tangible political change within Burma. Other factors, including the pace of internal liberalization and domestic negotiations between the ruling party and its opposition, can influence the results of transnational activism. In the case of the Free Burma campaign, Internet use was a necessary but certainly not a sufficient condition for effectiveness.[8]

- **Mediating factors: engaged exiles and the importance of the target country.**

Beyond Burma there has been considerable variance in both the presence and success of transnational campaigns against authoritarian regimes. A factor supporting such campaigns is the presence of an exile community strongly opposed to the regime in power, which is a feature of many of the cases we have examined here, including China, Cuba, Vietnam, Burma, and Saudi Arabia. A charismatic domestic leader, such as Aung San Suu Kyi in Burma, can also facilitate campaigns by acting as a focal point for transnational activism.

The mere existence of a high-profile dissident leader or a politically motivated online exile community is not enough to guarantee political impact. Since the success of a transnational activist campaign depends largely on influencing the policies of third parties (such as foreign governments or transnational corporations), the economic and strategic importance of the target country is a strong mediating factor. Internet-based campaigns against authoritarian regimes will be much more effective, for instance, when the country concerned is not a major trading or security partner of the United States. Burma's lack of strategic importance to the United States may be part of the reason that the transnational campaign to shame investors has been so successful. Likewise, Internet-based campaigns that target the strategic partners of the United States may fare less well. Transnational campaigns to highlight human rights abuses in Saudi Arabia have found less purchase because of the economic importance of the country's oil reserves and its status as an ally of the United States.

- **Online diasporas can be politically significant.**

The other major international users of the Internet are diasporas, a broader group than those made up of the political exiles who often run transnational activist campaigns. The members of diasporas, who tend to be better off and better educated than most of the public at home, may have more opportunities to air their views online. Their use of the Internet can both support and oppose the regime at home. Different diaspora communities, such as Middle Eastern and Chinese groups, contribute strongly to nationalist discourse on the Internet. Nationalist sentiment may serve to further regime goals, but it may also be critical of the regime, usually for its perceived weakness in dealing with other countries.[9] Since diaspora members are unconstrained by the censorship that those in their home country experience, they may feel freer to express their views online. Thus, diaspora discourse is often more extreme than that found at home.

The direct political impact of diaspora Internet use is, however, difficult to quantify. Its primary effect may be in amplifying domestic political sentiment, whether favorable to the regime or opposed to it. To the extent that online diasporas can interact with sufficient Internet users at home, they may also serve to inform domestic populations and catalyze political resistance.

Implications for Policy and Policy Makers

Using information technology to encourage specific foreign policy outcomes is not a new idea. Yet it has undergone something of a revival recently, particularly as the United States engages in global public diplomacy to complement its war on terrorism. American politicians have been stressing the need to "speak past the regimes and the elites and directly to the people themselves," whether in broad programs to tout American values abroad or by specific attempts to promote democratization in closed societies.[10] In this context the use of the Internet is seen as an important, if hazily conceptualized, component of America's renewed outreach effort.

We did not initially set out to isolate a neat list of prescriptions for policy makers interested in the intersection of technology and political change. Attempting to devise an equation of "Internet plus (specific) usage equals regime change" would be worthless and against the spirit of this study. Nonetheless, the conclusions we have drawn from the case studies in this volume have implications for those who are interested in thinking innovatively about Internet use in authoritarian regimes.

First, politicians and pundits alike should be wary of making heavy-handed pronouncements that link the Internet to democratization. While optimism is admirable, it may contribute to the perception that ending authoritarian rule is simply a matter of wiring enough people. Not only do such pronouncements imply a simple task for those who wish to promote democracy, but they may inspire false hopes among the citizens of authoritarian countries, who are led to believe that political change is only an e-mail away. Technology alone cannot accomplish miracles, and the Internet itself has no inherent political value. It is only a tool, and its specific uses by political, economic, and societal actors must be carefully weighed and considered. As a result of a general euphoria over the Internet and its applications, policy makers unfortunately may feel that the mere presence of the Internet in any given country will be enough to spur change and outweigh individual programs that promote specific uses of the technology.

That said, a reliance on such programs should also be kept in proportion. United States policy makers should take care not to succumb to the belief that the Internet will prove disproportionately important in the promotion of democracy. Conventional wisdom contributes to the general idea that anything with a URL is more sophisticated and more effective than, say, face-to-face meetings with key officials to discuss judicial reform. This notion has important implications for the future of democracy-assistance programs. In reality, the use of the Internet may be but a small factor in any democratic transition. Traditional (albeit less glamorous) forms of democracy assistance, such as bolstering local governments, aiding political parties, and promoting civic education, are vital ways to support liberalization in the long term. In fact, it may be helpful to think of the Internet as primarily facilitating work in these other areas rather than playing a starring role itself.[11]

Many also hold the belief that the Internet is spreading of its own accord into closed regimes, wreaking havoc with authoritarian practices once inside. This view ignores the fact that authoritarian states still control the pace and nature of the Internet's diffusion within their own borders. This does not mean that influencing Internet diffusion within authoritarian countries is impossible. Rather than focusing primarily on end users of the technology, however, policy makers interested in democracy promotion may also wish to consider how to accomplish their aims through international organizations such as the WTO, by encouraging certain kinds of national telecommunication and Internet policies in authoritarian regimes. Since even authoritarian countries are under pressure to conform to global economic norms, pushing for more liberal access and content policies in the context of economic development may be an effective if less tangible way to influence Internet diffusion and use in authoritarian countries.

At the same time, policy makers need to realize that encouraging foreign investment and e-commerce will not on its own engender a positive environment for political change in authoritarian regimes. As we have noted, domestic and foreign investment in authoritarian countries has not automatically led to more liberal government policies regarding the free flow of information. In fact, regional organizations such as ASEAN are encouraging authoritarian member states to create business-friendly but politically sanitized Internet infrastructure. Absent international pressure to the contrary, many authoritarian regimes will adopt such models. Moreover, U.S. policy makers should remember that the mere presence of U.S. investment in authoritarian regimes, particularly in the media sector, does not automatically lead to a more open information environment or to the promotion of American free-speech ideals. If policy makers consider these to be desirable goals, they will need to work concretely toward achieving them, whether through direct diplomatic initiatives focusing on core human rights and free expression, public-private partnerships, or other methods.[12]

United States policy makers should also be aware that not all antiregime Internet activity in authoritarian countries necessarily carries a pro–U.S. or pro-democracy bias. Militant nationalist and religious movements can use the Internet just as easily as those demanding peaceful transition. In China, the Internet is being used to stoke nationalism, which is in turn being used to justify, as well as inform, the foreign policy decisions of the country's leaders. Should this online nationalism eventually coalesce into a significant opposition movement, the consequences are unlikely to be favorable for U.S. policy. Likewise, militant Islamist movements and dissident groups that use ICTs to oppose authoritarian rule in the Middle East may well have goals that conflict with U.S. foreign policy objectives. The notion of freedom-loving cyberdissidents sweeping away a harsh ruler is romantic but not always realistic. Consequently, U.S. policy makers should scrutinize exactly who is using the Internet, and to what purpose.

This leads to a final point. Internet-facilitated political change need not spring solely from the realm of grassroots opposition, nor must its goal always be the complete collapse of a regime. Policy makers generally concentrate on supporting "people power" opposition movements in authoritarian regimes, often by attempting to facilitate communication. As Catharin Dalpino points out, U.S. policy often ignores immediate opportunities to push for gradual, liberalizing changes in authoritarian regimes, relying instead on cold war–style policies that seek rapid democratization or authoritarian collapse.[13] This approach has fed the perception that a nimble, fleet-footed technology like the Internet is crucial in successfully mobilizing grassroots opposition, itself viewed as a necessary ingredient for political change. Given a renewed emphasis on public diplomacy programs that directly target overseas publics, this view has gained urgency and legitimacy.

Yet political change in authoritarian regimes does not always happen in Internet time. In many cases much institutional groundwork needs to be laid beforehand, often by regime elites themselves. Focusing chiefly on Internet-facilitated democratization from below may not only be counterproductive, it may also fail to take stock of the spectrum of other ways that Internet use may contribute to liberalization, if not democratization.

Innovative e-government measures that genuinely try to address citizen concerns may indeed help strengthen the state, but they also better the lives of those living under authoritarian rule. Reform-minded elites in certain authoritarian countries may also want to use the Internet to increase transparency, reduce corruption, and make government more responsive. If the Internet can contribute to increased openness and liberalization in authoritarian regimes, that in itself may be a political impact worthy of support. Policy makers may wish to think creatively about how Internet use can support existing liberalizing trends, including those at the elite level, rather than focusing mainly on the technology's potential to catalyze grassroots opposition.

Ultimately, such refocusing may bring down some cherished, long-held notions about the Internet's political impact. Yet this is no call for pessimism. Rather, what is needed is a clear-eyed realism that separates facts about the technology's potential from the froth of wishful thinking. In turn, this may lead to a more informed, and thus more useful, optimism about what the Internet can accomplish in opening closed regimes.

Notes

Chapter 1: The Conventional Wisdom

1. Debate between candidates for the Republican Party primary, Phoenix, Arizona, December 7, 1999; confirmation hearings before the Senate Foreign Relations Committee, January 17, 2001.

2. Clinton's comments on the Internet and democracy are numerous. In particular, see his March 8, 2000, speech at the Paul H. Nitze School of Advanced International Studies, Johns Hopkins University, Washington, D.C., where he made the oft-quoted statement that China's attempt to crack down on the Internet "is sort of like trying to nail Jell-O to the wall."

3. Wriston, "Bits, Bytes, and Diplomacy"; Wright, "Gaining Freedom by Modem."

4. Barlow, "Declaration."

5. See www.eff.org/~barlow/Declaration-Final.html.

6. Lessig, *Code.*

7. See Lerner, *The Passing of Traditional Society;* Lipset, *Political Man;* Pye, *Communications and Political Development.*

8. See Huntington, *The Third Wave,* pp. 101–2; Diamond, "The Globalization of Democracy"; Schmitter, "The Influence of the International Context"; Linz and Stepan, *Problems of Democratic Transition,* p. 76.

9. See Carey, "Mass Media and Democracy"; Fox, *Media and Politics in Latin America;* Lawson, *Building the Fourth Estate;* Lee, *Voices of China;* Lichtenberg, *Democracy and the Mass Media;* Lynch, *After the Propaganda State;* Randall, "The Media and Democratisation"; Skidmore, *Television, Politics, and Transition;* Zhao, *Media, Market, and Democracy in China.*

10. Lynch, *After the Propaganda State*, p. 227. Lynch's study is, of course, an important exception to his own characterization of the literature, as are Ferdinand's *Internet, Democracy, and Democratization* and Simon, Corrales, and Wolfensberger's *Democracy and the Internet*.

11. See Bimber, "The Internet and Political Transformation"; Budge, *The New Challenge of Direct Democracy*; Coleman, "Can the New Media Invigorate Democracies?"; Davis, *The Web of Politics*; Hague and Loader, *Digital Democracy*; Grossman, *The Electronic Commonwealth*; Norris, *A Virtuous Circle*; Rash, *Politics on the Nets*; Schwartz, *Netactivism*; Tsagarouisanou, Tambini, and Bryan, *Cyberdemocracy*.

12. See Blanchard and Horan, "Virtual Communities"; Glogoff, "Virtual Connections"; Katz, "The Digital Citizen"; Nie and Erbring, *Internet and Society*; Putnam, *Bowling Alone*, chap. 9; Rich, "American Voluntarism"; Uslaner, "Social Capital and the Net"; Wellman and Gulia, "Virtual Communities."

13. The literature on Internet policy issues is enormous. For a sample, see Bar et al., "Access and Innovation Policy"; Benkler, "Free as Air"; Drake, *The New Information Infrastructure*; Lemley and Lessig, "The End of End-to-End"; Lessig, *Laws of Cyberspace*; Lessig, *The Future of Ideas*; Marsden, *Regulating the Global Information Society*; Speta, "Handicapping the Race"; Swire and Litan, *None of Your Business*.

14. In a study of 144 countries, Christopher Kedzie found a statistically significant relationship between access to e-mail networks and the level of democracy (measured by Freedom House's scores for civil and political liberties). However, his most recent data are from 1993, before the Internet was much of a presence in the developing world. In a more recent study of 179 countries, Pippa Norris found a statistically significant relationship between the Freedom House scores and the number of Internet users per capita, but the effect disappears when controlling for economic development. Hill and Hughes have analyzed the political content of postings to newsgroup discussions of authoritarian countries (such as soc.culture.cuba), but since few postings come from within the country in question, their predictions of democratic impact seem questionable.

Furthermore, the direction of causality between democracy and Internet diffusion remains a matter for debate. Kedzie suggests that access to e-mail is a cause of democratization, but Norris reverses the relationship, hypothesizing that democracy is a determinant of Internet diffusion. As Kedzie acknowledges, one cannot conclusively determine the nature of causality with nonexperimental data. See Kedzie, *Communication and Democracy*; Norris, *Digital Divide*; Hill and Hughes, "Is the Internet an Instrument of Global Democratization?"

15. See Franda, *Launching into Cyberspace*; Wilson, *The Information Revolution*; various studies by the Mosaic Group, available at http://mosaic.unomaha.edu/gdi.html.

16. See Goldstein, *The Internet in the Mideast and North Africa;* Reporters sans Frontières and Transfert.net, *Enemies of the Internet;* Sussman, *The Internet in Flux.*

17. In addition to previous studies of the cases examined in this book (which are cited in the corresponding chapters), several individual case studies deserve mention here: Hill and Sen, "The Internet in Indonesia's New Democracy," and Rohozinski, "Mapping Russian Cyberspace."

18. Another factor influencing Internet use in any given country is the international political economy of Internet diffusion. International factors have meant greater Internet bandwidth for Asia than for the Middle East, for instance, and such disparities will obviously influence how the Internet is used in each region. In the future, policies to bridge the global digital divide will matter for Internet access in the developing world, including most authoritarian regimes. While we acknowledge the importance of international factors as determinants of Internet diffusion and Internet use, we do not actively consider them in this study, for reasons of space and because of our desire to focus on the national context of each country. For an overview of these issues as they relate to developing countries, see Drake, *From the Global Digital Divide.*

19. See Lynch, *After the Propaganda State;* Taubman, "A Not-So World Wide Web."

20. See Keck and Sikkink, *Activists beyond Borders.*

21. Diasporas are a broader category than are political exiles; the latter may be active in transnational advocacy networks but are less likely to be engaged in general political discourse with those at home.

22. See Olcott and Ottaway, "The Challenge of Semi-Authoritarianism."

23. The authors' previous publications on these cases include Boas, "www.cubalibre.cu? The Internet and Its Prospects"; Boas, "The Dictator's Dilemma?"; Drake, Kalathil, and Boas, "Dictatorships in the Digital Age"; Kalathil and Boas, "The Internet and State Control"; Kalathil, "Chinese Media"; Kalathil, "Community and Communalism."

24. See Hill and Sen, "The Internet in Indonesia's New Democracy"; Rohozinski, "Mapping Russian Cyberspace"; Arquilla and Ronfeldt, "Emergence and Influence."

25. See Norris, *Digital Divide;* Corrales, "Lessons from Latin America."

26. Dalpino, *Deferring Democracy.*

Chapter 2: Wired for Modernization in China

1. "China Decides It's Internet Crazy," Reuters, August 21, 2000.

2. Several articles on China's experience with the information revolution have broadly informed this chapter. They include: Foster and Goodman, *The Diffusion of the Internet in China;* Hachigian, "China's Cyber-Strategy"; Hartford,

"Cyberspace with Chinese Characteristics"; Harwit and Clark, "Shaping the Internet"; Keller, "China's Impact on the Global Information Society"; Lynch, *After the Propaganda State;* Qiu, "Virtual Censorship in China"; and Tipson, "China and the Information Revolution." Off-the-record interviews with Chinese scholars, business executives, and officials in 2001 and 2002 have also provided information for this chapter.

3. Former vice president Hu took over as general secretary of the Communist Party at the 16th National Congress of the Communist Party in November 2002. He is expected to assume the presidency in March 2003, although Jiang Zemin, who is stepping down after thirteen years in power, will likely retain significant behind-the-scenes influence. The transition of power in November 2002 paved the way for a new generation of leaders to assume top party positions.

4. World Bank, *World Development Report 2002: Building Institutions for Markets* (New York: Oxford University Press, 2002).

5. U.S. State Department, "Country Report, 2001: China."

6. Private entrepreneurs were officially welcomed into the party by Jiang Zemin in July 2001. Studies conducted within China have shown that the party's traditional working-class base has withered within the past decade. See Ching Cheong, "Changing Face of China's Ruling Party," *Straits Times,* May 14, 2002.

7. Amnesty International, "Asia/Pacific."

8. Pei, "Future Shock."

9. Lee, *Voices of China,* p. 5; Lynch, *After the Propaganda State,* p. 3.

10. Lynch, *After the Propaganda State.*

11. Ibid.

12. Because Internet content providers are seen as having the power to interpret information, they are treated as much more sensitive than are Internet service providers, which merely provide connections to the Internet. China is one of the few countries to separate content and service providers artificially in this fashion.

13. Zhao, *Media, Market, and Democracy,* p. 34.

14. Lynch, *After the Propaganda State.*

15. Beach, "Running in Place." See also Kalathil, "Chinese Media."

16. Zhao, "Caught in the Web."

17. Gao and Lyytinen, "Transformation."

18. Ibid.

19. Tipson, "China and the Information Revolution"; Gao and Lyytinen, "Transformation."

20. Gao and Lyytinen, "Transformation."

21. Mueller and Lovelock, "The WTO."

22. Harwit and Clark, "Shaping the Internet."

23. Tipson, "China."

24. The government agencies involved in Internet regulation include the Ministry of Information Industry; the Ministry of State Security; the Administration of Industry and Commerce; the Ministry of Culture; the State Press and Publica-

tions Administration; the State Administration of Radio, Film, and Television; the State Encryption Administration Commission; the China Securities Regulatory Commission; and the Internet News Administrative Bureau of the State Council's Information Office. For a full description of each agency's function, see U.N. Conference on Trade and Development, "Electronic Commerce."

25. Lynch, *After the Propaganda State*.

26. Especially outside the major cities, fierce battles have erupted between armed gangs representing various telecommunication interests. The physical manifestation of competition between bureaucracies may strike outsiders as bizarre, but it underlines the importance that various ministries place on staking out turf. See Zhao, "Caught in the Web."

27. There are now reports that the Chinese government is putting together a plan to eliminate the MII altogether, further centralizing the management of telecommunications and information networks within the State Development Planning Commission. Although this would supposedly eliminate the problem of MII–SARFT competition, placing regulation of the Internet, telecommunication networks, and cable television networks under one body, it remains unclear how this might work in practice.

28. In fact, it is unclear whether China has committed itself to dismantling the interconnecting network regime, and if so, when. For more, see Foster and Goodman, *Diffusion*.

29. CNNIC's figures and methodology are widely disputed; independent Chinese and overseas research firms often come up with vastly different numbers. An independent study conducted by the Hong Kong–based market research firm Interactive Audience Measurement Asia Ltd. concluded that the true number of Internet users in January 2001 was 25 percent lower than CNNIC's estimates.

30. "China To Rival Japan in Internet Users by 2004," Reuters, February 7, 2001.

31. Xiaodong Li, "Looking Ahead at the Development of the IT Industry in 2001," State Council Development and Research Center, available on Sinofile, Information Services, Ltd., www.sinopolis.com/Archives/TOPSTORY/ts_010302_01.htm.

32. Interviews with Chinese officials, 2001.

33. For instance, see Hachigian, "China's Cyber-Strategy."

34. Taubman, "A Not-So World Wide Web."

35. For instance, although Chinese television excised the portions of U.S. Secretary of State Colin Powell's August 2001 interview that dealt with human rights, the text of his full comments was soon found on the web site of *People's Daily*, China's foremost state media organ.

36. For instance, see Taubman, "A Not-So World Wide Web." In contrast, Lynch, *After the Propaganda State*, argues that, far from creating an independent sphere of ideas and activity, the Internet and other ICTs are helping to create a chaotic space filled with apolitical content and atomized individuals, a space that ultimately will not contribute to the formation of an independent civil society.

37. This term is commonly used by the government in describing its goal for the Internet environment. See Shanthi Kalathil, "Between the Lines: China's Dot-Communism," *Foreign Policy*, January/February 2001.

38. The government occasionally lifts some of these blocks when politically expedient; for example, before and during the 2001 APEC meeting in Shanghai, attended by U.S. President George Bush and three thousand foreign journalists. When the international leaders left, the sites were reblocked.

39. There is a common understanding, among both government officials and the private sector, that such regulations will not be enforced 100 percent of the time. Yet even without these regulations, portals have shied away from anything even remotely controversial, such as when Sohu.com indicated that in theory it would not report a Taiwanese declaration of independence, lest the act be seen as undermining national unity.

40. See Liu Yuan, "Café Crackdown: China Enlists the Public in Its Ongoing Campaign To Censor the Internet," *Asiaweek*, February 2, 2001. In June 2002, a fire at an unlicensed Internet café resulted in the death of several patrons, prompting the government to go on a café-closing spree (although many subsequently reopened).

41. Tyler Marshall and Anthony Kuhn, "China Goes One-on-One with the Net," *Los Angeles Times*, January 29, 2000.

42. Bell, Brown, Jayasuriya, and Jones, *Toward Illiberal Democracy*.

43. Some argue that while nationalism can be manipulated by Chinese officials, it may also, if properly directed, help to create a more vibrant public sphere. For more, see Qiu, "Chinese Opinions."

44. Proxy servers are often hailed as a weapon against censorship, but their use by the public in China is the subject of much debate. While some assert that the real numbers of proxy users are higher than survey results indicate, it is also true that they are often difficult to access, commercially unviable, and easily located and blocked by the government. There have also been rumors that the government itself deploys fake proxies, using them as data-gathering devices; such rumors cause further self-policing by would-be users. For more on this topic, see Tsui, "Internet in China."

45. Guo and Bu, *Survey*.

46. There is considerable debate about whether organizations ranging from the loose network of the Falun Gong spiritual movement to the Party-originated "mass organization" All-China Women's Federation constitute the foundation for an independent civil society. While acknowledging that organizations such as the ACWF retain a significant state component, we analyze them in a civil society context for the purposes of this chapter. For a detailed discussion of the changing role of organizations such as the ACWF, see White, Howell, and Xiaoyuan, "In Search of Civil Society"; and Moore, "China's Fledgling Civil Society."

47. Moore, "China's Fledgling Civil Society."

48. Bell and Boas, "Falun Gong."

49. Interviews with overseas Falun Gong spokespeople, May 7, 2001.

50. Maggie Farley, "Hactivists Besiege China," *Los Angeles Times,* January 4, 1999; Jasper Becker, "Review of Dissidents, Human Rights Issues," *South China Morning Post,* January 12, 1999.

51. Although the China Democracy Party did rely on Internet use during its early stages, it never achieved the status of a formal opposition party, and as such it is discussed in the section on civil society in this chapter.

52. Government surveillance and the monitoring of citizens do, of course, form a large part of government Internet use; however, such actions are taken in reaction to public use of the Internet, and as such, we categorize them under that section.

53. One question, taken from a visit to the web site in June 2001, pertained to how a recent university graduate from Shandong might go about moving his official residence to Beijing in order to take a job there. The answer provided on the web site cited specific regulations and gave advice on how to go about the relevant procedure.

54. "Much Achieved by Government Online Project in China," *People's Daily Online,* July 13, 1999; "The Complete Reference to the Web Sites of Chinese Government Agency," http://chinasite.com/government.html.

55. Michael Ma, "China Wants Net To Spread Propaganda," *South China Morning Post,* February 10, 2001.

56. "China To Build Own 'Superhighway,'" *Associated Press,* January 8, 2001.

57. All statistics taken from the presentation "The Information Technology Industry in China," by Wei Lu, deputy director-general, Technical Economics Department, Development Research Center, State Council, presented at the Twelfth Asia Forum, "The IT Revolution and Asian Economies: Growing Interdependence of the Global Economy," May 25, 2001.

58. John Markoff, "Silicon Valley's Primal Spirit Lives, in a Part of Beijing," *New York Times,* August 4, 2000.

59. Harwit and Clark, "Shaping the Internet."

60. See Craig S. Smith, "Little Anxiety over China Web Rules," *New York Times,* October 3, 2000. See also Kalathil, "Between the Lines."

61. "China's Internet Industry Wants Self-Discipline," *People's Daily,* March 27, 2002.

62. Interviews with numerous Internet executives, 2001–2002. For a detailed picture of the Chinese Internet industry and its rising entrepreneurs, see Sheff, *China Dawn.*

63. In one famed incident, after inflaming Chinese leaders in the early 1990s by characterizing satellite television as a threat to totalitarian regimes, News Corp.'s Rupert Murdoch subsequently dropped BBC news programming from his Star TV satellite network, reportedly in an attempt to mollify officials and curry favor.

64. Mark Landler, "AOL Gains Cable Rights in China by Omitting News, Sex, and Violence," *New York Times,* October 29, 2001; Michael Dorgan, "U.S. Firms Silent over Chinese Net Arrest," *San Jose Mercury News,* July 6, 2000.

65. Bell, Brown, Jayasuriya, and Jones, *Towards Illiberal Democracy,* p. 13.

66. After businessman Huang Qi was tried for posting articles about the Tiananmen massacre on his web site, New York–based Human Rights Watch posted a statement on its web site urging Western governments and Internet corporations to come to Huang's defense. (U.S. Internet corporations were silent when Human Rights Watch raised the same plea shortly after Huang's arrest.) See "Subversion Trial Set for Web Site Creator," *South China Morning Post,* February 10, 2001; and Dorgan, "U.S. Firms Silent."

67. Although some international groups do rely on e-mail to contact supporters in China, this practice is perhaps less widespread than is popularly perceived. The *China Labour Bulletin,* a newsletter from Hong Kong by exiled labor activist and dissident Han Dongfang, is dependent on e-mail to keep in touch with external supporters, but contacts within China are primarily made by phone and through a regular radio program. (Source: e-mail correspondence with *China Labour Bulletin* web master, May 5, 2000.)

68. Kevin McLaughlin, "China's Two-faced Internet Policies (and the People Who Skirt Them)," *Business 2.0,* August 14, 2000.

69. The project is financed from a congressional allocation of $5 million to improve broadcasting to China, including the Internet and radio. For more, see Jennifer 8. Lee, "U.S. May Help Chinese Evade Net Censorship," *New York Times,* August 30, 2001. Continued U.S. support of anonymizing software, particularly that which targets China, is likely to depend on several altered factors following the September 11 attacks on America. Given the changing dynamics of U.S.–China relations in light of cooperative efforts against terrorism, in tandem with a trend toward less, rather than more, online privacy in the United States and elsewhere, such efforts may suffer in a protracted war on terrorism.

70. Evidence exists that the group's international information dissemination and lobbying efforts translated into action at diplomatic levels: Canadian Prime Minister Jean Chretien voiced concern about the crackdown in talks with China's premier, Zhu Rongji, in February 2001. See "China Vows War against Falun Gong," Reuters, February 12, 2001.

71. Interviews with overseas Falun Gong practitioners, February 7, 2001. Also see Bell and Boas, "Falun Gong."

72. For a comprehensive look at China's military modernization, see Mulvenon and Yang, *The People's Liberation Army;* and Karmel, *China and the People's Liberation Army.*

73. Tipson, "China and the Information Revolution."

74. Stokes, "China's Strategic Modernization."

75. Zhang, "War without Rules."

76. Thomas, "Like Adding Wings to the Tiger."

77. In fact, many of the reported atrocities may not have been verified but served to inflame nationalist emotion nonetheless. For more on this phenomenon, see Hughes, "Nationalism."

78. Dai, "Chinese Politics."

79. Edward Tian, president and chief executive officer of the China Netcom Corporation, as quoted in World Economic Forum's "Envisioning China in 2006," available at www.weforum.org.

80. Hachigian, "China's Cyber-Strategy."

Chapter 3: Channeling a "Limited" Resource in Cuba

1. Hinchberger, "Netting Fidel"; "InCUBAdora."

2. "Cuba Tests Online Waters," *BBC News,* April 4, 2002; Laurie Goering, "Cubans Find Ways To Access Internet, E-mail," *Chicago Tribune,* February 22, 2001; Scott Wilson, "Web of Resistance Rises in Cuba," *Washington Post,* December 26, 2000, p. A1.

3. "Disinformation about Cuban Internet Access," Radio Havana Cuba, February 7, 2001; Felix Lopez, "La verdad bloqueada," *Granma,* February 7, 2001.

4. In addition to this chapter's lead quotation, see, for instance, "More Internet Access on the Way to Cuba," *San Antonio Express-News,* March 8, 2001, p. B6.

5. Norma Márquez González, "Acerca del nuevo ministerio," *Giga* no. 2 (2000) (authors' translation).

6. I. J. Toby Westerman, "Beijing Gives Boost to Fidel: China Helps Cuba Get Current on Communications Technology," WorldNetDaily.com, June 4, 2000.

7. Figures are from the *CIA World Factbook,* 2001.

8. United Nations, CEPA, and Fondo de Cultura Económica, *La economía cubana.*

9. Ibid.

10. Some commentators have suggested that at least the former event was a carefully calculated move by Castro, with no real promise of political change. For instance, see David Gonzalez, "Castro's Door: Both Opened and Closed," *New York Times,* May 16, 2002, p. A12.

11. As stated in the introduction, we adopt a broad definition of civil society and consider CSOs to include all organizations that operate at least semi-autonomously from the state, regardless of political orientation. In Cuba, this includes both officially licensed organizations and illegal dissident groups.

12. See Gunn, "Cuba's NGOs."

13. In 1996, for instance, the Center for Study of the Americas, a think tank originally created by the Communist Party, was purged of those researchers who held progressive ideas for political and economic reform and had established close

ties with U.S. academics. See Bengelsdorf, "Intellectuals under Fire"; and Giuliano, *El Caso CEA.*

14. Carol Rosenberg, "Cuban American Group Seeks U.S. Aid against Castro," *Miami Herald,* February 9, 2001.

15. The Helms-Lieberman bill is S. 894, Solidaridad Act of 2001. The companion bill introduced in the House of Representatives is H.R. 1271. As of April 2002, no action had been taken on either bill beyond referral to the Senate Foreign Relations and House International Relations Committees.

16. See Nichols and Torres, "Cuba"; Nichols, "Cuban Mass Media"; and Ripoll, "The Press in Cuba."

17. As detailed later in this chapter, Cuba's state-owned telephone company was partially privatized in the 1990s, but the Cuban government still retains majority control, with a 51 percent stake. See Peters, "Cuba Goes Digital."

18. See Nichols, "Cuban Mass Media."

19. Independent journalists generally dictate their stories over international telephone calls to their counterparts in the United States. From there they are transcribed and posted on the Internet or broadcast via Radio Martí. Restrictions on Internet access and the jamming of Radio Martí ensure a limited Cuban audience for independent journalism.

20. See Julia Scheeres, "Cuba Bans PC Sales to Public," *Wired News,* March 25, 2002.

21. See Nichols and Torres, "Cuba."

22. See Press, *Cuban Telecommunications;* and Mosaic Group, "The Global Diffusion of the Internet Project: An Initial Inductive Study," http://mosaic.unomaha.edu/GDI1998/GDI1998.html.

23. Peters, "Cuba Goes Digital."

24. These figures are from ETECSA and are cited in Peters, "Cuba Goes Digital."

25. "China To Help Cuba Revamp Communications, Electronics Systems," *CubaInfo* 12, no. 8 (2000); "Government Paints Bright Digital Future, But Money and Politics Stand in the Way," *CubaNews,* March 2001, p. 6.

26. "Cuba Sets Deadline on Telephone Income Dispute, Threatens Cutoff," *CubaInfo* 11, no. 3 (1999): 3–4.

27. In March 1999 a Florida judge ruled that long-distance payments to ETECSA could be garnished to pay for a $187.6 million judgment against the Cuban government for shooting down two private planes flown by members of the exile organization Brothers to the Rescue. In response, Cuba cut off service to the majority of U.S. carriers. Most companies began routing calls through third countries, and the ruling was eventually overturned by an appeals court, allowing service to resume. However, Cuba attempted to impose a 10 percent tax to cover lost revenues resulting from the garnishment decision, and the United States refused to pay the tax, leading to another cutoff in December 2000 (this time, calls

through third countries were blocked as well). Service resumed in the summer of 2001, but only through a Canadian firm that routed calls through Canada. See Chris Oakes, "Cuban Telephone Crisis," *Wired News,* March 2, 1999; "Canadian Fix Allows Calls To Go through More Easily," *CubaNews,* August 2001, p. 5.

28. See Nelson Valdés, "Cuba."

29. On the establishment of this interministerial commission, see Valdés, "Cuba."

30. As mentioned earlier, Cuba's consolidation of Internet-governance institutions was closely modeled on China's own bureaucratic reshuffling two years earlier, when it merged the Ministry of Electronics Industries and the Ministry of Posts and Telecommunications to create the MII. For more details, see chapter 2.

31. The MIC's resolutions licensing each Cuban ISP and setting ETECSA's prices can be obtained online through the Cuban government's web site, www.cubagob.cu/.

32. Reliable figures on the Internet in Cuba are hard to come by, and no outside estimates are available to compare with government statistics. The figures cited earlier here are from Patricia Grogg, "Communications, Cuba: Internet Access Growing, But with Limits," Inter Press Service, January 23, 2002. Government figures are also listed on MIC's web site, www.cubagob.cu/des_eco/mic/mic_indicadores/informatizacion_sociedad.htm; however, as of June 2002 they had not been updated in nearly a year. Earlier statistics on Internet diffusion in Cuba can be found in Jesús Martínez, "The Net in Cuba," *Matrix News* no. 901 (January 1999), www.mids.org/pay/mn/901/cuba.html; Patricia Grogg, "Communcations, Cuba: Government To Set up Public Internet Terminals," Inter Press Service, October 18, 2000; Dalia Acosta, "Cuban Cybercafe for Intellectuals, Artists," Inter Press Service, November 27, 2000; and a number of wire service reports on government figures released at a March 2001 press conference (e.g., "Limitaciones técnicas y no políticas impiden acceso masivo de cubanos a Internet," Agence France-Press, March 3, 2001). At this press conference a government official said there were twelve thousand accounts that had the capacity to browse the Internet, though it is unclear whether he meant full access to the Internet or access to Cuba's limited intranet.

33. Dalia Acosta, "Internet Overcomes Gov't Resistance," Inter Press Service, April 12, 2001.

34. Boas, "The Dictator's Dilemma?" See also Valdés, "Cuba"; and Mosaic Group, "Global Diffusion."

35. Gonzalez and Ronfeldt, *Cuba Adrift,* pp. 73–74.

36. Quoted in Geri Smith, "Yahoo, Stay Home," *Business Week,* November 29, 1999, p. 206.

37. See, for instance, Maria F. Durand, "Cuba Goes Online," ABCNews.com, July 24, 2000.

38. See Goering, "Cubans Find Ways"; Wilson, "Web of Resistance"; Acosta, "Cuban Cybercafe."

39. See MIC Resolution 23 of the year 2000, available through the Cuban government's web site, www.cubagob.cu/.

40. See Peters, "Cuba Goes Digital."

41. See Hinchberger, "The New E-Man."

42. See Lopez, "La verdad bloqueada."

43. On the importance of political trustworthiness in the granting of Internet access, see Seror and Arteaga, "Telecommunications."

44. Wilson, "Web of Resistance."

45. See, for instance, "Cuba Tests Online Waters"; Peters, "Cuba Goes Digital"; "Despite Strict Government Control, Clever Cubans Still Get Bootleg Internet," *San Jose Mercury News,* March 24, 2002.

46. Press, *Cuban Telecommunications.*

47. Boas, "www.cubalibre.cu? Transnational Networking."

48. While Caritas had no e-mail access at the time of the survey in September 1998, it now appears to have gained access.

49. See "Dissident Cuban Economists Launch Website," Reuters, December 7, 2001.

50. The site states that it is designed by "Grupo de Apoyo ICEI" (ICEI Support Group), which is identified as "a group of free Cubans who morally and materially support the Cuban Institute of Independent Economists" (authors' translation); see www.cubaicei.org/Grupo%20de%20Apoyo.htm.

51. "Objetivos estrategicos del Ministerio de la Informatica y las Comunicaciones para el periodo 2001–2003," www.cubagob.cu/des_eco/mic/mic_objetivos/objetivos_2001_2003.htm.

52. See www.cubagob.cu/.

53. In February 1996 the Cuban air force shot down two private planes piloted by members of the Cuban exile organization Brothers to the Rescue, which had a history of violating Cuban airspace and dropping antigovernment leaflets over Havana. The United States charged that Cuba had shot down the planes in international airspace, but Cuba disputed the claim. The recently established online edition of the state newspaper *Granma* was the only place where an international audience could read the Cuban government's point of view on the issue. See "InCUBAdora"; Hinchberger, "Netting Fidel."

54. Cited in "Limitaciones técnicas" (authors' translation).

55. See www.granma.cu.

56. A list of these and other online publications is available at www.cubaweb.cu/esp/categorias/subcategories.asp?categoryID=11.

57. "Granma International Online Sets New 'Hit' Record," *Granma International,* April 4, 2000.

58. See "InCUBAdora."

59. See Peters, "Cuba Goes Digital"; and "Cuba's Wired Generation," *BBC News,* April 5, 2002.

60. See "Cuba's Wired Generation."

61. See "InCUBAdora"; Hinchberger, "Netting Fidel."

62. See www.cubatips.com/ and www.camaracuba.cubaweb.cu/.

63. See Hinchberger, "The New E-Man."

64. For instance, see www.gocubaplus.com and www.cubalinda.com, which are the Cuban travel web sites run by Stephen Marshall and Philip Agee, respectively.

65. These include www.cubagiftstore.com and www.cuba-shop.com. See Vito Echevarria, "New E-Commerce Sites Are Latest Leak in U.S. Embargo against Cuba," *CubaNews,* August 2001.

66. The site is www.ccw.cu. See "InCUBAdora"; "Virtual Store for B2B Commerce Launched in Havana," Global News Wire, March 15, 2001.

67. Cited in Sokol, "E-Cuba."

68. See www.tourandmarketing.com/english/home.html.

69. The Cuban Democracy Act of 1992.

Chapter 4: Catching up and Cracking down in Singapore, Vietnam, and Burma

1. The academic treatment of Internet use during political transition in Asia has been limited; one of the more relevant examples is Hill and Sen, "Indonesia's New Democracy." For an examination of how one-party authoritarian states in Asia deal with the Internet, see Hachigian, "The Internet and Power."

2. "The eAsia Report Executive Summary," *eMarketer,* 2001, www.emarketer.com/.

3. World Bank, *World Development Indicators 2002.*

4. Others dispute the existence of Asian political values that cut across national, ethnic, and cultural lines, citing transitions from authoritarian rule and a lively engagement with pluralistic politics in places such as Taiwan and South Korea as evidence that the existence of such values at the very least deserves further examination. For some examples of writing on Asian values and Asian political constructs, see Bell, Brown, Jayasuriya, and Jones, *Towards Illiberal Democracy;* Heng, "Give Me Liberty"; Pye and Pye, *Asian Power;* Fukuyama, "Confucianism and Democracy"; Cotton, "East Asian Democracy"; and Moody, *Political Opposition.*

5. ASEAN includes Burma, Brunei, Cambodia, Indonesia, Laos, Malaysia, Philippines, Singapore, Thailand, and Vietnam.

6. The task force will encourage an ASEAN Information Infrastructure. It lists as one of its goals the creation of recommendations on "including the social and

cultural dimensions of ASEAN into e-space." For more details, see the e-ASEAN web site, www.e-aseantf.org/.

7. Ministerial meetings on regional integration, held in Hanoi in July 2001, ended with a declaration aimed at narrowing the development gap between ASEAN's core members and its four newcomers: Burma, Cambodia, Laos, and Vietnam. Specific initiatives are likely to focus in part on incorporating ICT in development. Singapore, for one, immediately announced it would establish ICT, English, and trade-promotion training centers in the four countries. See Margot Cohen, "Reality Bites," *Far Eastern Economic Review,* August 16, 2001.

8. A good explanation of the developmental state and its role in economic transformation can be found in Evans, *Embedded Autonomy.*

9. For examples of state control over other ICTs, see Wong, "Implementing the NII Vision"; and Atkins, *Southeast Asia's New Media.*

10. Although Burma's ruling military junta renamed the country Myanmar, many in the international community refuse to recognize the new name. The U.S. State Department refers to the country as Burma in its *Country Report on Human Rights Practices,* and we follow that custom here.

11. Olcott and Ottaway, "Semi-Authoritarianism."

12. Moreover, the PAP's share of the vote rose 19 percent from its 1997 figures to 75 percent, again despite an economic downturn. See Trish Saywell, "Token Contest," *Far Eastern Economic Review,* November 15, 2001.

13. Rodan, "The Internet."

14. World Bank, *World Development Indicators 2002.*

15. Minges, Ismail, and Press, *The E-City.*

16. "Infocomm Facts and Figures," Singapore government web site, www.ida.gov.sg.

17. Numbers on the percentage of Internet users vary according to who performs the study. A study released in September 2000, however, states that Singapore had the highest Internet penetration in Asia. Minges, Ismail, and Press, *The E-City.*

18. Rodan, "Information Technology."

19. Minges, Ismail, and Press, *The E-City.*

20. Hai, "Rapid Deployment.

21. Minges, Ismail, and Press, *The E-City.*

22. Speech by George Yeo, EMASIA '98, Los Angeles, June 4, 1998, Columbia International Affairs Online, https://wwwc.cc.columbia.edu/sec/dlc/ciao/conf/asoc_spch98/yeg01.html.

23. Ibid.

24. Rodan, "Asia."

25. Through use of the International Security Act, the government can place restrictions on publications that are thought to incite violence, counsel disobedience to the law, arouse tensions among segments of the population, or threaten

national interests, security, or public order. Although the wide-ranging act has not been invoked extensively in recent years, the mere threat of its use is enough to discourage many journalists and editors from testing implicitly or explicitly the delimited markers on speech. Not only do journalists hesitate to venture beyond these markers, they often shy from approaching them, creating a press climate that is even more restricted than the government has indicated is acceptable. For more on this subject, see Seow, *The Media Enthralled.*

26. The shareholding structure is detailed in Singapore's Newspaper Printing and Presses Act, available online, www.mita.gov.sg/NPPA.htm.

27. Committee To Protect Journalists, *Attacks.*

28. Hai, "Rapid Deployment.

29. "Singapore Government's Liberalization of the Telecom Sector, One Year On," U.S. embassy, Singapore, July 2001, www.usembassysingapore.org.sg/embassy/politics/Telecom2001.html.

30. U.S. State Department, "Singapore: Country Reports on Human Rights Practices, 2000," Bureau of Democracy, Human Rights, and Labor, 2001.

31. Rodan, "Singapore."

32. Minges, Ismail, and Press, *The E-City.*

33. From an AsiaOne press release, available online, www.asia1.com.sg/html/pr010524.html. Also see Minges, Ismail, and Press, *The E-City.*

34. According to an employee of one site, the amendments would have allowed politically themed sites to be charged with an offense for anonymous individual postings. The new rules also state that nonparty political sites should not "campaign for any party."

35. At the former site of Sintercom, www.sintercom.org, a link now redirects the user to a Singaporean food-appreciation site.

36. The freelancer, Robert Ho, was forced to undergo a psychiatric evaluation, found to be mentally ill, and released. See Committee To Protect Journalists, *Attacks.*

37. Bell, Brown, Jayasuriya, and Jones, *Towards Illiberal Democracy.*

38. Hai, "Rapid Deployment."

39. "The Singapore E-Government Action Plan," www.ida.gov.sg.

40. For more details, see the Singapore eCitizen web site, www.ecitizen.gov.sg.

41. "New Curbs on Net Political Campaigning," Associated Press, August 13, 2001.

42. Speech by George Yeo, 1998 (see n. 22).

43. Rodan, "Asia."

44. Rodan, "Singapore."

45. World Bank, *World Development Report 2002.*

46. Tim Kelly and Michael Minges, *Vietnam Internet Case Study* (Geneva: International Telecommunication Union, March 2002).

47. Transparency International, "Corruption Perceptions Index 2001," www.transparency.org/cpi/2001/cpi2001.html#cpi.

48. Dao, *Democracy in Vietnam*, p. ix.

49. "Economist.com Country Briefings: Vietnam," August 27, 2001, Economist Intelligence Unit, www.economist.com/countries/vietnam.

50. CIA, "World Factbook: Vietnam," www.cia.gov/cia/publications/factbook.

51. Kelly and Minges, *Vietnam*.

52. Human Rights Watch, "Human Rights Watch: World Report 2001, Vietnam," 2002, www.hrw.org/wr2k1/asia/Vietnam.html.

53. Ibid.

54. World Bank, *World Development Indicators 2002*.

55. Hoang-Giang Dang, "Internet in Vietnam: From a Laborious Birth into an Uncertain Future," *Informatik Forum* 13, no. 1, www.interasia.org/vietnam/dang-hoang-giang.html .

56. Although some anecdotes cite as many as five hundred sites blocked, the Open Society report found that sites such as ABC, Amnesty International, CNN, Dow Jones, GILC, Jennycam.com, Nasdaq, Planned Parenthood, Playboy, Penthouse, and Thule.org were all accessible. For more information, see the comprehensive report by the Open Society on the web, www.soros.org/censorship/eastasia/vietnam.html.

57. Jeffrey Sachs, Michael Porter, and Klaus Schwab, "Global Competitiveness Report 2001–2002," World Economic Forum, in collaboration with the Center for International Development, Harvard University, and the Institute for Strategy and Competitiveness, Harvard Business School (New York: Oxford University Press, 2001).

58. Anecdotal accounts note that many Internet café users spend their time on word processing or game playing rather than surfing the web. For more on this, see Pierre, "Vietnam's Contradictions."

59. Dang, "Internet in Vietnam."

60. From a letter sent by the Committee To Protect Journalists to Tran Duc Luong, the president of the Socialist Republic of Vietnam, April 29, 2002. The letter also notes that another man, dissident Tran Khue, had his computer and several documents confiscated after he circulated an open letter to Chinese president Jiang Zemin on the Internet.

61. "Vietnam: Intranet Development Model," *Vietnam Economic News,* January 18, 1999.

62. Singapore established a similar policy toward satellite television access several years ago.

63. Dang, "Internet in Vietnam."

64. This stems in part from the country's long experience with colonialism, war, and foreign intervention.

65. Dissident Nguyen Dan Que's writings continue to be available on such overseas Vietnamese-run political web sites as Vietnam Insight, although they are

generally inaccessible within Vietnam. These sites often rely on high-level sources inside Vietnam who provide information secretly.

66. One group's campaign claims to have prompted Hanoi to allow Nguyen Dan Que's family to visit him in prison. Eng, "A New Kind of Cyberwar."

67. Pierre, "Vietnam's Contradictions."

68. World Bank, *World Development Indicators 2002.*

69. Committee To Protect Journalists, *Attacks.*

70. The Computer Science Development Law, promulgated by the State Law and Order Restoration Council, Law 10/96 (the 8th Waxing of Tawthalin, 1358 M.E./20th September 1996). Available online, www.myanmar.com/gov/laws/computerlaw.html.

71. For example, Australian Leo Nichols was arrested in 1996 for the illegal use of a fax machine. He subsequently died in prison.

72. Brian Mockenhaupt, "Wordsmithery," *Far Eastern Economic Review,* September 20, 2001.

73. Neumann, "Burmese Journalism."

74. Kyaw Zwa Moe, "News of Attacks Hard To Find in Burma," *Irrawaddy,* September 17, 2001.

75. Gina Chon, "Waiting To Be Wired," *Asiaweek,* July 20, 2001.

76. See n. 71.

77. Peter Alford, "Internet Download Arrests," *Australian,* December 30, 1999.

78. "Burma Sets up National E-Task Force To Bridge Digital Divide," *Myanmar Times* (English version), December 13, 2000, from BBC Monitoring Asia Pacific.

79. China in particular is thought to have helped Burma with its signal intelligence capabilities. See Selth, "Burma's Intelligence Apparatus."

80. Danitz and Strobel, "The Internet's Impact on Activism."

81. The Open Society also sponsors the Burma Project, one of the first international campaigns to make strategic use of the web in attracting support and mobilizing.

82. In a recent example from October 2001, the Free Burma Coalition threatened to mount protests at outlets of the San Francisco–based Pottery Barn, an American home-furnishings chain that has imported items from Burma. Pottery Barn subsequently withdrew Burmese-made products from its collection, joining other firms such as Costco, Ikea, Sarah Lee, and Wal-Mart. For more, see "Pottery Barn Bins Burmese Goods," *Far Eastern Economic Review,* October 11, 2001.

83. Rodan, "The Internet."

Chapter 5: Technology and Tradition in the United Arab Emirates, Saudi Arabia, and Egypt

1. While this chapter's opening quotation is an example of such speculation, Thomas Friedman has expressed more nuanced views in recent statements on the

political impacts of ICTs in the Middle East. See, for instance, "The Hidden Victims," *New York Times,* May 1, 2002, www.nytimes.com/2002/05/01/opinion/01FRIE.html.

2. Lerner, *The Passing of Traditional Society;* Alterman, *New Media.*

3. All these figures are from Ajeeb Research Unit, March 15, 2001, http://eit.ajeeb.com/ViewArticle.asp?Article_ID=28132, as well as the accompanying article "Over 3.5 Million Arabs Accessing the Net, According to Ajeeb.com Survey," March 25, 2001, http://eit.ajeeb.com/ViewArticle.asp?Article_ID=27643.

4. Ibid.

5. Alterman, "Mid-Tech Revolution."

6. See Ajami, "What the Muslim World Is Watching"; and Fandy, "Information Technology."

7. See Amin and Gher, "Digital Communications"; Fandy, "Information Technology"; and Salhi, "Information Technology."

8. As used here, the term *Islamist* refers to fundamentalist Islamic political movements; *Islamic* refers more generally to the religion.

9. The figures are from CIA, *The World Factbook* (Washington, D.C.: 2001), www.cia.gov/cia/publications/factbook/index.html.

10. See Rugh, "The United Arab Emirates: What Are the Sources of Its Stability?" *Middle East Policy 5,* no. 3 (September 1997): 14–24.

11. See Rugh, "The United Arab Emirates."

12. Al-Sayegh, "Diversity in Unity."

13. U.S. State Department, *Country Reports.*

14. Rosenthal, "Information Technology," www.american.edu/carmel/lr2962a/uae.htm.

15. Ajeeb Research Unit, "3.5 Million Arabs Accessing the Net," http://eit.ajeeb.com/ViewArticle.asp?Article_ID=27643.

16. See Goldstein, *The Internet;* and Rosenthal, *Information Technology in the UAE.* A 1998 report by the Mosaic Group states that proxy servers were required for all accounts (including leased lines) after 1997. It is unclear from these reports when this requirement was lifted for businesses with leased-lined access. See Mosaic Group, "The Global Diffusion of the Internet Project: An Initial Inductive Study," http://mosaic.unomaha.edu/gdi.html.

17. The discussion forum is now officially closed; see http://ddg.hypermart.net.

18. Goldstein, *The Internet;* U.S. State Department, *Country Reports.*

19. The web site http://etisalat.charges.too.much.net (based abroad but accessible in the UAE) features some technical information on bypassing the country's censorship mechanism, including the URLs of foreign-based proxy servers, though such servers are undoubtedly blacklisted themselves as soon as they are posted.

20. Deutsche Presse-Agentur, April 29, 2001.

21. While the IT Education Project benefits all the country's schools, the initiative was spearheaded by Sheik Mohammed of Dubai.

22. *Gulf News,* August 23, 2000.

23. Sheik Mohammed even has his own web site, where he promotes various IT–related initiatives; see www.sheikmohammed.co.ae/.

24. See Meena S. Janardhan, "United Arab Emirates E-Government Service Gets Glowing Reviews," Inter Press Service, January 22, 2002.

25. See Rosenthal, *Information Technology.*

26. "New Economy, Old Rules?" *PC Magazine Middle and Near East,* June 2000, www.mafhoum.com/press/52T1.htm.

27. Even without Dubai's economic diversification strategies, the depletion of oil reserves might not prove to be of significant political concern. Other emirates with minimal oil reserves also remain economically solvent and politically stable, buttressed by subsidies from Abu Dhabi and Dubai.

28. These figures are from the CIA, *World Factbook.*

29. See Fandy, *Saudi Arabia;* Gause, *Oil Monarchies;* and Wilson and Graham, *Saudi Arabia.*

30. See Gause, *Oil Monarchies.*

31. U.S. State Department, *Country Reports.*

32. Gause, *Oil Monarchies.*

33. U.S. State Department, *Country Reports.*

34. Even after public Internet access debuted in Saudi Arabia, some users continued dialing into Bahrain for access that was uncensored and, depending on use, sometimes cheaper.

35. See Mosaic Group, "Global Diffusion" and "An Update: The Internet in the Kingdom of Saudi Arabia," both at http://mosaic.unomaha.edu/gdi.html.

36. Ajeeb Research Unit, March 15, 2001.

37. "Saudi Telecom Selects Compaq TeMIP for Network and Services Management," Compaq press release, February 5, 2002. See also *Middle East Times,* June 1, 2001.

38. Mosaic Group, "An Update," p. 2. Several thousand of the most commonly accessed approved sites are cached on local servers; when a user requests one of these, it can be delivered more rapidly than if it had to be screened in real time. Requests for sites not stored in the cache are checked against a blacklist of forbidden URLs and, if not already banned, are passed through a filtering mechanism that can eliminate the site based on keywords. See Brian Whitaker and Patrick Barkham, "Sites Caught in Saudis' Web," *Manchester Weekly Guardian,* May 24, 2000.

39. Goldstein, *The Internet,* p. 53.

40. "Saudi Arabia Says It Will Ban Two Hundred Thousand Internet Sites," Associated Press, April 29, 2001.

41. Jennifer Lee, "Companies Compete To Provide Saudi Internet Veil," *New York Times,* November 19, 2001.

42. *Jedda Arab News,* March 30, 2001.

43. "Saudi Arabia Says It Will Ban Two Hundred Thousand Internet Sites."

44. "Saudi Censors Try To Stay a Step ahead of Net Surfers," Associated Press, September 23, 2000.

45. See Yamani, *Changed Identities*.

46. Fandy, *Saudi Arabia*.

47. See Teitelbaum, "Dueling for *Da'wa*."

48. "Saudi Launches Web Portal for Pilgrimage Services," Agence France-Presse, July 2001.

49. See a list of ministry homepages, www.saudiembassy.net/links/gov.htm.

50. "eCommerce Saudi Arabia," www.recexpo.com/new/ecom/ecom_index.asp.

51. Indeed, in response to a subsequent and much bolder Islamist petition, the Memorandum of Advice, the king had religious authorities denounce the petition, and he dismissed members of the 'ulama who refused to sign the denunciation. See Gause, *Oil Monarchies*.

52. Serwer and Key, "Tech Is King."

53. See Gause, *Oil Monarchies,* p. 58.

54. Saudi Arabia's most famous exiled dissident, Osama bin Laden, has less influence within the country than has CDLR or MIRA; the impact of his al-Qaeda network (including its use of ICTs) is more significant at the international level. For this reason, we consider the example of Bin Laden and al-Qaeda in the conclusion to this chapter rather than examining it here.

55. Fandy, *Saudi Arabia*.

56. Fandy, "Information Technology."

57. Gause, *Oil Monarchies*.

58. Figures from CIA, *The World Factbook*.

59. See Olcott and Ottaway, "Semi-Authoritarianism."

60. Kassem, *Guise of Democracy*.

61. See Diana Digges, "Rights Groups Recoil at Egypt Law," *Christian Science Monitor* 91, no. 131 (June 3, 1999), p. 6.

62. The center's director, Saad Eddin Ibrahim, had been an outspoken critic of irregularities in the 1995 parliamentary elections as well as the treatment of Egypt's Coptic Christian minority. See Weaver, "Mubarak Regime."

63. Many of the officially foreign publications sold in Egypt are published exclusively for the Egyptian market but are printed in Cyprus because they cannot obtain a domestic license. See "Egypt: A Sign of the Times," *Global News Wire,* February 1, 2001.

64. El-Nawawy, however, reports that commercial service existed in a "legal gray area" until 1996. See El-Nawawy, "Profiling Internet Users."

65. Kelly, Girardet, and Ismail, *Internet on the Nile: Egypt Case Study.*

66. Kamel, "Information Technology"; Kamel, "Internet Commercialization."

67. Ajeeb Research Unit, March 15, 2001.

68. "Cyber Cafés Hit the Road," *PC World Middle East,* April 2001, www.pcworldegypt.com/archive/ton_cybercafe_April2001.htm.

69. Jetiana C. Anderson, "Egypt's Cyber Cafes for the Poor," *Choices* (June 2000): 22–23, www.undp.org/dpa/choices/2000/june/p22-23.htm.

70. "USAID/Egypt: The Information and Communications Technology Project (ICT)," www.usaid.gov/regions/ane/ict/ict-egypt.htm.

71. See Alterman, "Information Revolution"; Thomas Friedman, "Censors Beware," *New York Times,* July 25, 2000; and *Middle East Times,* www.metimes.com.

72. "Banned Islamist Paper Now on the 'Net," Reuters, February 21, 2001. See also http://alarabnews.com/alshaab/.

73. "Egypt Holds Three over Homosexual Web Site," Reuters, April 5, 2001; "Two Jailed for Three Months for Gay Website," Agence France-Presse, April 12, 2001.

74. "Poet's Son Held by 'Web' Police in Egypt," Africast.com, November 26, 2001; "Web Cats," *al-Ahram Weekly Online,* November 29, 2001, www.ahram.org.eg/weekly/2001/562/eg6.htm.

75. Alexander Stille, "Egypt: Internet Arrest," *Correspondence: An International Review of Culture and Society* no. 9 (spring 2002): 38–39.

76. Alterman, "Egypt: Stable."

77. See www.ibnkhaldun.org/.

78. Examples include the Arab Women's Solidarity Association, http://awsa.net/, and the Legal Research and Resource Center for Human Rights, www.geocities.com/~lrrc/.

79. See Nidumolu et al., "Information Technology."

80. See "The Dawn of Egyptian E-Government, *PC World Middle East,* June 2001, www.pcworldegypt.com/archive/ton_egov_june2001.htm. Online telephone bill payments can be made at www.mcitel.gov.eg.

81. See Ahmed Fekry, "Egypt Upgrades State IT with Microsoft Help," *Middle East Times,* April 13, 2001, http://metimes.com/2K1/issue2001-15/bus/egypt_upgrades_state.htm.

82. See, for example, www.addustour.com, www.alahali.com/, and www.alwafd.org/.

83. Fatih M. Yilmaz, "Muslim Brotherhood Looks at Internet for Effective Campaign," IslamiQ.com, October 3, 2000, www.islamiqdaily.com/world/art_wld1_03102000.php4.

84. See Samir, "Egypt's Cyber Agenda."

85. See "Egypt Slashes ISP Line Costs, Plans 'Smart Villages,' " Reuters, September 14, 2000; and "Investors Raise Capital of Smart Village Project in Egypt to US$40 million," DITnet, June 21, 2000, www.dit.net/ITNews/newsjune2000/newsjune21.html.

86. Examples include the IDSC's TourismNet, www.tourism.egnet.net, and the Ministry of Tourism's site, www.touregypt.net.

87. Alterman, "Egypt: Stable."

88. Olcott and Ottaway, "Semi-Authoritarianism."

89. See the Copts' web site, www.copts.com/, as well as Rowe, "Four Guys."

90. www.ummah.org.uk/ikhwan/.

91. Salhi, "Information Technology"; Fandy, "Information Technology."

92. For example, see Dahan, "Internet Usage."

93. Kamrava and Mora argue that many governments in the Middle East have not undertaken the type of extensive economic liberalization that has shifted power to nonstate actors in other parts of the world. This observation is particularly true of rentier states. See Kamrava and Mora, "Civil Society."

94. See Wheeler, "Global Culture."

95. See Mosaic Group, "Global Diffusion."

96. Anderson, *Arabizing the Internet*.

97. Alterman, "Counting Nodes."

98. Fandy, "Information Technology."

99. See Alterman, "Information Revolution"; and Anderson, *Arabizing the Internet*.

Chapter 6: Beyond Blind Optimism

1. See, for instance, Friedman, *Lexus;* Kobrin, "Back to the Future"; and Wriston, *Twilight.*

2. For example, see Arquilla and Ronfeldt, *Networks;* and Arquilla and Ronfeldt, *Swarming.*

3. See, for instance, Florini, *Third Force;* Mathews, "Power Shift"; Simmons and Oudraat, *Managing Global Issues;* Warkentin, *Reshaping World Politics.*

4. Dalpino, *Deferring Democracy*, p. 52.

5. In fact, state regulation and control of the Internet are becoming more prevalent in the democratic world as well. In contrast to its anarchic beginnings, the Internet is increasingly being regulated and overseen by governmental, intergovernmental, and nongovernmental organizations. National governments are pressing for a greater say in determining acceptable content within their borders (as in the French case against Yahoo). Authoritarian regimes that favor strongly delineated national borders online may therefore find greater resonance with a global audience than they have in the recent past. Moreover, the post–September 11 security environment has placed more emphasis on the control of information infrastructure, which could translate into a more tightly regulated Internet in general.

6. This dovetails with the argument that authoritarian regimes are more efficient than democratic ones since they can implement policy unfettered by opposition. The flip side of this view is that authoritarian regimes are also more susceptible to making large mistakes since checks on authority do not exist. See Maravall, "Authoritarian Advantage."

7. In Malaysia, for instance, what began as a grassroots movement protesting the arrest and imprisonment of the deputy prime minister eventually became, in part owing to online momentum, a formal opposition party. This example is frequently cited as evidence that a potential opposition movement simply needs Internet access to get the ball rolling. Yet national context is always important. Malaysia's semi-authoritarian government, for instance, was arguably more vulnerable to opposition than were some of the stronger authoritarian governments surveyed here.

8. Note that a nearly complete lack of Internet access within Burma did not prevent key dissidents from passing information to transnational networks, either by smuggling printed matter out of the country or by placing covert phone calls. Although Internet access would undoubtedly facilitate the efforts of dissidents to communicate with activists abroad, the lack of access has not prevented them from finding other ways to get information out.

9. Kalathil, "Community and Communalism."

10. Speech by Henry Hyde, member, U.S. House of Representatives (R–IL), and chair, House International Relations Committee, to the Council on Foreign Relations, June 17, 2002.

11. Such U.S. democracy-promotion organizations as the National Democratic Institute and the International Republican Institute have been active in using the Internet to support specific activities, such as linking democracy-assistance groups with local parliaments or with one another. See "The Internet and Democracy-Building: The NED Experience," presentation by Carl Gershman, president of the National Endowment for Democracy, at an international workshop organized by the U.K. Foreign and Commonwealth Office, April 27–28, 2001.

12. The idea of the private sector, nongovernmental organizations, and governments working jointly to promote human rights–friendly business practices has been implemented in other sectors. The U.S. State Department, in conjunction with the U.K. Foreign and Commonwealth Office, worked with oil and mining companies in the late 1990s to establish voluntary and nonbinding principles on security and human rights. See Freeman, "Drilling." For examples of the industry's role in regulating information privacy, see Haufler, *Public Role.*

13. Dalpino, *Deferring Democracy.*

Glossary

Definitions are drawn (in most cases slightly modified) from the following sources: *The American Heritage Dictionary of the English Language,* 4th edition; *The Free Online Dictionary of Computing;* techdictionary.com; webopedia.com; and whatis.com.

anonymizer

A privacy service that allows users to visit web sites without allowing anyone to gather information about which sites they visit and without allowing a visited web site to gather information about them.

backbone

A set of high-speed paths to which local or regional networks connect for long-distance traffic on the Internet.

broadband

A type of transmission that shares the bandwidth of a medium such as copper or fiber-optic cable, to carry more than one signal at high speed.

bulletin board system

A computer and associated software that typically provides an electronic message database where people can log in and leave messages.

chat room

A real-time electronic forum where visitors can meet one another and engage in online conversations.

circuit switching

A type of communication in which a dedicated path or circuit is established for the duration of a transmission between the sender and receiver. The telephone system is an example of a circuit switched network.

digital signature

A coded message added to a document or data that guarantees the identity of the sender.

domain name

An Internet address in alphanumeric form, naming the corresponding organization (the part of the address to the left of the dot), the type of organization (such as ".com" for commercial; ".edu" for educational, etc.), and/or the country in which it is registered (such as ".fr" for France or ".uk" for the United Kingdom).

encryption

Putting data into a secret code so it is unreadable except by authorized users.

FIDOnet

A system for exchanging e-mail, discussion groups, downloads, and other files among users of over 30,000 bulletin board services. Started in 1984.

firewall

A security system that enforces a boundary between two or more networks to monitor or control access and transfers of information.

gateway

A device that enables data to flow between different networks.

Internet content provider (ICP)

An organization that provides online content but not necessarily Internet access.

Internet service provider (ISP)

An organization that provides other organizations or individuals access to, or presence on, the Internet.

intranet

A network that is not necessarily connected to the Internet but provides similar services.

landline

Traditional wired telephone service.

leased line

A dedicated line that is leased exclusively to connect two points, twenty-four hours a day, seven days a week.

local area network (LAN)
A network connecting computers that are close to each other, usually in the same building.

newsgroup
A discussion group on the Internet that focuses on a particular topic.

open source
A method and philosophy for software licensing and distribution, designed to encourage use and improvement of software by ensuring that anyone can copy the source code and modify it freely.

packet switching
A technology that divides messages into standard-sized packets and transmits them to their destination by the most expedient route. Not all packets traveling between the same two hosts, even those from a single message, will necessarily follow the same route.

peer-to-peer
A type of transient Internet network that allows a group of computer users with the same networking program to connect with one another and directly access files from one another's hard drives.

portal
A web site that aims to be an entry point to the World Wide Web, typically offering a search engine, links to useful pages, and possibly news or other services.

proxy server
A computer and associated software that will pass on a URL request from a World Wide Web browser and return the results. The proxy server acts as an intermediary between a user and the Internet, allowing for security, administrative control, and caching service.

short message service
A feature of wireless phones that allows users to receive and sometimes transmit short text messages.

spam
Unsolicited e-mail sent indiscriminately to multiple mailing lists, individuals, or newsgroups.

teletext
An electronic communications system in which printed information is broadcast by television signal to sets equipped with decoders.

trunk line

A communication channel between two points, usually the large-band-width telephone channels between switching centers that handle many simultaneous voice and data signals.

Usenet

A public messaging system that uses a computer network, usually the Internet, to transfer messages organized in thematic groups.

Works Cited

Ahmad, Mumtaz, and I. William Zartman. "Political Islam: Can It Become a Loyal Opposition?" *Middle East Policy* 5, no. 1 (1997): 68–84.

Ajami, Fouad. "What the Muslim World Is Watching." *New York Times Magazine,* November 18, 2001.

Al-Sayegh, Fatma. "Diversity in Unity: Political Institutions in Civil Society." *Middle East Policy* 6, no. 4 (1999): 14–16.

Alterman, Jon B. "Counting Nodes and Counting Noses: Understanding the New Media in the Middle East." *Middle East Journal* 54, no. 3 (2000): 355–61.

———. "Egypt: Stable, But for How Long?" *Washington Quarterly* 23, no. 4 (2000): 107–18.

———. "Focus on the New Media: Shrinking the World and Changing the News." *Middle East Insight* 14, no. 2 (1999): 29–61.

———. "The Middle East's Information Revolution." *Current History* 99, no. 633 (2000): 21–26.

———. "Mid-Tech Revolution." *Middle East Insight* 5, no. 1 (2001).

———. *New Media, New Politics? From Satellite Television to the Internet in the Arab World.* Washington, D.C.: Washington Institute for Near East Policy, 1998.

Amin, Hussein Y., and Leo A. Gher. "Digital Communications in the Arab World: Entering the Twenty-first Century." In *Civic Discourse and the Digital Age: Communications in the Middle East,* ed. Hussein Y. Amin and Leo A. Gher. Stamford, Conn.: Ablex, 2000.

Amnesty International. "Asia/Pacific: Highlights of Amnesty International Report 2002 Covering Events from January to December 2001." Amnesty International Publications, 2002.

Anderson, Jon W. "Arabizing the Internet." *Emirates Occasional Papers,* no. 30. Emirates Center for Strategic Studies Research, Abu Dhabi, United Arab Emirates, 1998.

Arquilla, John, and David Ronfeldt, eds. *Networks and Netwars: The Future of Terror, Crime, and Militancy.* Santa Monica, Calif.: RAND, 2001.

———. *Swarming and the Future of Conflict.* Santa Monica, Calif.: RAND, 2000.

Atkins, William. *The Politics of Southeast Asia's New Media.* Richmond, U.K.: Curzon Press, 2002.

Awad, Ibrahim. "The External Relations of the Arab Human Rights Movement." *Arab Studies Quarterly* 19, no. 1 (1997): 59–75.

Bahgat, Gawdat. "The Gulf Monarchies: Economic and Political Challenges at the End of the Century." *Journal of Social, Political, and Economic Studies* 23, no. 2 (1998): 147–75.

Bakkar, Piet. "New Nationalism: The Internet Crusade." Paper presented at the annual meeting of the International Studies Association, Chicago, February 20–24, 2001.

Bar, François, et al. "Access and Innovation Policy for the Third-Generation Internet." *Telecommunications Policy* 24 (2000): 489–518.

Barlow, John Perry. "A Declaration of the Independence of Cyberspace." World Economic Forum, Davos, Switzerland, February 8, 1996, www.eff.org/~barlow/Declaration-Final.html.

Beach, Sophie. "Running in Place." *Committee To Protect Journalists: Press Freedom Reports from around the World,* 2001, www.cpj.org/Briefings/2001/China_aug01/China_aug01.html.

Bell, Daniel A., David Brown, Kanishka Jayasuriya, and D. M. Jones. *Towards Illiberal Democracy in Pacific Asia.* New York: St. Martin's Press, 1995.

Bell, Mark R., and Taylor C. Boas. "Falun Gong and the Internet: Evangelism, Community, and Struggle for Survival." *Nova Religio* 6, no. 2 (2003).

Bengelsdorf, Carollee. "Intellectuals under Fire." *In These Times,* September 16, 1996, pp. 27–29.

Benkler, Yochai. "Free as the Air to Common Use: First Amendment Constraints on Enclosure of the Public Domain." *New York University Law Review* 74 (1999): 354–446.

Bimber, Bruce. "The Internet and Political Transformation: Populism, Community, and Accelerated Pluralism." *Polity* 31, no. 1 (1988): 133–60.

Blanchard, Anita, and Tom Horan. "Virtual Communities and Social Capital." *Social Science Computer Review* 16 (1998): 293–307.

Boas, Taylor C. "The Dictator's Dilemma? The Internet and U.S. Policy toward Cuba." *Washington Quarterly* 23, no. 3 (2000): 57–67, www.twq.com/summer00/boas.pdf.

———. "www.cubalibre.cu? The Internet and Its Prospects for a Democratic Society in Cuba." *Stanford Journal of International Relations* 1, no. 1 (1998): 30–41.

———. "www.cubalibre.cu? Transnational Networking and the Impact of the Internet on Non-Democratic Rule." Honors thesis, Stanford University Center for Latin American Studies, 1999.

Brown, Frederick Z. "Vietnam's Tentative Transformation." *Journal of Democracy* 7, no. 4 (1996): 73–87.

Budge, Ian. *The New Challenge of Direct Democracy*. Oxford: Polity Press, 1996.

Bunt, Gary R. *Virtually Islamic: Computer-mediated Communication and Cyber-Islamic Environments*. Cardiff, U.K.: University of Wales Press, 2000.

Carey, James W. "Mass Media and Democracy." *Journal of International Affairs* 47, no. 1 (1993): 1–21.

Carothers, Thomas. *Aiding Democracy Abroad: The Learning Curve*. Washington, D.C.: Carnegie Endowment for International Peace, 1999.

Chase, Michael, and James Mulvenon. *You've Got Dissent: Chinese Dissident Use of the Internet and Beijing's Counter-Strategies*. Santa Monica, Calif.: RAND, 2002.

China Foresight Project. *China's Internet in 2005: Six Scenarios*. Institute for the Future, Center for the Future of China, Menlo Park, Calif., 2000.

Clark, Janine A. "Private Voluntary Organizations in Egypt: Islamic Development, Private Initiative, and State Control." *Middle East Journal* 51, no. 2 (1997): 286–87.

Coleman, Stephen. "Can the New Media Invigorate Democracies?" *Political Quarterly* 70, no. 1 (1999): 16–22.

Committee To Protect Journalists. *Attacks on the Press in 2001: A World-wide Survey by the Committee To Protect Journalists.* New York, 2002.

Cotton, James. "East Asian Democracy: Progress and Limits." In *Consolidating the Third Wave of Democracies: Regional Challenges,* ed. Larry Diamond, Marc F. Plattner, Yun-han Chu, and Hung-mao Tien, pp. 95–119. Baltimore, Md.: Johns Hopkins University Press, 1997.

Cullen, Richard. "The Internet in China." *Columbia Journal of Asian Law* 13, no. 1 (1999): 99–134.

Cullen, Richard, and Hua Ling Fu. "Seeking Theory from Experience: Media Regulations in China." *Democratization* 5, no. 2 (1998): 155–77.

Dahan, Michael. "Internet Usage in the Middle East: Some Political and Social Implications." People across Borders Conference, Middle East Virtual Community, August 1–15, 2000, www.mevic.org/papers/inet-mena.html.

Dai, Xiudian. "Chinese Politics of the Internet: Control and Anti-Control." *Cambridge Review of International Affairs* 8, no. 2 (2000): 181–94.

Dalpino, Catharin E. *Deferring Democracy: Promoting Openness in Authoritarian Regimes.* Washington, D.C.: Brookings Institution Press, 2000.

Dang, Hoang-Giang. "Internet in Vietnam: From a Laborious Birth into an Uncertain Future." *Informatik Forum* 13, no. 1 (1999).

Danitz, Tiffany, and Warren Strobel. "The Internet's Impact on Activism: The Case of Burma." *Studies in Conflict and Terrorism* 22 (1999): 257–59.

Dao, Tang Duc. *On the Struggle for Democracy in Vietnam.* Springwood, New South Wales, Australia: Butterfly Books, 1994.

Davis, Richard. *The Web of Politics.* New York: Oxford University Press, 1999.

Diamond, Larry. "The Globalization of Democracy: Trends, Types, Causes, and Prospects." *Global Transformation and the Third World,* ed. In Robert Slater et al. Boulder, Colo.: Lynne Rienner, 1992.

Diamond, Larry, and Marc F. Plattner, eds. *Democracy in East Asia.* Baltimore, Md.: Johns Hopkins University Press, 1998.

Drake, William J. *From the Global Digital Divide to the Global Digital Opportunity: Proposals Submitted to the G–8 Kyushu-Okinawa Summit 2000—Report of the World Economic Forum Task Force on the*

Digital Divide. Geneva: World Economic Forum, 2000, www.ceip.org/
files/projects/irwp/pdf/wef_gdd_statement.pdf.

Drake, William J., ed. *The New Information Infrastructure: Strategies for
U.S. Policy.* New York: Twentieth Century Press, 1995.

Drake, William J., Shanthi Kalathil, and Taylor C. Boas. "Dictatorships
in the Digital Age: Some Considerations on the Internet in China and
Cuba." *IMP: The Magazine on Information Impacts* (2000),
www.ceip.org/files/Publications/dictatorships_digital_age.asp?p=5
&from=pubdate.

Dunn, Michael Collins. "Is the Sky Falling? Saudi Arabia's Economic Problems and Political Stability." *Middle East Policy* 3, no. 4 (1995): 29.

Eickelman, Dale F., and Jon W. Anderson, eds. *New Media in the Muslim
World: The Emerging Public Sphere.* Bloomington: Indiana University
Press, 1999.

El-Nawawy, Mohamed A. "Profiling Internet Users in Egypt: Understanding the Primary Deterrent against Their Growth in Number." Paper
presented at the annual meeting of the Internet Society, Yokohama,
Japan, July 18–21, 2000, www.isoc.org/inet2000/cdproceedings/8d/
8d_3.htm.

El-Nawawy, Mohamed A., and Magda M. Ismail. "Overcoming Deterrents and Impediments of Electronic Commerce in Light of Globalization: Egypt, a Case in Point." Paper presented at the annual meeting of
the Internet Society, San Jose, Calif., June 22–25, 1999.

Eng, Peter. "A New Kind of Cyberwar." *Columbia Journalism Review*
(September/October 1998).

Evans, Peter B. *Embedded Autonomy: States and Industrial Transformation.* Princeton, N.J.: Princeton University Press, 1995.

Fandy, Mamoun. "CyberResistance: Saudi Opposition between Globalization and Localization." *Comparative Studies in Society and History*
41, no. 1 (1999): 124–47.

———. "Information Technology, Trust, and Social Change in the Arab
World." *Middle East Journal* 54, no. 3 (2000): 378–418.

———. *Saudi Arabia and the Politics of Dissent.* New York: St. Martin's
Press, 1999.

Ferdinand, Peter, ed. *The Internet, Democracy, and Democratization.*
London: Frank Cass, 2000.

Ferenz, Michele N. "Civil Society in the Middle East." *Nonprofit and Voluntary Sector Quarterly* (1999): 83–99.

Florini, Ann M. *The Third Force: The Rise of Transnational Civil Society.* Washington, D.C.: Carnegie Endowment for International Peace, 2001.

Foster, William, and Seymour E. Goodman. *The Diffusion of the Internet in China.* Stanford, Calif.: Center for International Security and Cooperation, 2000.

Fox, Elizabeth, ed. *Media and Politics in Latin America.* London: Sage, 1988.

Franda, Marcus. *Launching into Cyberspace: Internet Development and Politics in Five World Regions.* Boulder, Colo.: Lynne Rienner, 2002.

Freeman, Bennett. "Drilling for Common Ground." *Foreign Policy* (July/ August 2001).

Friedman, Edward. *The Politics of Democratization: Generalizing East Asian Experiences.* Boulder, Colo.: Westview Press, 1994.

Friedman, Thomas L. *The Lexus and the Olive Tree: Understanding Globalization.* New York: Farrar, Straus and Giroux, 1999.

Fukuyama, Francis. "Confucianism and Democracy." *Journal of Democracy* 6, no. 3 (1997): 20–33.

Gao, Ping, and Kalle Lyytinen. "Transformation of China's Telecommunications Sector: A Macro Perspective." *Telecommunications Policy* no. 24 (2000): 719–30.

Garnham, David, and Mark Tessler. *Democracy, War and Peace in the Middle East.* Bloomington: Indiana University Press, 1995.

Gause, F. Gregory III. "The Gulf Conundrum: Economic Change, Population Growth, and Political Stability in the GCC States." *Washington Quarterly* 20, no. 1 (1997): 145–65.

———. *Oil Monarchies: Domestic and Security Challenges in the Arab Gulf States.* New York: Council on Foreign Relations Press, 1994.

Giuliano, Maurizio. *El caso CEA: Intelectuales e inquisidores en Cuba— Perestroika en la isla?* Miami: Ediciones Universal, 1998.

Glogoff, Stuart. "Virtual Connections: Community Bonding on the Net." *First Monday* 6, no. 3 (2001), http://firstmonday.org/issues/issue6_3/ glogoff/.

Goldstein, Eric. *The Internet in the Mideast and North Africa: Free Expression and Censorship.* New York: Human Rights Watch, 1999.

Gonzalez, Edward, and David Ronfeldt. *Cuba Adrift in a Postcommunist World.* Santa Monica, Calif.: RAND, 1992.

Goodson, Larry P., and Soha Radwan. "Democratization in Egypt in the 1990s: Stagnant or Merely Stalled?" *Arab Studies Quarterly* 19, no. 1 (1997): 1–21.

Green, Jerrold D. "The Information Revolution and Political Opposition in the Middle East." *Middle East Studies Association Bulletin* 33, no. 1 (1999): 21–27.

Grossman, Lawrence. *The Electronic Commonwealth*. New York: Penguin, 1995.

Gunn, Gillian. *Cuba's NGOs: Government Puppets or Seeds of Civil Society?* Cuba Briefing Paper Series No. 7. Washington, D.C.: Georgetown University Caribbean Project, 1995.

Guo, Liang, and Wei Bu. *Survey on Internet Usage and Impact*. Center for Social Development, Chinese Academy of Social Sciences, 2001.

Hachigian, Nina. "China's Cyber-Strategy." *Foreign Affairs* 80, no. 2 (March/April 2001): 118–33.

———. "The Internet and Power in One-Party East Asian States." *Washington Quarterly* 25, no. 3 (2002): 41–58.

Hague, Barry N., and Brian D. Loader. *Digital Democracy: Discourse and Decision Making in the Information Age*. New York: Routledge, 1999.

Hai, Ernie Quah Cheng. "Rapid Deployment of the Internet by the Singapore Government." Paper presented at the sixth annual meeting of the Internet Society, Montreal, June 24–28, 1996.

Hammond, Andrew. "A New Political Culture Emerges in Egypt." *Middle East* no. 255 (1996): 5–7.

Harding, Harry. *Organizing China: The Problem of Bureaucracy, 1949–1976*. Stanford, Calif.: Stanford University Press, 1981.

Hartford, Kathleen. "Cyberspace with Chinese Characteristics." *Current History* 99, no. 638 (2000): 255–62.

Harwit, Eric, and Duncan Clark. "Shaping the Internet in China: Evolution of Political Control over Network Infrastructure and Content." *Asian Survey* 41, no. 3 (2001): 337–408.

Hashem, Sherif. *The Evolution of Internet Services in Egypt: Towards Empowering Electronic Commerce*. Cairo: Cabinet Information and Decision Support Center, 1998.

———. *Technology Access Community Centers in Egypt: A Mission for Community Empowerment*. Cairo: Cabinet Information and Decision Support Center, 1998.

Haufler, Virginia. *A Public Role for the Private Sector: Industry Self-Regulation in a Global Economy.* Washington, D.C.: Carnegie Endowment for International Peace, 2001.

Heng, Russell. "Give Me Liberty or Give Me Wealth." In *Debating Singapore: Reflective Essays,* ed. Derek da Cunha, pp. 9–21. Singapore: Institute of Southeast Asian Studies, 1994.

Hill, David T., and Krishna Sen. "The Internet in Indonesia's Democracy." *Democratization* 7, no. 1 (2000): 119–36.

Hill, Kevin A., and John E. Hughes. "Is the Internet an Instrument of Global Democratization?" In *Cyberpolitics: Citizen Activism in the Age of the Internet.* Lanham, Md.: Rowman and Littlefield, 1998; and *Democratization* 6, no. 2 (summer 1999): 99–127.

Hinchberger, Bill. "Netting Fidel." *Industry Standard* (April 17, 2000), www.thestandard.com/article/article_print/1,1153,13759,00.html.

———. "The New E-Man." *Industry Standard* (April 17, 2000), www.thestandard.com/article/display/0,1151,13765,00.html.

Huff, Tobe E. "Globalization and the Internet: Comparing the Middle Eastern and Malaysian Experience." *Middle East Journal* 55, no. 3 (2001): 439–58.

Hughes, Christopher Rene. "Nationalism in Chinese Cyberspace." *Cambridge Review of International Affairs* 13, no. 2 (spring/summer 2000): 195–209.

Human Rights Watch. "Nipped in the Bud: The Suppression of the China Democracy Party." *China* 12, no. 5 (2000), www.hrw.org/reports/2000/china/index.htm.

Huntington, Samuel P. *The Third Wave: Democratization in the Late Twentieth Century.* Norman: University of Oklahoma Press, 1991.

Ibrahim, Awad. "The External Relations of the Arab Human Rights Movement." *Arab Studies Quarterly* 19, no. 1 (1997): 59–76.

Ibrahim, Saad Eddin. "From Taliban to Erbakan: The Case of Islam, Civil Society, and Democracy." In *Civil Society and Democracy in the Muslim World,* ed. Elizabeth Ozdalgee and Sune Persson. Istanbul: Swedish Institution, 1997.

———. "Reform and Frustration in Egypt." *Journal of Democracy* 7, no. 4 (1996): 125–35.

"InCUBAdora." *Punto-Com* no. 7 (February 2001): 26–33.

Ismail, Salwa. "Confronting the Other: Identity, Culture, Politics, and Conservative Islamism in Egypt." *International Journal of Middle East Studies* 30, no. 2 (1998): 199–226.

Kalathil, Shanthi. "Chinese Media and the Information Revolution." *Harvard Asia Quarterly* 6, no. 1 (winter 2002): 27–30.

———. "Community and Communalism in the Information Age." *Brown Journal of World Affairs* 9, no. 1 (2002).

Kalathil, Shanthi, and Taylor C. Boas. "The Internet and State Control in Authoritarian Regimes: China, Cuba, and the Counterrevolution." Working Paper No. 21. Washington, D.C.: Carnegie Endowment for International Peace, 2001.

Kamel, Ramsey. *The Information Technology Landscape in Egypt.* Washington, D.C.: American University, Kogod School of Business, 1999.

Kamel, Tarek. "Internet Commercialization in Egypt: A Country Model." Paper presented at the seventh annual meeting of the Internet Society, Kuala Lumpur, June 24–27, 1997, www.isoc.org/isoc/whatis/conferences/inet/97/proceedings/E6/E6_2.HTM.

Kamrava, Mehran. "Frozen Political Liberalization in Jordan: The Consequences for Democracy." *Democratization* 5, no. 1 (December 1998): 138–57.

Kamrava, Mehran, and Frank O' Mora. "Civil Society and Democratisation in Comparative Perspective: Latin America and the Middle East." *Third World Quarterly* 19, no. 5 (1998): 893–916.

Karmel, Solomon M. *China and the People's Liberation Army: Great Power or Struggling Developing State?* New York: St. Martin's Press, 2000.

Kassem, May. *In the Guise of Democracy: Governance in Contemporary Egypt.* Reading, U.K.: Ithaca Press, 1999.

Katz, John. "The Digital Citizen." *Wired* 5, no. 12 (1997).

Kechichian, Joseph A. "Saudi Arabia's Will To Power." *Middle East Policy* 7, no. 2 (2000): 47–60.

Keck, Margaret E., and Kathryn Sikkink. *Activists beyond Borders: Advocacy Networks in International Politics.* Ithaca, N.Y.: Cornell University Press, 1998.

Kedzie, Christopher R. *Communication and Democracy: Coincident Revolutions and the Emergent Dictator's Dilemma.* Santa Monica, Calif.: RAND, 1997.

Keith, Ronald C. "Chinese Politics and the New Theory of 'Rule of Law.'" *China Quarterly* no. 125 (1991): 109–19.

Keller, Perry. "China's Impact on the Global Information Society." In *Regulating the Global Information Society,* ed. Christopher T. Marsden. London: Routledge, 2000.

Kelly, Jim, Guy Girardet, and Magda Ismail. *Internet on the Nile: Egypt Case Study.* Geneva: International Telecommunication Union, 2001.

Khalifa, Ali Mohammed. *The United Arab Emirates: Unity in Fragmentation*. Boulder, Colo.: Westview Press, 1979.

Kienle, Eberhard. "More Than a Response to Islamism: The Political Deliberalization of Egypt in the 1990s." *Middle East Journal* 52, no. 2 (1998): 219–35.

Kirby, Owen H. "Want a Democracy? Get a King." *Middle East Quarterly* (2000): 3–12.

Kobrin, Stephen. "Back to the Future: Neomedievalism and the Postmodern Digital World Economy." *Journal of International Affairs* 51, no. 2 (1998): 361–86.

Kubba, Laith. "The Awakening of Civil Society." *Journal of Democracy* 11, no. 3 (2000): 84–90.

Lawson, Chappell. *Building the Fourth Estate: Democratization and the Rise of a Free Press in Mexico*. Berkeley: University of California Press, 2002.

Lee, Chin-Chuan, ed. *Voices of China: The Interplay of Politics and Journalism*. New York: Guilford Press, 1990.

Lemley, Mark A., and Lawrence Lessig. "The End of End-to-End: Preserving the Architecture of the Internet in the Broadband Era." *UCLA Law Review* 28 (2000).

Lerner, Daniel. *The Passing of Traditional Society: Modernizing the Middle East*. Glencoe, Ill.: Free Press, 1958.

Lessig, Lawrence. *Code and Other Laws of Cyberspace*. New York: Basic Books, 1999.

———. *The Future of Ideas: The Fate of the Commons in a Connected World*. New York: Random House, 2001.

Li, Cheng. *China's Leaders: The New Generation*. Lanham, Md.: Rowman and Littlefield, 2001.

Li, Cheng, and Lynn White. "Elite Transformation and Modern Change in Mainland China and Taiwan: Empirical Data and the Theory of Technocracy." *China Quarterly* no. 121 (1990): 1–35.

Lichtenberg, Judith, ed. *Democracy and the Mass Media*. New York: Cambridge University Press, 1990.

Linz, Juan J., and Alfred Stepan. *Problem of Democratic Transition and Consolidation: Southern Europe, South America, and Post-Communist Europe*. Baltimore, Md.: Johns Hopkins University Press, 1996.

Lipset, Seymour Martin. *Political Man: The Social Bases of Politics*. Garden City, N.Y.: Doubleday, 1960.

Lu, Wei. "The Information Technology Industry in China." Paper presented at a conference on the IT revolution and Asian economies, "Growing Interdependence of the Global Economy," May 25, 2001.

Lynch, Daniel C. *After the Propaganda State: Media, Politics, and "Thought Work" in Reformed China.* Stanford, Calif.: Stanford University Press, 1999.

Mann, Catherine L., Sue E. Eckert, and Sarah Cleeland Knight. *Global Electronic Commerce: A Policy Primer.* Washington, D.C.: Institute for International Economics, 2000.

Maravall, José María. "The Myth of the Authoritarian Advantage." In *Economic Reform and Democracy,* ed. Larry Jay Diamond and Marc F. Plattner. Baltimore, Md.: Johns Hopkins University Press, 1995.

Marsden, Christopher T., ed. *Regulating the Global Information Society.* London: Routledge, 2000.

Mathews, Jessica. "Power Shift." *Foreign Affairs* 76, no. 1 (January/February 1997): 50–77.

Minges, Michael, Magda Ismail, and Larry Press. *The E-City: Singapore Internet Case Study.* Geneva: International Telecommunication Union, 2001.

Moody, Peter R. *Political Opposition in Post-Confucian Societies.* New York: Praeger, 1988.

Moore, Rebecca. "China's Fledgling Civil Society: A Force for Democratization?" *World Policy Journal* 18, no. 1 (spring 2001): 56–66.

Mosaic Group. *The Global Diffusion of the Internet Project: An Initial Inductive Study.* 1998, http://mosaic.unomaha.edu/gdi.html.

————. *An Update: The Internet in the Kingdom of Saudi Arabia.* 1999, http://mosaic.unomaha.edu/gdi.html.

Moustafa, Tamir. "Conflict and Cooperation between the State and Religious Institutions in Contemporary Egypt." *International Journal of Middle East Studies* 32, no. 1 (2000): 3–23.

Mueller, Milton, and Peter Lovelock. "The WTO and China's Ban on Foreign Investment in Telecommunications Services: A Game Theoretic Analysis." *Telecommunications Policy* 24 (2000): 731–59.

Mulvenon, James, and Richard Yang, eds. *The People's Liberation Army in the Information Age.* Santa Monica, Calif.: RAND, 1999.

Murphy, Richard W., and F. Gregory Gause III. "Democracy and U.S. Policy in the Muslim Middle East." *Middle East Policy* 5, no. 1 (1997): 58–67.

Neumann, Lin A. "The Survival of Burmese Journalism." *Harvard Asia Quarterly* 6, no. 1 (winter 2002): 20–26.

Nichols, John Spicer. "Cuban Mass Media: Organization, Control, and Functions." *Journalism Monographs* 78 (1982): 1–35.

Nichols, John Spicer, and Alicia M. Torres. "Cuba." In *Telecommunications in Latin America,* ed. Eli M. Noam. New York: Oxford University Press, 1998.

Nidumolu, Sarma R., Seymour E. Goodman, Douglas R. Vogel, and Ann K. Danowitz. "Information Technology for Local Administration Support: The Governorates Project in Egypt." *MIS Quarterly* 20, no. 2 (June 1996): 197–223.

Nie, Norman, and Lutz Erbring. *Internet and Society: A Preliminary Report.* Stanford, Calif.: Stanford Institute for the Quantitative Study of Society, Stanford University, 2000.

Norris, Pippa. *Digital Divide: Civic Engagement, Information Poverty and the Internet Worldwide.* New York: Cambridge University Press, 2001.

———. *A Virtuous Circle: Political Communication in Post-Industrial Democracies.* New York: Cambridge University Press, 2000.

Norton, Richard Augustus. "The Future of Civil Society in the Middle East." *Middle East Journal* 47, no. 2 (1993): 205–16.

Okruhlik, Gwenn. "Rentier Wealth, Unruly Law, and the Rise of Opposition: The Political Economy of Oil States." *Comparative Politics* 31, no. 3 (1999): 295–315.

Olcott, Martha Brill, and Marina Ottaway. "The Challenge of Semi-Authoritarianism." Working Paper No. 7. Washington, D.C.: Carnegie Endowment for International Peace, 1999.

Pei, Minxin. *Future Shock: The WTO and Political Change in China.* Policy Brief, no. 3. Washington, D.C.: Carnegie Endowment for International Peace, 2001.

Peters, Philip. *Cuba Goes Digital.* Washington, D.C.: Lexington Institute, 2001.

Pierre, Andrew J. "Vietnam's Contradictions." *Foreign Affairs* 79, no. 6 (November/December 2000).

Press, Larry. *Cuban Telecommunications, Computer Networking, and U.S. Policy Implications.* Santa Monica, Calif.: RAND, 1996.

Putnam, Robert D. *Bowling Alone: The Collapse and Revival of American Community*. New York: Simon and Schuster, 2000.

Pye, Lucian, ed. *Communications and Political Development*. Princeton, N.J.: Princeton University Press, 1963.

Pye, Lucian W., and Mary W. Pye. *Asian Power and Politics: The Cultural Dimensions of Authority*. Cambridge, Mass.: Harvard University Press, 1985.

Qiu, Jack Linchuan. "Chinese Opinions Collide Online: U.S.–China Plane Collision Sparks Civil Discussion on Web." *USC Annenberg Online Journalism Review* (April 12, 2001), http://ojr.usc.edu/content/story.cfm?id=561.

———. "Virtual Censorship in China." *International Journal of Communications Law and Policy* 4 (winter 1999/2000), www.ijclp.org/4_2000/pdf/ijclp_webdoc_1_4_2000.pdf.

Randall, Vicky. "The Media and Democratisation in the Third World." *Third World Quarterly* 14, no. 3 (1993): 625–46.

Rash, Wayne, Jr. *Politics on the Nets: Wiring the Political Process*. New York: W. H. Freeman, 1997.

Reporters sans Frontières and Transfert.net. *Enemies of the Internet: Attempts to Block the Circulation of Information on the Internet*, Report 2001. Paris: Éditions 00h00, 2001, www.00h0.com.

Rich, Paul. "American Voluntarism, Social Capital, and Political Culture." *Annals of the American Academy of Political and Social Science* 565 (September 1999): 15–34.

Ripoll, Carlos. "The Press in Cuba, 1952–1960: Autocratic and Totalitarian Censorship." In *The Selling of Fidel Castro: The Media and the Cuban Revolution*, ed. William E. Ratliff. New Brunswick, N.J.: Transaction Books, 1987.

Rodan, Garry. "Asia and the International Press: The Political Significance of Expanding Markets." *Democratization* 5, no. 1 (1998): 125–54.

———. "Information Technology and Political Control in Singapore." Working Paper No. 26. Japan Policy Research Institute, 1996.

———. "The Internet and Political Control in Singapore." *Political Science Quarterly* 113, no. 1 (1998): 63–90.

———. "Singapore: Information Lockdown, Business as Usual." In *Losing Control: Freedom of the Press in Asia,* ed. Louise Williams and

Roland Rich, pp. 169–89. Canberra: Asia Pacific Press, 2000.

Roberts, Walter R., and Harold R. Engle, "The Global Information Revolution and the Communist World." *Washington Quarterly* 9, no. 2 (spring 1986): 141–49.

Rohozinski, Rafal. "Mapping Russian Cyberspace: Perspective on Democracy and the Net." Paper presented at the Conference on Information Technologies and Social Development, June 22–24. Geneva: United Nations Research Institute for Social Development, 1998, www.unrisd.org/infotech/conferen/russian/toc.htm.

Rosenthal, Lisa. *Information Technology in the UAE.* Washington, D.C.: American University, Kogod School of Business, 2000.

Rowe, Paul S. "Four Guys and a Fax Machine? Diasporas, New Information Technologies and the Internationalization of Religion in Egypt." *Journal of Church and State* 43, no. 1 (winter 2001): 81–92.

Rugh, William A. "The United Arab Emirates: What Are the Sources of Its Stability?" *Middle East Policy* 5, no. 3 (1997): 14–24.

Sahli, Hamoud. "Information Technology and Its Impact on Social and Political Change: The Case of the Gulf Arab States." Paper presented at the annual meeting of the International Studies Association, Chicago, February 20–24, 2001.

Samir, Said. "Egypt's Cyber Agenda." *Pharaohs* (September 2000): 62–66.

Sarsar, Saliba. "Arab Politics: Can Democracy Prevail?" *Middle East Quarterly* 7, no. 1 (March 2000): 39–48.

Schmitter, Philippe C. "The Influence of the International Context upon the Choice of National Institutions and Policies in Neo-Democracies." In *The International Dimensions of Democratization: Europe and the Americas,* ed. Laurence Whitehead. New York: Oxford University Press, 1996.

Schwartz, Edward. *Netactivism: How Citizens Use the Internet.* Sebastapol, Calif.: Songline Studios, 1996.

Selth, Andrew. "Burma's Intelligence Apparatus." *Burma Debate* 4, no. 4 (September/October 1997).

Seow, Francis T. *The Media Enthralled: Singapore Revisited.* Boulder, Colo.: Lynne Rienner, 1998.

Seror, Ann C., and Juan Miguel Fach Arteaga. "Telecommunications Technology Transfer and the Development of Institutional Infrastructure: The Case of Cuba." *Telecommunications Policy* 24 (2000): 203–21.

Serwer, Andy, and Angela Key. "Tech Is King; Now Meet the Prince." *Fortune* 140, no. 11 (1999): 104–16.

Sheff, David. *China Dawn: The Story of a Technology and Business Revolution.* New York: HarperCollins, 2002.

Shue, Vivienne. *The Reach of the State: Sketches of the Chinese Body Politic.* Stanford, Calif.: Stanford University Press, 1988.

Simmons, P. J., and Chantal de Jonge Oudraat, eds. *Managing Global Issues: Lessons Learned.* Washington, D.C.: Carnegie Endowment for International Peace, 2001.

Simon, Leslie David, Javier Corrales, and Donald R. Wolfensberger. *Democracy and the Internet: Allies or Adversaries?* Washington, D.C.: Woodrow Wilson Center Press, 2002.

Singapore Government's Liberalization of the Telecom Sector: One Year On. Singapore: U.S. Embassy, 2001, www.usembassysingapore.org.sg/embassy/politics/Telecom2001.html. .

Skidmore, Thomas E., ed. *Television, Politics, and the Transition to Democracy in Latin America.* Baltimore, Md.: Johns Hopkins University Press, 1993.

Smith, Barbara. "A Survey of Egypt: Sham Democracy." *Economist* (March 20, 1999): 16–17.

Sokol, Brett. "E-Cuba: One Guess Who'll Control Access to the Internet." *Miami New Times,* July 27, 2000.

Speta, James B. "Handicapping the Race for the Last Mile? A Critique of Open Access Rules for Broadband Platforms." *Yale Journal on Regulation* 17 (2000): 39–91.

Sreberny-Mohammadi, Annabelle. "The Media and Democratization in the Middle East: The Strange Case of Television." *Democratization* 5, no. 2 (1998): 179–99.

Stokes, Mark A. *China's Strategic Modernization: Implications for the United States.* Strategic Studies Institute, U.S. Army War College, 1999.

Sullivan, Denis J., and Sana Abed-Kotob. *Islam in Contemporary Egypt: Civil Society vs. the State.* Boulder, Colo.: Lynne Rienner, 1999.

Sussman, Leonard R. *Censor Dot Gov: The Internet and Press Freedom.* New York: Freedom House, 2000.

———. *The Internet in Flux: Press Freedom Survey 2001.* Washington, D.C.: Freedom House, 2001.

Swire, Peter P., and Robert E. Litan. *None of Your Business: World Data Flows, Electronic Commerce, and the European Privacy Directive.* Washington, D.C.: Brookings Institution Press, 1998.

Taubman, Geoffry. "A Not-So World Wide Web: The Internet, China, and the Challenge to Nondemocratic Rule." *Political Communication* 15 (1998): 255–72.

Teitelbaum, Joshua. "Dueling for Da'wa: State vs. Society on the Saudi Internet." *Middle East Journal* 56, no. 2 (2002): 222–39.

Thomas, Timothy L. "Like Adding Wings to the Tiger: Chinese Information War Theory and Practice." Fort Leavenworth, Kans.: Foreign Military Studies Office, 2000, http://call.army.mil/call/fmso/fmsopubs/issues/chinaiw.htm.

Tipson, Frederick S. "China and the Information Revolution." In *China Joins the World: Progress and Prospects,* ed. Elizabeth Economy and Michel Oksenberg. New York: Council on Foreign Relations, 1999.

Tsagarouisanou, Rosa, Damian Tambini, and Cathy Bryan. *Cyberdemocracy.* London: Routledge, 1998.

Tsui, Lokman. "Internet in China: Big Mama Is Watching You." Master's thesis, University of Leiden, 2001, www.lokman.nu/thesis/.

United Nations, Comisión Económica para América Latina y el Caribe (CEPAL), and Fondo de Cultura Económica. *La Economía Cubana: Reformas Estructurales y Desempeño en Los Noventa.* 2nd ed. Mexico City, 2000.

United Nations, Conference on Trade and Development. "The Electronic Commerce and Development Report 2001." New York, 2001.

U.S. State Department. *Country Report on Human Rights, 2001.* Bureau of Human Rights Democracy and Labor, 2002, www.state.gov/g/drl/rls/hrrpt/2001/eap/8289.htm.

Uslaner, Eric M. "Social Capital and the Net." *Communications of the ACM* 43, no. 12 (December 2000): 60–64.

Valdés, Nelson. "Cuba, the Internet, and U.S. Policy." Cuba Briefing Paper Series No. 13. Washington, D.C.: Georgetown University Caribbean Project, 1997.

Warkentin, Craig. *Reshaping World Politics: NGOs, the Internet, and Global Civil Society.* Lanham, Md.: Rowman and Littlefield, 2001.

Weaver, Mary Anne. "Muburak Regime Is Now on Trial in Egypt." *New York Times Magazine,* June 17, 2001.

Weiner, Jed. "Jordan and the Internet: Democracy Online." *Middle East Insight* 13, no. 9 (May/June 1998): 49–50.

Wellman, Barry, and Milena Gulia. "Virtual Communities as Communities: Net Surfers Don't Ride Alone." In *Communities in Cyberspace,* ed. Marc A. Smith and Peter Kollock. New York: Routledge, 1999.

Wheeler, Deborah. "Global Culture or Culture Clash: New Information Technologies in the Islamic World—A View from Kuwait." *Communication Research* 25, no. 4 (1998): 359–76.

———. "In Praise of the Virtual Life? New Media, Democratization, International Development, Human Rights, and the Protection of Middle East Cultural Spaces." *Monitors: A Journal of Technology and Human Rights* 1, no. 1 (autumn 1996): 1–32.

White, Gordon. *Riding the Tiger: The Politics of Economic Reform in Post-Mao China.* Stanford, Calif.: Stanford University Press, 1993.

White, Gordon, Jude Howell, and Xiaoyuan Shang. *In Search of Civil Society: Market Reform and Social Change in Contemporary China.* Oxford: Clarendon Press, 1996.

Wilson, Ernest J. III. *The Information Revolution and Developing Countries.* Cambridge, Mass.: MIT Press, Forthcoming.

Wilson, Peter W., and Douglas F. Graham. *Saudi Arabia: The Coming Storm.* Armonk, N.Y.: M. E. Sharpe, 1994.

Wong, Poh-Kam. "Implementing the NII Vision: Singapore's Experience and Future Challenges." In *National Information Infrastructure Initiatives: Vision and Policy Design,* ed. Brian Kahin and Ernest Wilson. Cambridge, Mass.: MIT Press, 1997.

World Bank. *World Development Indicators 2002.* Washington, D.C.: International Bank for Reconstruction and Development, 2002.

———. *World Development Report 2000–2001: Attacking Poverty.* New York: Oxford University Press, 2000.

———. *World Development Report 2002: Building Institutions for Markets.* New York: Oxford University Press, 2002.

Wright, Robert. "Gaining Freedom by Modem." *New York Times,* January 28, 2000.

Wriston, Walter. "Bits, Bytes, and Diplomacy." *Foreign Affairs* 76, no. 5 (September/October 1997): 172–82.

———. *The Twilight of Sovereignty: How the Information Revolution Is Transforming Our World.* New York: Scribner, 1992.

Yamani, Mai. *Changed Identities: The Challenge of the New Generation in Saudi Arabia.* London: Royal Institute of International Affairs, 2000.

Zahlan, Rosemarie Said. *The Making of the Modern Gulf States: Kuwait, Bahrain, Qatar, the United Arab Emirates and Oman*. Reading, U.K.: Ithaca Press, 1998.

Zakaria, Fareed. "The Rise of Illiberal Democracy." *Foreign Affairs* 76, no. 2 (November/December 1997): 22–43.

Zhang, Ming. "War without Rules." *Bulletin of the Atomic Scientists* 55, no. 6 (November/December 1999): 16–18.

Zhao, Yuezhi. "Caught in the Web: The Public Interest and the Battle for Control of China's Information Superhighway." *Info* 2, no. 1 (February 2000): 41–65.

———. *Media, Market, and Democracy in China: Between the Party Line and the Bottom Line*. Urbana: University of Illinois Press, 1998.

Index

About the Authors

Shanthi Kalathil is a Carnegie associate in the Information Revolution and World Politics Project at the Carnegie Endowment. Before joining the Endowment, she was a Hong Kong-based staff reporter for the *Asian Wall Street Journal*. She has written extensively on the information revolution and political change in developing countries. Ms. Kalathil holds an M.Sc. from the London School of Economics and a B.A. from the University of California, Berkeley.

Taylor C. Boas is pursuing a Ph.D. in political science at the University of California, Berkeley. He was previously a project associate in the Information Revolution and World Politics Project at the Carnegie Endowment. He holds an M.A. from the University of California, Berkeley, and a B.A. from Stanford University.